Limits to Globalization

Limits to Globalization

Disruptive Geographies
of Capitalist Development

Eric Sheppard

OXFORD
UNIVERSITY PRESS

OXFORD
UNIVERSITY PRESS

Great Clarendon Street, Oxford, OX2 6DP,
United Kingdom

Oxford University Press is a department of the University of Oxford.
It furthers the University's objective of excellence in research, scholarship,
and education by publishing worldwide. Oxford is a registered trade mark of
Oxford University Press in the UK and in certain other countries

First Edition published in 2016
Impression: 3

Published in the United States of America by Oxford University Press
198 Madison Avenue, New York, NY 10016, United States of America

British Library Cataloguing in Publication Data
Data available

Library of Congress Control Number: 2015960978

ISBN 978–0–19–968116–7

Printed by CPI Group (UK) Ltd, Croydon, CR0 4YY

This book is dedicated to my father Norman Sheppard (FRS), 1921–2015: A tirelessly critical thinker who wished for a better world.

Contents

Contents

List of Figures

Preface: Understanding Globalizing Capitalism

As a socio-economic system, capitalism has been globalizing, undergoing metamorphosis along the way, at least since rudimentary local capitalist economies, scattered through the coastal trading cities of Asia, Africa, and Europe by the thirteenth century CE, were overwhelmed in the eighteenth century by the European variant enabled by European states' colonial exploitation. While seemingly ubiquitous and neoliberal, capitalism still is globalizing; its prevalence around the world remains uneven and variegated. How are we to understand this always incomplete, geographical process and project? In this book I assay a geographical answer.

To many potential readers, this question will seem naïve if not dated. For the last twenty-five years, Anglophone geographical and development economists have taken unprecedented interest in the relationship between geography, economics, and development. They offer the familiar theory of market capitalism articulated in mainstream economics: an explanatory framework that reduces capitalism to market equilibrium. In this view, the essence of capitalism is the perfectly competitive market, in which equally powerless autonomous individuals make rational, self-interested choices about what to sell and consume. This is triply reductive (Fine and Milonakis, 2009): to economic processes alone, to the economic actor as an individual, and to abstract universal laws, devoid of history and geography and implying a particular theoretical aesthetic: explanations derivable via the seemingly apolitical and scientific language of mathematics.

In this view, capitalism is capable in principle of benefiting all bodies and places, as the market enables goods supplied to align with consumers' preferences. Its focus on the rationality of choice further implies an approach that can account for all realms of social and cultural behaviour, making economic theory applicable across the social sciences. In the past three decades, economists have further extended its applicability by acknowledging and identifying conditions under which the presuppositions for perfect competition do not hold (and geography emerges as important), such as increasing returns, information asymmetry and transactions costs. Socio-economic structures, norms and habits can now be explained by economists as strategic responses to 'market imperfections', 'inspiring a whole range of "new" fields straddling other disciplines such as new economic history, new institutional economics, new political economy, new economic geography and so on' (Fine and Milonakis, 2009: 9).

Mainstream economists acknowledge, of course, that really existing globalizing capitalism looks little like their abstract models. Comforted by Milton Friedman's (1953) claim that it does not matter how unrealistic your assumptions are, as long as your conclusions seem plausible, these models are presented as discursive ideals, against which the real world always is to be found wanting and in need of improvement. In this view, there is a capitalist path to growth and prosperity, a teleological development trajectory for all, which people and places neglect at their peril. As I write this (August 2015), the European Union is taking Greece's Syriza party behind the woodshed, applying the rod of austerity against their sin of seeking to contest the models. Such punishments are not confined to the national scale, nor are they new. Detroit is similarly castigated for its profligacy and economic irrationality; poverty in Jakarta's kampungs is blamed on ill-defined property rights, kampung residents' sub-rational economic behaviour, and an incompetent developmental state. From a Keynesian perspective, by contrast, capitalist economic crisis in a territory is due to its government's reluctance to undertake the requisite deficit spending.

Geographers' delight in gaining such attention from economists and their fellow travellers has been tempered by the quandary this places them in. Economic geography is gaining unprecedented attention from those who long dismissed it, but not in ways that the bulk of economic geographers would endorse. In this book I show how a geographical perspective on globalizing capitalism sheds a very different light on its potential and pitfalls. Anthropomorphic globalization cannot be reduced to globalizing capitalism, of course: It is a multifaceted process that dates back to the first movement of humans beyond what we now call Africa. The version of globalization whose limits are identified here is the currently hegemonic capitalist variant and its teleological developmentalist narrative of prosperity for all. These limits, derived from taking seriously the geography of globalizing capitalism, disrupt this developmentalist narrative. On the one hand, the historical geography of the co-evolution of European capitalism with colonialism and slavery implies that capitalism, as we know it, does not play out in the flat, individualist world of mainstream economic theory; its already existing patterns of uneven development shape future possibilities for differently positioned bodies and places. On the other hand, and the focus of this book, the geography of globalizing capitalism makes it inherently incapable of delivering on proponents' promise of benefits for all. The spatialities produced by and productive of capitalist development (including asymmetric and uneven connectivities) mean that uneven geographical development is the norm, not the exception (Chapters 1–7). Beyond this, acknowledging that economic processes co-evolve with political, cultural/identity and biophysical/material processes (Chapter 8) further destabilizes globalizing capitalism and disrupts its developmentalist narrative.

From a geographical perspective, economists' tendency to blame poverty and stagnation on people and places that fail to align themselves with its models reflects their limited, place-based geographical imaginary. Globalizing capitalism is in continual spatio-temporal disequilibrium, riven by socio-spatial unevenness and conflict and confounded by more-than-economic processes. It is not capable of bringing prosperity to all, even in principle. Instead of reducing socio-spatial inequality, globalizing capitalism tends to reproduce prosperity and precarity. The wealth and prosperity that concentrate in certain bodies and places is in good part due to unequal, asymmetric connectivities that simultaneously impoverish other bodies and places. Given these limits to capitalist globalization, impoverished bodies and places cannot prosper by simply following the capitalist development trajectory imposed on them. Rather, they should experiment with alternative socio-spatial imaginaries and practices.

A glance at public discourse reveals that the mainstream economic vision, presented as a triumphalist narrative of intellectual progress and logical superiority, trumps its alternatives. Economics gained influence through the texts of Scottish and English political economy in the eighteenth and nineteenth century when England, in particular, was beginning its transition from an agricultural, mercantile economy to a global industrial capitalist one, underwritten by its colonial empire (Blaut, 1993). Adam Smith was just the most prominent of a group of political economists providing advice about how markets and states are inter-related, and how their nation-state could enhance the prosperity of its citizen-subjects. This trajectory of scholarship, classical political economy, culminated in the writings of Karl Marx. Marx' trenchant analysis of capitalism's limitations, while acknowledging its political and economic superiority to pre-existing European political economic systems, and particularly his belief in capitalism's eventual demise through a socialist revolution, proved too controversial (Pasinetti, 1977). These were times of political unrest, stretching from the French and American revolutions to the short-lived revolutions of 1848, and Marx' theoretical analysis formed the basis for Marx and Engels' 1848 *Communist Manifesto*.

By the late nineteenth century, an alternative economic theory was emerging in England, Austria, and France, against classical political economy: the marginalism of William Stanley Jevons, Carl Menger, and Léon Walras. Instead of asking macro-scale questions about economics, politics, and growth, the marginalists reframed economic theory around the utility-maximizing choices of autonomous individuals and the role of markets in coordinating these. Methodologically, this entailed a turn from more qualitative macro-historical analysis to mathematical modelling. This became the basis for the mainstream economic theory of capitalism, through the signal contributions of the Englishman Alfred Marshall's 1890 *Principles of Economics*, the American Frank Knight's 1921 *Risk, Uncertainty and Profit*, and the American-led neoclassical economics of the mid-twentieth century. ('Neoclassical', because these views could also be traced back to another aspect of Adam Smith's *Wealth of Nations*: his discussion of the invisible hand of the market.) It is through this revolution that the mainstream vision of capitalism seemingly has triumphed. Indeed, under this flag 'political economy' was redefined in terms of public choice economics, trumping the critical analysis of classical political economy.

From the perspective of mainstream economists, others' views fall outside the canon of respectable theory. Indeed, they increasingly are found outside economics altogether, in the liminal spaces of such other social sciences as economic geography as yet unconquered by economics imperialism. Yet this triumphalist narrative glosses over ongoing, unresolved disputes even among European and American economists cutting across more than a century. These include Ludwig Von Mises and the Austrians vs. Oscar Lange in the 1930s, on the question of socialist calculation (Schumpeter, 1954); Joan Robinson, Piero Sraffa and Cambridge, UK economists vs. Paul Samuelson, Robert Solow and Cambridge, MA in the 1960s, on the theory of capital (Harcourt, 1972); John Maynard Keynes and the New Deal vs. Friedrich von Hayek and neoliberalism, particularly after the 1980s (Mirowski and Plehwe, 2009); and current disputes about austerity as the solution to economic crisis and state indebtedness after the global economic 2008 crisis (itself inexplicable from a mainstream perspective, except as a regulatory failure).

Claims of scientific superiority must always be subject to the most rigorous scrutiny, as I undertake here. Too often, apparent academic consensus is a result of debate having been foreclosed by the dominant perspective, rather than a legitimate debate drawing on the knowledge of all parties—engaged pluralism (Barnes and Sheppard, 2010). In this spirit, I seek to challenge how mainstream (geographical) economics has foreclosed debate about globalizing capitalism. For mainstream economists geography is 'out there': 'as exogenous a determinant as an economist can ever hope to get' (Rodrik, Subramanian, and Trebbi, 2004: 134), reduced to place-based characteristics and distance. There are no substantial socio-political differences between the individual economic actors whose rational choices shape market outcomes: individuals may differ in terms of endowments and preferences, but under perfect competition no one has the power to bend markets to her/his interests. Yet for economic geographers, geography is, in mainstream economists' terms, endogenous: continually subject to transformation by the economic processes it shapes. It is also relational—there is far more to spatiality than place-based characteristics and fixed distance metrics. Indeed, the world of globalizing capitalism is already socio-spatially unequal. These inequities do not predetermine outcomes, but do imply unequal conditions of possibility for livelihood practices.

Before proceeding, I wish to dispel two potential misconceptions. First, I do not seek to set geographers' thinking against that of economists. Contemporary differences are inherent to neither discipline, but reflect the different spatio-temporal positionalities of those protagonists who shaped the current state of thinking in each. Mainstream economics emerged from a globally influential United States after 1945, with its new-found belief in the power of markets and at a time when quantification was seen as the *sine qua non* for value free social science. Contemporary Anglophone human geography was shaped in the Anglophone world during the 1960s and 1970s, influenced by the political visions of these times and places. The disagreement, then, is ontological/ideological rather than strictly disciplinary. Second, I do not seek to place qualitative and quantitative theory languages in mutual opposition, a stance too often found on both sides of this interdisciplinary debate. Mainstream Economics is relentlessly mathematical, whereas mainstream human geographers emphasize the limits of quantification, with rigour defined differently in each case. Although I desist from doing so here the bulk of my arguments can be (and have been) developed mathematically (albeit in the twenty-first century mathematics of complex dynamics rather than the nineteenth century mathematics of equilibrium), drawing conclusions that align better with those of qualitative economic geographers than of quantitative mainstream economists. Many aspects cannot and should not be quantified, but mathematics can be bent to the purpose of both visions of globalizing capitalism and its geographies.

Acknowledgements

This book could not have been written without the many graduate students with whom I have had the privilege to work over the years. Five stand out, whose scholarship is closely bound up with various parts of this monograph. Trevor Barnes, of course: our book *The Capitalist Space Economy* remains foundational for the arguments developed here. Paul Plummer, Luke Bergmann, Jun Zhang, and Claire Pavlik made key contributions to the development of ideas appearing in various parts of this book, and will recognize some of their writing in my own. But so many other former advisees have influenced me in various ways. It is impossible to tease this all out, so I simply list them with gratitude (you know who you are!): Anant, Andrea, Bill, Bongman, Byron, Catherine, Chris, Dai, Dmitrii, Gaby, Jim, Josh, Kate, Leila, Lutalo, Marion, Mary, Michael, Mickey, Moira, Morgan, Padraig, Raj, Renata, Ryan, Sam, Sookjin, Steve H, Steven S, Taekyung, Theano, Yeongki, Yu, and Yvette.

During the years of its gestation, I have had very substantial institutional support that has materially contributed to this monograph. In particular, I thank the University of Minnesota (especially its Interdisciplinary Center for the Study of Global Change), the Center for Advanced Study of the Social and Behavioral Sciences at Stanford, UCLA, the Rockefellar Bellagio Center, and the National Science Foundation. Conversations, seminars, and debates with colleagues and friends (abrogated of all responsibility for what follows) have also been vital, including: John Adams, Ron Aminzade, Ragui Assaad, Jim Blaut (RIP), Bruce Braun, Leslie Curry (RIP), Bud Duvall, David Faust, Kathy Gibson, Vinay Gidwani, Michael Goldman, Julie Graham (RIP), David Harvey, George Henderson, Allen Isaacman, Fred Lukermann (RIP), MJ Maynes, Richa Nagar, Jamie Peck, Dick Peet, Phil Porter, Ananya Roy, Rachel Schurman, Neil Smith (RIP), Ed Soja (RIP), Joan Tronto, and Dick Walker. At OUP, I thank my editor David Musson for some sage advice, Clare Kennedy for gentle pushes when needed, and Kim Allen for her meticulous copy-editing.

But Helga stands out, of course: my muse; my inspiration; my love; my most trenchant critic.

I am grateful to Luis Felipe Alvarez León for thoughtfully reading and commenting on the penultimate draft, and to Matt Zebrowski for drawing the figures. Parts of Chapters 2 and 3 draw closely from previously published articles: 'The spaces and times of globalization' *Economic Geography* (2002) 78: 307–30, 'Geography matters: Agency, structures and dynamics' (with P. Plummer) *Journal of Economic Geography* (2006) 6: 619–37, and 'Geographical political economy' *Journal of Economic Geography* (2011) 11: 319–31. Chapters 6 and 7 are heavily indebted to 'Trade, globalization and uneven development' *Progress in Human Geography* (2012) 36: 44–71. The discussion of evolutionary economic geography in Chapter 5 is taken from an as-yet unpublished manuscript with Jun Zhang: 'Politicizing evolutionary economic geography'. For the figures in Chapter 8, I am indebted to Luke Bergmann for permission to use data based on his calculations, and to Guy Abel and Nikola Sander for the data based on their calculations, published in *Science*.

1

Geography, Economy, Development

Geographical economists and economic geographers tend to conceptualize and mobilize geography very differently. For the former it is an exogenous state of the world: a given, largely place-based set of biophysical features, or a calculable cost of doing business (transport or communications costs). For the latter group, geography in its multifaceted aspects (including both 'nature' and spatialities—for example, place, scale, accessibility, connectivities, positionality) is produced through economic (and other) processes: a constructed geography. Yet these constructed geographies feed back to shape how geographical unevenness and inequality are reproduced and recreated through capitalist economic relations—uneven geographical development. Associated with each of these conceptualizations of geography is a distinct opinion about the capacity of globalizing capitalism to engender economic development. In this chapter, I compare and contrast these views. To appreciate their genealogy, I begin with a brief overview of the emergence of Anglophone geography (cf. Barnes, 2000; Scott, 2000a). Sections 1.2 and 1.3 summarize how the relation between geography and economy is (very differently) conceptualized in geographical economics and economic geography. Finally, I turn to analyse the implications of these differences for what is meant by economic development.

1.1 Economic Geography: A Brief Genealogy

The field of economic geography emerged as a separate area of study, as quasi-imperial commercial geography, in Europe and the United States at the turn to the twentieth century. This was toward the end of a 'long' nineteenth century—the high point of European colonialism and of globalizing capitalism's first (post-1846) phase of free trade-led globalization. Commercial geographers sought to catalogue and map the world's geological and biological resources, and associated economic activities. They were 'concerned with empirical detail, global geographical categorization based upon commodity specialization, and the spatial patterns and conditions of commercial trade' (Barnes, 2000: 18), producing cartographic catalogues of vital import for the Euro-American elites running colonial empires, investing in them, and settling new spaces. For them, geography was the biophysical background shaping both differentiated conditions of production in different parts of the world and the means of transportation connecting them.

In the early 1960s, with human geography seeking to punch its weight as one of the newly scientific social sciences (Barnes, 2004), North American and British scholars pioneered a distinct, theoretical/explanatory economic geography, rather than the descriptive approach of commercial geography. Drawing on German predecessors (von Thünen, Alfred Weber, Palander, Christaller, Lösch), and armed with new tools from mathematics, operations research, computing and inferential statistics, the goal was to deduce the location of economic activities on the basis of capitalists' profit-maximizing choices. The geographic background was artificially simple: Archetypically a featureless isotropic plain. The only differentiating factor, on the basis of which land use patterns and agglomerations of industrial and retail activities could be derived, was transport costs. This cluster of achievements, gathered under the rubric of location theory, could explain why economic patterns emerged even in the absence of any biophysical differentiation: morphogenesis. On a flat plain, geographical differentiation is reduced to relative location, defined as the cost of overcoming distance. This exemplified geography's attempt to present itself as the spatial science, with its own morphological laws (Schaeffer, 1953; Bunge, 1966). Over time, in collaboration with mainstream urban and regional economists, tools of increasing technical sophistication were deployed in the name of modelling the space-economy in terms of general economic equilibrium. This catalysed a whole new discipline, regional science (Isard, 1999), but geographers became increasingly disenchanted with this project.

By the early 1970s, a very different intellectual revolution was underway in Anglophone economic geography, taking it away from neoclassical equilibrium-oriented regional science toward Marxian political economy, ironically led by early pioneers of logical empiricist human geography and location theory (compare Harvey, 1969, 1973, 1982b). This shift reflected scepticism both about the possibility of morphological laws, which were plagued by the 'pattern-process problem' (i.e. the same morphological pattern can be generated from very different processes), and about whether capitalism could solve problems of poverty and inequality as implied in neoclassical economics. At the centre of this rejection of location theory was a critique of its 'spatial fetishism'. Neil Smith (1981: 112) defines spatial fetishism as treating space as sufficiently autonomous of social processes that 'no change in the social process or spatial relations could alter the fundamental structure of space'. As Ed Soja (1980: 100) put it: 'Social space is thus interpreted as physical space'. Against this, Henri Lefebvre (1991 [1974]) had argued that space is produced, taking distinct forms under different economic systems.[1]

Smith took the position that space can have no independent causal effect because it is endogenous to (produced by) the economy, denying the distinct role for space in economic geography asserted by location theorists. This complete rejection did not stand the test of time, however. According to Soja (1980: 81): 'social relations of production are both space-forming and space-contingent', a conceptualization he dubbed the socio-spatial dialectic. Others agreed: 'Substance laws and analyses of social processes might be different were they to make integral the fact of their necessarily spatial character' (Massey, 1984: 53); 'The prevailing assumption in the social sciences is that society and economy have geographical outcomes but not geographical foundations. We disagree' (Storper and Walker, 1989: 226).

Since the 1980s, economic geographers have brought an increasingly diverse set of conceptualizations to the understanding of globalizing capitalism. These include a 'cultural turn' (drawing on post-structural accounts of capitalism), an institutional turn (stressing issues of governance and institutions), feminist economic geography, a 'relational turn' (emphasizing capitalism's increasingly networked nature), diverse economies perspectives (stressing the persistence of non-capitalist economic activities in the face of globalizing capitalism), post-colonial approaches, and evolutionary economic geography (Sheppard, Barnes, and Peck, 2012). Notwithstanding this diversity, including some deep disagreements about the relative merits of these approaches, a broad consensus exists with respect to the question of geography and economy that resonates with Soja's position (also shared across Anglophone human geography): although socioeconomic processes 'produce' geography (conceptualized as space and/or nature), those produced geographies reciprocally shape socio-economic processes. With this in mind, I turn to comparing mainstream economic and geographic perspectives, beginning with the former.

1.2 Exogenous Geographies: The View from Economics

For geographical economists and their mainstream fellow travellers, geography is conceptualized as prior to the economy: 'as exogenous a determinant as an economist can ever hope to get' (Rodrik et al., 2004: 134). Exogenous

---

[1] Smith (1984) made the same point about nature.

factors play a vital role in any universal model, including that aspired to by mainstream economics. Contrasting universal with local models, Stephen Gudeman (2008: 15–16) describes how universal models banish 'ontological angst' 'by positing an independent bottom level . . . from which the remaining "facts," "variables," or institutions of social life can be derived' (see also Gudeman and Penn, 1982). Economists' universal models are bounded by exogenous variables that do not respond to market incentives, and by externalities whose effects fall outside market exchange (although attempts to extend their range entail endogenizing both of these, cf. Fine and Milonakis, 2009). Exogenizing geography can provide such a foundation.

There is disagreement among economists, however, about how to define geography. One view, propagated by Jeffrey Sachs (and resonating with that of commercial geography), treats geography as 'first nature': The physical world of climate, topography, and river basins. The more influential alternative, propagated by Paul Krugman, aligns with spatial science and location theory: the geographic background is a uniform backcloth of homogeneous space, with mobility limited by transportation costs. Processes of morphogenesis, driven by economic laws, account for a 'second nature': agglomerations of population and economic activities, and flows of people and commodities between places (Krugman, 1993: 129).

1.2.1 *Sachs and Physical Geography*

Utilizing fine resolution geospatial data measuring population density, and Gross Domestic Product (GDP) per capita and per square mile worldwide, Sachs and his colleagues compute a regression in which tropicality and distance from navigable water are statistically significant predictors of levels and rates of growth of GDP (and population density) (Gallup, Sachs, and Mellinger, 1999). The regression specification is derived in reduced form from a standard neoclassical single sector economic growth model in dynamic equilibrium, augmented with possibilities of increasing returns, in which differences in transport costs (measured by distance to navigable water) and lower productivity (measured by tropicality) are hypothesized to reduce equilibrium growth rates, *ceteris paribus*. In Ricardo Hausmann's (2001: 45) felicitous term, places are 'prisoners of [their] geography'. Differences in natural endowments prevent rates of economic growth from equalizing across space, requiring intervention by development institutions (e.g. the World Bank, the United Nations) to level an economic playing field tilted by its pre-existing uneven biophysical geography.

In this view, physical geography constitutes a given backcloth (so slow moving, by comparison to the dynamics of societal change, that it can be taken as fixed) 'resolutely external to society' (cf. Krugman, 1993; Castree and

Braun, 1998: 7). Sachs' argument has generated a minor industry of econo-
metric studies seeking to estimate the statistical effects of tropicality and
distance to navigable water on mean rates of GDP growth; these are largely
at the international but also at the subnational scale (focusing on access to
water, cf. Démurger et al., 2002; Sachs, Bajpal, and Ramiah, 2002).

Other development economists have contested this 'first nature' version of
geography and economy, however, arguing that the key determinant is not
physical but political geography. Thus Acemoglu, Johnson, and Robinson
(2002) argue that institutions rule: that the eventual prosperity of more temperate colonies by comparison to tropical colonies is explained by differences
in institutions. European colonizers brought exploitative institutions to colonies in the Middle East, Asia, Africa, and the tropical Americas, whereas the
right (European) institutions were installed in the white settler colonies
(North America, South Africa, the southern cone of South America, Australia,
and New Zealand) where indigenous populations were dominated (and eliminated). In short, European superiority is the key—an argument fraught with
(presumably unintended) stereotypes about Europeans civilizing the backward tropics. Rodrik et al. and Easterly and Levine reach a similar conclusion
(Easterly and Levine, 2003; Rodrik Subramanian, and Trebbi, 2004). By contrast, others find that 'geography' (first nature) trumps institutions (Faye,
McArthur, and Sachs., 2004; Olsson and Hibbs Jr, 2005; Nordhaus, 2006;
Presbitero, 2006).

Although Adam Przeworski (2004a, 2004b) argues that neither geography
nor institutions are an exogenous cause of poverty or prosperity, the geography vs. institutions debate circulates widely in the public domain: compare
Sachs' *The End of Poverty* and Paul Collier's *The Bottom Billion* with Acemoglu
and Robinson's *Why Nations Fail* (Sachs, 2005; Collier, 2007; Acemoglu and
Robinson, 2012). Yet there is common ground. Notwithstanding disagreement about the relative importance of physical or political geography, the
consensus is that geographies of poverty and plenty can be explained by
inherited (exogenous) place-based characteristics—not by capitalism's own
limitations.

1.2.2 *Krugman and Morphogenesis*

Whereas development economists seek to explain geographies of economic
inequality in terms of differences in non-economic place-based characteristics, geographical economists begin with a homogeneous geographical backcloth: a 'flat' world in which no place has an initial locational advantage
(usually, two locations at either end of a line, or points equally separated
around a circle). They thus identify with the location theoretic tradition in
economic geography. This is by far the more popular approach among

mainstream economists, who see Sachs as tackling the much easier but mundane task of explaining why geographical inequality begets economic inequality.[2] Utilizing Dixit–Stiglitz mathematical models of monopolistic competition, Krugman and his followers derive stable equilibrium outcomes in which either spatial differentiation emerges (some places become industrial clusters whereas others remain agricultural), or there is no specialization. The key, determining which equilibrium outcome holds, is the exogenous factor of transportation costs. If transport costs are minimal or very high, there is no economic incentive for geographical specialization. For intermediate transport costs, some regions become industrial whereas others remain agricultural. For this case multiple equilibria are possible: For a two-region model either region might industrialize, and economic theory cannot settle the where question. Minor differences in initial conditions can push industry initially toward one region rather than the other, igniting a path-dependent process of spatial economic differentiation. Geography matters, but how it matters depends on prior events (Krugman, 1991, 1996).

This multiple-equilibrium approach to understanding the relation between geography and economy proved controversial among mainstream economists. They were uncomfortable with the possibility of more than one equilibrium—with the notion that equilibrium outcomes do not depend entirely on economic reasoning. Nevertheless, Krugman received the Nobel Medal in Economics in part for his contributions to reviving geographical economics, catalysing what is by now a broad, rapidly evolving research agenda, extending also into fields where geographers have had little to say such as trade theory (Brakman, Garretsen, and von Marrewijk, 2009) (but see Chapters 6 and 7).

Applying this approach to the global scale, Krugman's framework offers an alternative explanation of wealth and poverty to the geography vs. institutions debate. Redefining the two regions of Krugman's original model as world regions, a north–south model is constructed to account for industrialization of the north (Krugman and Venables, 1995). In this view, both the global polarization of industrialization and wealth of the late nineteenth to mid-twentieth century, and the shift of industrialization toward Asia and Latin America in the last twenty years, represent equilibrium outcomes that reflect falling transport costs (Crafts and Venables, 2001; Baldwin, 2006; Venables, 2006). According to this narrative, historically high transport costs precluded specialization at the global scale, implying a relatively equal world. As transport costs fell between the seventeenth and nineteenth centuries, however, during

---

[2] In an entry for the *New Palgrave Encyclopedia of Economics*, Sachs persists in trying to persuade his colleagues to integrate agglomeration economies with 'physical geography' (Sachs and McCord, 2008).

'globalization 1' (Williamson, 2005), specialization became the stable equilibrium outcome. In this formulation, either region might have 'won', with unspecified historical contingencies shaping the north's 'victory'. After a 'counter-globalization' interregnum (1929–45), 'globalization 2' has unleashed a combination of further falling communications costs and spatially disaggregated global production networks. Transport costs have fallen to the point where regional specialization no longer is the equilibrium outcome, so the world is currently experiencing industrialization in the south with the emergence of the BRICS.[3] In this culminating phase of globalizing capitalism, where the world has flattened, the theory predicts that industrialization will finally diffuse to all world regions as the new equilibrium outcome.

1.2.3 Shared Presuppositions

There is little love lost between proponents of 'first' and 'second' nature versions of geographical economics, yet they share a common set of presuppositions about geography and economy. First, they agree that the geographic backcloth (the geographical characteristics of places and communications and transport costs) can be treated as *exogenous* to the economy. As a consequence, they agree that state actions may be necessary to redress market imperfections associated with geography. As noted above, Sachs argues for global interventions to compensate for 'bad geography' and level the playing field. With respect to 'second nature', Ottaviano and Thisse (2004) derive the 'spatial impossibility theorem' for the case of a flat backcloth: neoclassical competitive equilibria cannot exist in a capitalist space economy. In this spirit, the World Bank's *World Development Report 2009: Reshaping Economic Geography* argues that transitional state action may be necessary to flatten geography and enable market-oriented development to reduce spatial inequality (World Bank, 2009).[4] Similarly, Anthony Venables (2006: 74) argues that 'geography' implies that 'trade is not necessarily a force for convergence of incomes', an argument even acceptable to the inveterate free trader Douglas Irwin (2006). Thus, in important ways mainstream geographical economics calls market triumphalism into question. If such geographical characteristics can be commodified, however, making them endogenous to the economy, this would revive the possibility that the market can modulate such differences through participants' rational choices (Chapter 8).

---

[3] Brazil, Russia, India, China, South Africa.
[4] Like Krugman, this report stresses communications infrastructure, confining consideration of Sachs' 'first nature' to the transport costs of a landlocked nation (Sheppard, Maringanti, and Zhang, 2009a).

Second, they share what Brenner (2004) has dubbed *methodological territorialism*: Geography is presented as being about places and their characteristics, implying that territorial entities can be treated as bounded, homogeneous and quasi-independent units of analysis. Place-based characteristics (climate, navigability, governance, being landlocked, population size, ethnic diversity) shape local possibilities of wealth or poverty (Sachs, 2005; Collier, 2006, 2007; Venables, 2006). For Krugman et al., place-based characteristics are endogenous ('second nature'), emerging as equilibrium outcomes. Nevertheless, in a flat world with no locational advantage the difference between industrialization and agriculture is entirely contingent ('path dependent'), and the focus of analysis still is what happens in place.

Yet, and this is the third commonality, *one geographical scale causally dominates* all others: That of the human body. Mainstream economists' commitment to micro-foundations, duplicated in geographical economics, reduces economic explanation to methodological individualism (Levine, Sober, and Wright, 1987; Barnes and Sheppard, 1992; Arrow, 1994; Hodgson, 2007). In this view, economic outcomes are to be explained as the consequence of individuals' autonomous rational actions, aggregated to account for macro-economic outcomes (e.g. aggregate production functions, or factor endowments). They are thereby also presumed to adequately account for the dynamics of territorial (urban, regional, and most commonly national) economies. In this view, geographical scales are given, nested, and inter-related through a bottom-up causal logic. This duplicates hierarchy theory in ecology, where it is argued that objects at any scale are shaped by events at smaller scales, albeit constrained by the slower moving characteristics of larger scales (Wu, 1999). Geographical detail is then attached to this scalar ontology in the form of attributes characterizing each scaled unit of analysis (body, region, nation). These might include individual attributes (given preferences and endowments), place-based attributes (resources, climate, culture, etc.), and relative location (accessibility to other such units, defined by given communications costs).

Fourth, to the extent that there is sustained discussion of the interactions between places and their consequences, this theoretical framework implies that *interdependencies are mutually beneficial* for the places they connect. This is most trenchant in the free trade doctrine's claim that market-based trade is beneficial for all places (see Chapter 6), but similar arguments are made about factor mobility. Migration, capital flows, direct investment, knowledge and resources flow from places of net surplus to those of net deficit, eliminating geographical imbalances and equalizing opportunity (e.g. Ohlin, 1933; Samuelson, 1954; Borts and Stein, 1964; Siebert, 1969; O'Brien, 1992; Borjas, 2001).

8

1.3 The View from Geography

Whereas thinking in economics readily can be characterized as hewing to a hegemonic mainstream canon, geography is the opposite. Anglophone economic geography is currently dominated by variegated versions of geographical political economy (Sheppard, 2011a), a very diverse body of knowledge, rife with philosophical, theoretical, and methodological disagreement (Sheppard and Barnes, 2000; Barnes, Peck, and Sheppard, 2012). Nevertheless, there is a shared understanding of geography and economy that differs in critical ways from that of geographical economics. In contrast to economists' Cartesian ontology, that is, a given geography of quasi-autonomous individuals and territories supplemented by distance vectors (measured in economic terms), geographers favour a relational or, I would insist, dialectical approach.[5] At the centre of this is Soja's socio-spatial dialectic: neither geography nor economy are fixed; each is heterogeneous and continually shifting and shaping the other (in non-convergent ways) through processes of co-constitution.

1.3.1 Nature–Economy Relations

Economic geographers have paid less attention than they should to the more-than-human, biophysical world at the centre of Sachs' thinking (the sub-fields of agriculture, political ecology, and resource geography remain dominated by the economic geography of industry and services). Yet geographers also approach this relationally, conceptualizing the biophysical environment as co-evolving with, partially constituted through, and inseparable from socio-economic processes, producing hybrid or more-than-human geographies (Whatmore, 2001). From this perspective, Sachs' account is redolent of environmental determinism. Sachs, and Jared Diamond (1997, 2005), rightly protest that they do not endorse the cultural racism that made environmental determinism notorious (Semple, 1911; Huntington, 1922; Peet, 1985). Nevertheless Sachs, like Semple and Huntington, conceptualizes the more-than-human world as more-or-less external to and determinant of society and economy (Blaut, 1999; Peet, 2006).[6] Yet his principal surrogates of 'geographical' disadvantage, the geographical distribution of malaria (for tropicality) and access to navigable waters, have long been shaped by societal change: the

---

[5] The relational turn has defined itself as new, and in opposition to Marxism (Bathelt and Glückler, 2003; Yeung, 2005). Yet Marxian dialectical thinking is profoundly relational in its thinking (Harvey, 1996: ch. 2), and relational thinking can be traced back to spatial science. Consider Waldo Tobler's (1970: 936) 'first law of geography': 'Everything is related to everything else, but near things are more related to distant things.'

[6] Economists' resistance to Sachs' version of economic geography may be because they share geographers' leeriness of environmental determinism.

elimination of malaria from subtropical regions of the first world, and the colonial geopolitics shaping transportation systems, navigational improvements, and national boundaries. Gaza remains desperately poor, not-withstanding its temperate, coastal location, and Switzerland, Austria, or Botswana prosper by comparison to less land-locked countries.

This does not mean, of course, that biophysical processes are irrelevant: temperate climates are better suited for producing grain-based annual agricul-tural surpluses, third world environmental health problems like malaria receive inadequate attention, and tropical conditions pose very specific chal-lenges that local agricultural knowledge and practices, and cultural norms, have found ways to address (Sheppard et al., 2009b). Nevertheless, recogniz-ing more-than-human geographies implies, in technical terms, that Sachs' and others economists' statistical models are mis-specified; they fail to account for such reciprocal causal effects by treating 'first nature' as if it were exogenous. I return to these issues in Chapter 8.

1.3.2 *Spatialities*

'Spatialities' has become a catch-all term for the various aspects constituting the spatial organization of society. A variety of these have been discussed and theorized within the Anglophone literature on socio-spatial theory, including economic geography, with the emphasis shifting over time. These include, but certainly should not be restricted to, distance, place, scale, connectivity, and positionality (with feminist and non-US/UK geographers arguing for other spatialities, for example Rose, 1993; Chaturvedi, 2003; Yiftachel, 2003; O'Neill and McGuirk, 2005).[7] As we have seen, geographical economists emphasize place and distance, as exogenous features. Distance (as a surrogate for transport costs) was already central to 1960s location theory. Place gained particular attention in Krugman-style geographical economics. In what follows, I offer a brief chronology of these spatialities within eco-nomic geography.

1.3.2.1 PLACE
A powerful body of research developed in the 1980s around questions of locality, place, and territorial economies, taking empirical inspiration from the emergence of dynamic industrial clusters in Europe and North America, in places ranging from California's Silicon Valley to the 'third Italy' towns of

---

[7] Unlike some scholars, I do not suggest that spatiality can be subdivided into separable categories: These overlap, complicate, and complement one another, representing alternative starting points from which to also contemplate the others (compare Leitner, Sheppard, and Sziarto, 2008; Jessop, Brenner, and Jones, 2008).

Emilia-Romagna (Murgatroyd et al., 1985; Piore and Sabel, 1986; Scott, 1988, 1998; Storper and Walker, 1989; Massey, Quintas, and Wield, 1992; Saxenian, 1994; Cooke and Morgan, 1998). This coincided with post-Fordist technological shifts away from standardized mass production toward flexible specialization, favouring the emergence of Marshallian industrial districts. Conceptually, instead of treating place-based characteristics as fixed, place and economy are theorized as co-constitutive (e.g. Harvey, 1982b, 1994). According to Allen Scott (2000b: 87), prevalent economic conditions implied that transactions costs matter primarily at the local scale; for those requiring close physical proximity 'the spatial costs of transacting are . . . extremely high', whereas longer distance transactions costs are 'extremely low'. Firms in sectors dominated by the former agglomerate into global city-regions. For firms in sectors characterized by the latter type, both relative location and spatial agglomeration are of little importance; they operate within an undifferentiated space of flows whose structural logic is 'placeless' (Castells, 1996: 413), a 'pure flow economy' (Storper, 1997: 28), or a field of transactions of 'unlimited geographical range' (Scott, 2000b: 88).

Beyond the co-constitution of flexible specialization and economic agglomerations, a variety of place-based 'relational assets' are argued to be key to the success of such clusters in the face of the centripetal forces of globalizing capitalism. Key assets, facilitating local technological dynamism and local competitiveness, can be grouped into reduced transactions costs, tacit knowledge, and the local political, social, and cultural milieu (Amin and Thrift, 1992; Leyshon and Thrift, 1997; Storper, 1997). These have been identified through their presence in successful agglomerations (Signorini, 1994; Malmberg, Sölvell, and Zander, 1996; Malmberg and Maskell, 2002)—although this is rarely confirmed by establishing their absence from unsuccessful ones.

This focus on how place-based relational assets co-evolve with economic agglomeration and clustered geographies of technological change and innovation, creating territorial economies, is a place-based account of the geography of globalizing capitalism. In this view, territories prosper or stagnate on the basis of their co-evolving local conditions. Territorial specialization in the right sectors generates growth; specialization in the wrong sectors results in undesirable 'lock-in'. The capacity to reinvent a territorial economy when it runs into trouble is a positive sign of resilience. Little attention was paid to the putative significance of relations extending beyond territorial boundaries—a neglect that became the subject of significant criticism (Markusen, 1996; Bathelt and Taylor, 2002; Oinas, 2002; Bathelt, Malmberg, and Maskell, 2004). The shift away from a 1970s concern for economic decline and spatial restructuring of older industrial regions toward a 1980s celebration of the dynamism of new industrial districts, critics argue, has encouraged economic geographers to neglect both the role of broader forces of uneven geographical development in shaping local possibilities (Smith, 1984; Sheppard, 2002), including developments in struggling peripheral localities (Werner, 2012b).

1.3.2.2 SCALE

Turning their attention to making sense of uneven geographies of globalization in the 1990s, economic geographers began to theorize the relationship between economy and geographic scale (ranging from the body to the globe). This scholarship supplemented research on place, interrogating how change in any territorial economy is also affected by change at other geographic scales. Beyond this, and drawing more broadly on theorizations of scale in human geography, it challenged conventional notions of scale. The existence of a vertical hierarchy of scales, from the body to the globe, had generally been taken for granted, with certain kinds of activities associated with particular scales (trade with the global, trade unions with the national, services with the local, and caring work with the home). Scale theorists emphasize that scales are socially constituted, however, conceptualizing how scales are made, their shifting relative influence, and how events at one scale are shaped by shifting relationships with other scales (Smith, 1992; Leitner, 1997; Marston, 2000; Brenner, 2001; Leitner and Miller, 2007).

The study of globalizing capitalism requires attending to these issues: The production of new scales (e.g. the European Union or ASEAN), the changing importance of different scales (e.g. the global relative to the national), and shifting relations between scales (e.g. how global scale processes influence, but also are influenced by, local events). Again, rather than conceptualizing scale as exogenous to the economy, geographic scale and economic processes are co-constitutive of one another. Stimulated by Bob Jessop's (1994) speculations on the hollowing out of the nation-state, Erik Swyngedouw (1997b) and Neil Brenner (1999) pioneered a scalar theory of globalization. In this view, between 1945 and the early 1970s, with the dissolution of supra-national colonial empires and under the intellectual hegemony of Keynesian theory and policy (Fordism), there was consensus that the nation-state should be the dominant geographical scale at which economic relations were organized and governed. This ushered in an era of state-led development. As North Atlantic Fordism entered a crisis in the late 1970s, triggered by declining national productivity (particularly in the United States and Britain), by organized labour's ability to demand more of the surplus, but also by intensified international competition undermining key Fordist industrial regions in North America and Europe, other scales became more influential.

There has been much attention to the growing influence of the global scale, of course, but scale theorists offer a more nuanced analysis of shifts at and across multiple scales. Thus observers of transnational corporations note that their global reach has not resulted in a loss of either national identity or attachment to localities (Ruigrok and van Tulder, 1995; Dicken, 2003); they engage in strategic localization, with global competitiveness also rooted in close relationships with particular localities (Mair, 1997). Similarly, nation-states not only actively participate in supra-national organizations and agreements (harmonizing market regulation, dismantling national barriers to commodity and capital flows, erecting barriers to undocumented immigration, etc.), but also promote their local (particularly metropolitan) economies as vital to national economic competitiveness (Jessop, 2001):

> [T]he contemporary round of globalization has radically reconfigured the scalar organization of territorialization processes under capitalism, *relativizing* the significance of the national scale while simultaneously *intensifying* the role of both sub- and supra-national forms of territorial organization. . . . Processes of territorialization remain endemic to capitalism, but today they are jumping at once above, below, and around the national scale upon which they had converged throughout much of the last century. (Brenner, 1999: 52–3)

In short, political economic processes can be simultaneously globalizing and localizing: glocalization. But this is not a zero-sum game in which influence is reallocated from one scale to another. Nation-states encourage localization, whereas metropolitan economies depend on nation-states to champion them and their products in global markets. 'The globalization of urbanization and the glocalization of state territorial power are two deeply intertwined moments of a single process of global restructuring . . . since the early 1970s. . . . From this point of view, globalization must be understood as a re-scaling of global social space, not the subjection of localities to the deterritorializing, placeless dynamics of the "space of flows"' (Brenner, 1998: 27). Jessop (1999) highlights how conflicts also emerge between the national and the local scale, as a result of cities engaging in global strategies for enhancing their own competitiveness: glurbanization (see also Smith, 2004).

Theorizing scale goes beyond the place-based accounts of industrial districts and city-regions discussed above, by emphasizing how local economic dynamism both catalyses and is shaped by events at other scales. For example, the dynamism of the industrial clusters of Emilia-Romagna proved important to Italian and EU-scale economic growth, catalysing national and EU policies to facilitate the development of such clusters in many regions in order to enhance territorial economic competitiveness.[8] By the same token, these larger-scale initiatives affected local economic dynamism by publicizing and promoting such places as exemplary of a new phase of globalizing capitalism (at least in core capitalist economies).

---

[8] The dynamism of these towns was partly an emergent consequence of actions at smaller scales, of course: individual firms and economic agents, local collaborations of various kinds, etc.

The co-constitution of economy and scale in the context of globalization is not simply in the hands of states and firms. Andy Herod emphasizes the active role of labour, demonstrating how unions engage in multi-scalar labour organizing strategies that can shape the scalar nature of capital–labour relations and firms' responses (Herod, 2001). Those examining other forms of political resistance to the negative economic impacts of globalizing capital also emphasize the politics of scale. Such action cannot just occur locally, even though local experiences often motivate collective action. To have broader impact, local social movements must engage in scale jumping (Smith, 1992; Leitner, 1997; Swyngedouw, 1997a; Harvey, 2000; Leitner, Sheppard, and Sziarto, 2008).

Summarizing, economic geographers theorizing scale share with those focusing on place an emphasis on territorial economies in relation to globalizing capital. Their important addition is to show how the trajectories of places at a particular scale also depend on how they articulate with changes at other scales; globalization and localization are not independent processes but need to be considered in relation to one another (Brenner, 2001). Further, scales (like other spatialities) are not given features of the world, shaping economic processes, but co-evolve with globalizing capitalism. Through the co-constitution of economy and geography, scales can shift in importance in unexpected ways. New scales may emerge, with significant consequences: a far more complex geography of globalizing capitalism than that found in the widely circulating accounts of global homogenization, a flat world, and the disappearing nation-state (e.g. O'Brien, 1992; Ohmae, 1995; Friedman, 2005).

1.3.2.3 NETWORKS AND CONNECTIVITY
Local networks are a central feature of place-based accounts of industrial districts and city-regions. Drawing on scholarship in economic sociology and organizational economics, theorizing alternative market structures, local networks are argued to be key to the dynamic competition/collaboration/ learning characterizing such clusters, as superior to hands-off market exchange or hierarchical corporate decision-making (Granovetter, 1973; Williamson, 1985; Scott, 1988, 1989; White, 1988; Powell, 1990). This focus on local and place-based networks (Amin and Thrift, 1994) reinforces place-based perspectives, but there is more to networks than this.

Actor-network theory (ANT) has been influential in geographical conceptions of networks, and also in economic geography. ANT emphasizes the relational, flattened, and emergent nature of networks.[9] Positioning itself against social network analysis (SNA), an influential body of sociological

[9] This resonates with other calls for a 'flat' ontology, devoid of hierarchy or scale (cf. Marston, Jones III, and Woodward, 2005; Anderson and McFarlane, 2011).

scholarship stressing persistent structures of power and influence within social networks (cf. Hargittai and Centeno, 2001),[10] ANT conceptualizes networks not as structures that shape action, but as simply a 'summing up' of interactions. A network's 'actants'—humans, animals, resources, machines, etc.—all have a broadly equivalent potential to shape the network's emergent order.[11] It follows that power is an outcome rather than a pre-existing condition.

'[I]ntentionally oxymoronic' (Law, 1999: 5), seeking to by-pass the long-standing discussion of structure vs. agency in social theory (cf. Giddens, 1984), actants are theorized as deriving their intentionality, identity. and morality from the network, rather than as independent agents (Latour 1999: 17). Once actor-networks are 'successfully established, if all the elements act in concert, then they will take on the properties of actors' (Murdoch, 1997: 361). Actor-networks can become stable and persistent features of society, exhibiting emergent order around 'centers of calculation', but their stability and structure is more apparent than real. Even long-standing networks are continually subject to disruption—a step away from disaster.

In Latour's hands, ANT undermines what have become commonsense distinctions in the social sciences: between humans and nature, between science and its objects of study, between modernity and tradition, but also between global and local—denying the coherence of geographical scale:

> Is a railroad local or global? Neither. It is local at all points, since you always find sleepers and railroad workers, and you have stations and automatic ticket machines scattered along the way. Yet it is global, since it takes you from . . . Brest to Vladivostok. . . . [A]s concepts, 'local' and global' work well for surfaces and geometry, but very badly for networks and topology. . . . One branch of mathematics has been confused with another! (Latour, 1993: 117–19)

This conception of networks reinforces a territorial approach to the spatialities of globalizing capitalism: broad-ranging but flattened networks invoke a socio-spatial ontology resonating with mainstream geographical economics' presumption of a flat geographical backcloth on which all actors are equally empowered, notwithstanding their invocation of a relational rather than a methodologically individualist explanation. Path dependence is the key to emergent centres of calculation, not pre-existing inequality. Broader-scale networks are a defining feature of globalizing capital, of course, ranging from trade networks, to those of foreign direct investment, global finance

---

[10] A geographical counterpart to social network analysis played an important role in economic geography's 'spatial science' phase, building on Kansky's (1963) study of the transport networks of Königsberg (Immanuel Kant's home town) (Chorley and Haggett, 1974).

[11] Suspicious of causal explanation and categorical thinking, Bruno Latour's (2005) epistemology is resolutely empirical, seeking to follow and describe rather than evaluate actor-networks (Haraway, 1997).

markets, technological know-how, migration, telecommunications, labour unions and social movements. After 2000, invoking a relational turn, economic geographers began to highlight the increasingly disintegrated nature of global production in terms of global production networks, rather than commodity chains or value chains (Hopkins and Wallerstein, 1994; Gereffi, 1996; Kaplinsky, 2000; Coe et al., 2004; Hess and Yeung, 2006). Yet it is a big stretch to describe these in ANT terms as flattened, fragile, and emergent networks, with no systematic internal power differentials and offering equivalent conditions of possibility for all actants (Dicken et al., 2001).

Even as networks spread, connecting previously separated actants and places in surprising and unexpected ways, it does not follow that this shrinking world (Kirsch, 1995) is one where relative locational advantage disappears: Space annihilated by time. Consider the leading edge of a putatively flattened globalizing capitalism: The economic geography of cyberspace. Imaginaries of cyberspace emphasize flatness: Anyone with a computer can participate, the wisdom of crowds predominates knowledge production, and the most powerful centres of calculation are vulnerable to a smart kid in his bedroom in Nairobi. Yet the Internet, like all networks, reflects as much as it challenges pre-existing power relations. Its space-transcending technologies can produce profoundly new patterns of connectivity. Yet too often they also reproduce pre-existing unequal political economies of globalizing capitalism. The telecommunications networks that Castells and Thomas Friedman envisioned as catalysing a flat space of flows retain a strong internal socio-spatial differentiation (Figure 1.1), reminiscent of those associated with pre-existing methods of communication and transportation (Dodge and Kitchen, 2001; Graham and Marvin, 2001; Aoyama and Sheppard, 2003). Fifty years after the formal end of colonialism, flying between Dakar and Kampala still requires a stopover in Johannesburg, and Internet connectivity within Africa utilizes cable systems that take information offshore, along the coast of Africa, and back in, like colonial era steamship routes (http://www.telegeography.org/telecom-resources/submarine-cable-map/index.html accessed March 11, 2016).

The choice is not between ANT and SNA—two extremes on the continuum of conceptualizing networks. Really existing networks are not particularly flat, but structured in ways that position some actants favourably relative to, and able to exert power over, others. But they are also not the rigid structures conceptualized in SNA: There is both structure and emergence, a unexpected shift in network positionality and possible power. Their internal networked spatial structure also maps into geographical space, albeit in increasingly complex ways. Networks span geographical space without covering it (Leitner, 2004). In network space, proximity between nodes is measured by their connectivity—the ease and intensity of the flows along links directly and indirectly connecting them. This connectivity may have little to do with

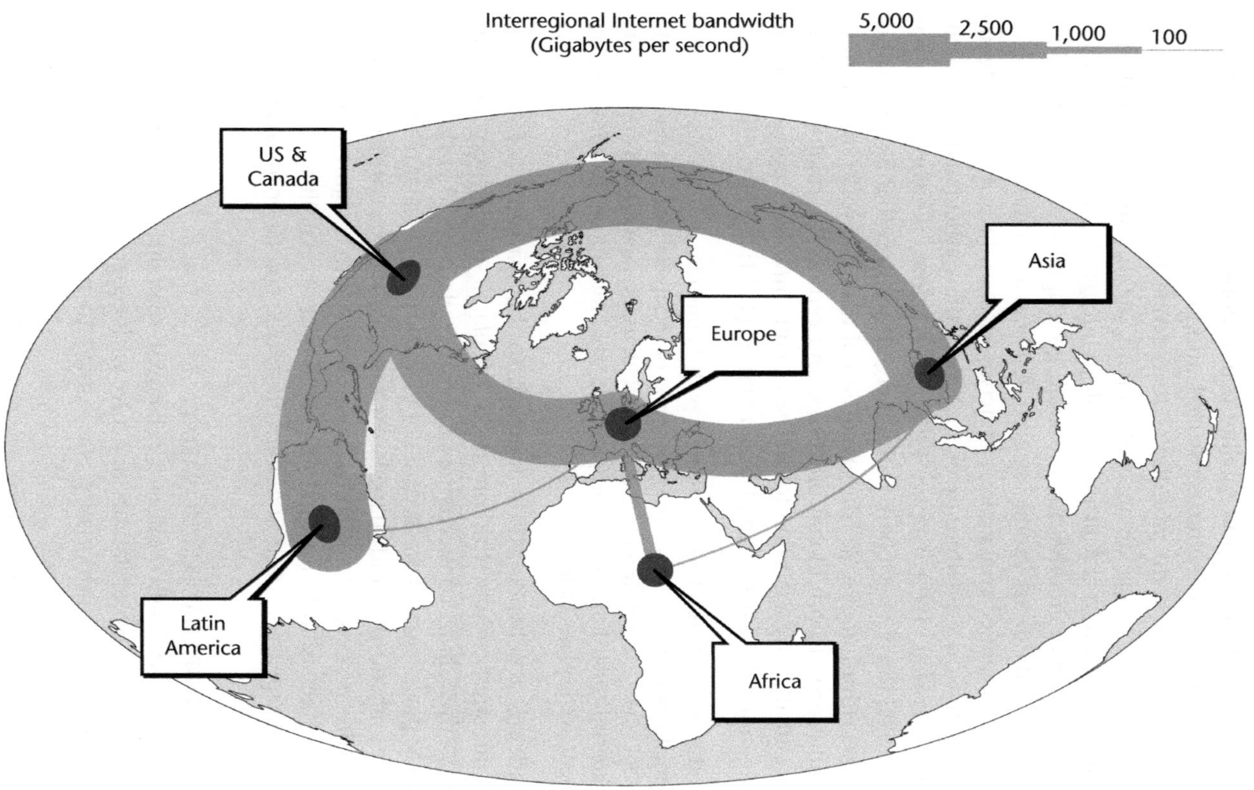

Figure 1.1 Global cyberconnectivity, 2014

Source: Redrawn from a figure presented by Mauldin (2015).

geographic proximity (the distance between places). In network space, Los Angeles can be much closer to London than are smaller European cities. The profitability of connecting Los Angeles with London is higher, resulting in more flights, phone calls, cable and satellite connections, broader band Internet connections, larger and better connected airports, larger router farms, etc. I have borrowed the term wormholes to describe these intense economic connectivities across long distances (Sheppard, 2002). This is all part of an economic sector vital to globalizing capitalism but greatly neglected as such by both geographical economists and economic geographers: transportation logistics and communications, producing accessibility as a commodity (Chapter 2).

Such over-simplified conceptions of networks stem, in part, from attempts to present networks as alternatives to, rather than articulated with, other spatialities (Powell, 1990; Latour, 1993). *Pace* Latour, networks are always already scaled (local vs. global), with emergent features that also contribute to the reconstitution of scale (the expansion of trade networks contributes to the significance of both global processes, and certain key trading localities, such as Dubai).[12] By the same token, *pace* Scott, inter-local networking and place are mutually constitutive. Doreen Massey (1991: 28) puts this well:

> Instead ... of thinking of places as areas with boundaries around, they can be imagined as articulated moments in networks of social relations and understandings, but where a larger proportion of those relations, experiences and understandings are constructed on a far larger scale than what we happen to define for that moment as the place itself.

Summarizing, a network-centric approach to the spatialities of globalizing capitalism stresses how the prospects of places depend on horizontal relations—their direct connectivities with other places—rather than limiting analysis to place-based characteristics or to vertical inter-scalar relations (how places are embedded in and shape larger and smaller scale entities). A further spatiality deserves consideration, however, if we are to account for how ever-shifting but persistently unequal geographies of accessibility, connectivity, and power shape the evolution of networks: socio-spatial positionality.

1.3.2.4 SOCIO-SPATIAL POSITIONALITY
Socio-spatial positionality offers a relational spatiality that acknowledges how pre-existing power relations co-evolve with geographies of connectivity. In feminist theory, positionality was coined to make sense of the social

---

[12] Latour has backed off from some of his agnosticism and critiques of spatiality, accepting that truth is not simply a social construct as conservative critics of science now influentially suggest (Latour, 2004), and acknowledging that 'It's not that there is no hierarchy, no ups and downs, no rifts, no canyons, no high spots. It is simply that if you wish to go from one site to another, then you have to pay the full cost of relation, connection, displacement, and information' (Latour, 2005: 176).

situatedness of subjects 'in terms of gender, race, class, sexuality and other axes of social difference' (Nagar and Geiger, 2007: 267). In this view, differently positioned subjects have distinct identities, experiences, and perspectives, shaping their understanding of and engagement with the world, their ontological and epistemological stance (situated knowledge: Haraway, 1988), and their actions. Yet, as Mohanty (2003) also has noted, positionality is socio-*spatial* because the social and the spatial are mutually constitutive: in her terms, third world women are distinctly positioned by comparison to their first world counterparts, undermining facile claims for a global feminism. As in network thinking, socio-spatial positionality is a relational concept emphasizing the connections and interactions between subjects who are not only differently positioned but also unequally empowered. Positionality thus addresses both difference and inequality. Beyond this, it also questions the generality and normative status of any particular positionality. For example, empowering women in a patriarchal society entails undermining the taken-for-grantedness of masculine norms and practices. Finally, socio-spatial positionality is continually re-enacted through its uneven connectivities. Re-enactments routinely reproduce pre-existing positionalities, giving them a durability that seemingly naturalizes them. Nevertheless, through subjects' relationally constituted practices and imaginaries, relations of power and situated understandings can be contested and re-negotiated, occasionally radically reshaping the power-geometry of socio-spatial positionalities.

Applying this framework to economic geography requires identifying where agency is located, and how it operates relationally. With respect to human subjects engaging in economic activities, actors who are differently positioned, in terms of their role in the economy and social and geographic location, have uneven possibilities of making the world. With respect to place and region, the positionality of a territorial economy influences its future possibilities. Core regions are advantaged relative to peripheral ones: the uneven economic geographies of connectivity that reflect such power hierarchies also reproduce them. At the same time, however, and notwithstanding the persistence of positional differences, globalizing capitalism is replete with examples where long-standing patterns of uneven development give rise to key moments when positional hierarchies are turned upside down, reflecting emergent contradictions of globalizing capitalism (Wallerstein, 1979; Harvey, 1982b). Our understanding of the exact conditions under which such restructuring occurs is imperfect, but is vital to improving our understanding of the out-of-equilibrium dynamics of a capitalist space-economy. This requires that we take into account the uneven connectivities between bodies and territories, not just place-based characteristics.

Positionality also has a scalar aspect: economic actants functioning at different scales have distinct, differently empowered positionalities. By dint of conventions of nation-state sovereignty, national economies can exert powers unavailable to sub-national regions (e.g. issuing currencies, controlling the flow of commodities, capital, and humans across their borders). Yet such positionalities/power relations are subject to contestation. Localities seek to challenge ways in which they are constrained by the nation-state, developing their own extra-national connectivities with offshore places. Nation-states and localities may contest the capacity of supra-national scales to intervene behind national borders (consider current anti-austerity disputes in the European Union, or protests against WTO directives), or may abrogate their sovereignty by acceding to the agendas of supra-national institutions. It is by no means the case that power simply operates top-down, in a scalar hierarchy (Leitner and Miller, 2007); indeed, such presumptions must be challenged (Nagar et al., 2002). Yet power is unevenly located at various scales—and can function to create or alter inter-scalar power relations. Extending positionality to scaled spatialities helps make sense of the complex political economies of scale.

1.4 Development in Question

The contrasting conceptions of geography and economy summarized in the previous two sections engender contrasting views of development, and of the possibilities associated with globalizing capitalism. These can be summarized in terms of whether globalizing capitalism is able to eliminate socio-spatial inequality by redressing place-based characteristics that block its wealth-creating potential—intervening to right the capitalist ship (Section 1.4.1), or whether globalizing capitalism (re)produces socio-spatial inequality by its very nature implying that alternatives to it must be explored (Section 1.4.2). The former view is characteristic of mainstream and geographical economics, underwriting a view of development as a process whereby poorer people and places can attain capitalist prosperity by following the lead and expertise of the more developed. The latter, dominant among economic geographers, implies scepticism about the possibility of any universal 'best practice' path to development under globalizing capitalism.

1.4.1 *Economics' Developmentalism*

In mainstream economics, by far the dominant view of economic development is that it constitutes a shared teleological sequence of stages that territories (typically, nations) should go through. Walt Rostow's (1960) self-styled 'non communist manifesto' remains influential; he argued that all societies follow the US through a series of capitalist stages from 'traditional' to 'beyond mass consumption'.[13] Sachs explicitly accepts Rostow's position that US style capitalism is the best available model for economic development, and the corollary that other ways of organizing economic systems are inferior and should be abandoned (Sachs, 2005). Acknowledging the immense difficulties that ensued from implementing this imaginary through his 'shock therapy' programme, for transitioning state socialism into capitalism in the former Soviet realm, Sachs now recognizes that local conditions can result in very different trajectories from those predicted by free market proponents. This 'prison of geography' necessitates supranational intervention into markets, leveling the global playing field so that capitalism can realize its potential as the ubiquitous development tide that can lift all boats.[14]

In this view colonialism is at best an intervening factor between 'first nature' and development, notwithstanding its demonstrated history of unequal exploitative relations advancing Europe relative to the rest of the world. Indeed, the division of the world into colonizers and the colonized is itself in good part a consequence of the natural disadvantages of tropical and distant places. Colonialism may have enhanced impoverishment across Asia, Africa, and Latin America but is not an 'ultimate cause' (Acemoglu, Johnson, and Robinson, 2002, 2003). The effects of colonialism are seen as having little relevance in a contemporary world of sovereign nation-states, accorded the autonomy, and responsibility, to make the choices that determine their residents' wellbeing.

While geographical and development economists are cautious about the beneficence of market-based outcomes, this has catalysed no significant rethinking of Rostow's developmentalist imaginary. This reflects their conceptualization of geography and economy: of territory, distance, and connectivity. First, national political borders are taken as exogenous to the economy, with nation-states presumed to be natural, fixed territorial economic units—a position that socio-spatial theorists have extensively critiqued as the national territorial trap or methodological nationalism (Agnew, 1994; Brenner, 2004). This implies that nation-states can be taken as autonomous, equivalent, and coherent units of analysis. Size does not matter: the United States and Vanuatu are simply two observations. Nor does history: as soon as new nation-states come into existence (the production of scale) they become a coherent territorial economy, characterized in terms of place-based national attributes—a new observation to be added to the analysis.

[13] Rostow's optimism about bringing capitalism to all aligned with a broader trend in post Second World War US social science, including geography: that of modernization theory (Bernstein, 1971).
[14] Shock therapy remains a valuable tool for Sachs under certain circumstances, however—including China (Sachs 2005, 160).

Invoking methodological nationalism enables analysts to account for the performance of each territorial economy in terms of presumed causal place-based territorial attributes: Average Gross Domestic Product (GDP) per capita, aggregate production functions, governance measures or temperature, etc. The regression specifications utilized in the debates about geography and development that I summarized above are of exactly this kind. This is a place-based statistical specification: Territories' performance scores are regressed against other place-based indicators, with all units of analysis presumed to be from the same population and subject to identical laws. The explanatory task becomes accounting for how a single measure of economic well-being varies across (in this case) national territories, by identifying other national attributes that 'cause' performance differences (causality being defined as a significant partial correlation, backed up by a general equilibrium theory rationalizing causation).[15]

This approach effectively ranks territories based on their performance—a sequential ranking from worst to best (typically, the West), determining which attributes predict success. This is indeed Rostowian logic, creating a single trajectory of development along which all territories are aligned.[16] The policy implication is that other territories can only match the success of the highest performers by altering local conditions to match those of the leaders. The leaders are then presented as the experts, whose advice should be followed (the philosophy driving 1980s Structural Adjustment Policies of the Washington Consensus). This place-based specification also is the norm in mainstream statistical analysis of the performance of subnational regional economies (with some exceptions, e.g., Fingleton, 2000; Yamamoto, 2008; Basile, Capello, and Caragliu, 2012; Doran and Fingleton, 2013), even though geographical economists readily concede, at this scale, that these are not autonomous territorial economies. Quantitative geographers have long pointed out that such methodological territorialism is highly problematic, because place-based regressions cannot account for the many ways in which territorial economies are interconnected and affect one another (not to mention inter-scalar relations).[17]

Development economists increasingly take into account international distance-related effects. Discussions of landlocked countries, for example, note that their performance will depend on a variety of attributes of the neighbouring countries through which their imports and exports must be

---

[15] Such analysis seems unaware of the severe logical problems with such macroeconomic concepts as the aggregate production function (Chapter 2).

[16] Recently, development economists have joined others in questioning the validity of such economistic indices as a measure of development (Waring, 1988; Stiglitz, Sen, and Fitoussi, 2010), albeit without questioning this place-based approach to explaining performance.

[17] Statistically, these models are mis-specified: they do not attend to the possibility of spatial auto-regressive relations.

shipped to reach the sea (Collier, 2006; Venables, 2006). Geographical economists also have reinvented an old geographers' trick, the gravity model, to
predict trade flows (Chapter 6). Yet, as for Krugman, economic distance is
assumed to be independent of the economy. Further, when attention does
turn to such connectivities, it is presumed that unfettered spatial economic
interdependencies (trade, foreign direct investment, portfolio capital flows,
migration) are mutually beneficial for the places they connect together. If this
were the case, then the neglect of such interdependencies, while problematic
in the details, does not undermine the validity of the Rostowian developmental imaginary. Interconnections only hasten the diffusion of well-being from
prosperous to impoverished places, creating a flatter world in which efficient
markets can more readily realize their putative benefits, with lower transport
costs accelerating the progress of 'backward' territories along the path to
development (World Bank, 2009).

In this view, with a Walrasian auctioneer to clear markets, globalizing
capitalism can help realize a benevolent and harmonious space-economy in
which all appropriately behaving places are equally positioned and
empowered to succeed. To be developed is to realize high levels of median
per capita GDP and the like, which immanent capitalist accumulation is
imagined to make possible—blocked only by the wrong geography: bad latitude, bad attitude (Hart, 2002) or poor governance. Jim Blaut (1987, 1993)
dubs this a diffusionist developmental imaginary, a historical narrative pre-
senting the developmental histories of western Europe and North America as
the norm against which all are judged (with most found wanting).

1.4.1.1 CRITIQUING NEOLIBERAL DEVELOPMENTALISM: 'NEW' DEVELOPMENT ECONOMICS

As noted above, a particularly trenchant application of Rostow's teleology was
the prosecution of Structural Adjustment Policies (SAPs) beginning in the
1980s. These were squarely neoliberal policies, with a Washington Consensus,
centred on the Washington DC triangle of the US government, the IMF, and
the World Bank, driving a pro-market, anti-state approach to development.
This has been criticized not only by economic geographers and critical development scholars, but also by a currently influential generation of (largely
US-based) development economists. Shared critiques do not amount, however, to agreement about what to do.

Sachs, Joseph Stiglitz, and Dani Rodrik have led this critique (notwithstanding disagreements between Sachs and Rodrik over geography vs. institutions),
arguing for forms of Keynesianism as an alternative to neoliberal SAPs. As
noted above, Sachs calls for a big push of multilateral state intervention to
overcome geographical disadvantage and other extra-economic shortcomings. Stiglitz, emphasizing the lack of transparency of the Bretton Woods

institutions and the failure of free trade to achieve its promise in an unequal world, calls for a variety of reforms to empower disadvantaged nations. He argues against structural adjustment and biopiracy, and for policies promoting global equity, forgiving national debts, and stimulating aggregate demand in the global South (Stiglitz and Charlton, 2005; Stiglitz, 2006). Rodrik (1997, 2007) highlights how globalization undermines economically desirable aspects of national sovereignty: workers are disadvantaged due to their low mobility, and legitimate national cultural preferences and norms are suppressed. Since national-scale interventions no longer suffice, he seeks modifications to the norms governing global trade.

William Easterly and Hernando de Soto are similarly critical of the Bretton Woods institutions, but favour Hayek not Keynes. Easterly divides the world into planners (such as Sachs and the World Bank) and seekers (the entrepreneurial spirit in us all). In his view, global development policies of all kinds are Big Push initiatives that are doomed to fail: 'The White Man's Burden emerged from the West's self-pleasing fantasy that 'we' were the chosen ones to save the Rest. . . . The Enlightenment saw the Rest as a blank slate—without any meaningful history or institutions of its own—upon which the West could inscribe its superior ideals' (Easterly, 2006: 23). De Soto, credited with converting Peruvian president Alberto Fujimori from Keynesianism to neoliberalism, sees poorly demarcated property rights as the principal cause of poverty. He argues that a vital source of capital for small entrepreneurs is self-finance, from equity accumulated in their homes and businesses (de Soto, 2000). Lacking property rights, the poor cannot take advantage of such potential sources of capital (which he estimates as worth over US$9 trillion worldwide). To address this the global South should copy the United States in order to move from a 'pre-capitalist' to a 'capitalist' property system (de Soto, 2000: 172).

Notwithstanding inter-personal and theoretical differences that can seem irreconcilable (geography vs. institutions, Keynes vs. Hayek), these critics of structural adjustment agree, along with with Hayek, Keynes, and geographical economists, that impoverishment and uneven geographical development are not inherent to globalizing capitalism. Rather, they are a consequence of its inappropriate implementation (Sheppard, 2011b). This endorses Rostow's teleological 'west is best' model of capitalist development, a model that locates expertise about development squarely within the global north. Cowen and Shenton (1996) distinguish between immanent and intentional development: that is, between development as an emergent process and strategic efforts to create development. Stageist thinking about development invokes a teleological path of immanent development for all. If this path seems blocked for those not yet developed, the expertise developed in wealthy countries (whose prosperity seemingly confirms their success in solving development problems) must be passed down, as intentional development policy (adjusted to local context). There have been profound shifts in consensus among northern 'experts' about the correct path, shifting over the decades from Keynesianism to neoliberalism (the Washington Consensus) and then back to a 'post-Washington consensus' where the state matters after all, yet socio-spatial inequality has persisted—even increased. Notwithstanding the repeated failure of these different prescriptions, the institutions of the global North and those trained therein remain the recognized global location of expertise (Sheppard and Leitner, 2010). Geographers arrive at very different conclusions, however.

1.4.2 *Geographers' Critiques*

As I elaborate in Chapters 2 and 3, geographers' relational/dialectical approach to the relationship between geography and economy implies that uneven geographical development is endemic to capitalism, as are disequilibrium and periodic crisis. In this view, globalizing capitalism entails no straightforward diffusion of prosperity from north to south as implied by Rostow's teleology. Differences in socio-spatial positionality, a historical legacy of social hierarchies and geopolitical power inequalities mediated through shifting geographies, act to reproduce such inequalities, notwithstanding periodic spatial restructuring. *Prima facie* evidence in support of this argument is that this most recent phase of rapid, neoliberalizing globalization, like that of the nineteenth century, has been accompanied by persistent and intensifying socio-spatial inequalities, even before the 2008 global crisis (Milanovic, 2005; Piketty, 2014 [2013]). In this view, Rostow's teleological view of capitalist development is neither realizable nor desirable.

An example of this difference in perspectives can be found in debates about the origins and implications of Europe's capitalist industrial revolution. In line with Max Weber's (2003 [1902]) *The Protestant Ethic and the Spirit of Capitalism,* and a generation of European and North American economic historians (Blaut, 2000), both Sachs and Douglass North (2005) explain European prosperity in terms of northwestern European territorial attributes (climate, topography, politics, culture, religion). In this view, Europe was uniquely positioned to become capitalist and lead the world down this path. From this place-based perspective, Europe's geohistorical ascent relative to once more prosperous Asia can only be explained by a lack of such attributes in the latter region (including China's decision to end global exploration in 1433, just as Europe was beginning). Yet such place-based explanations overlook Europe's key relational advantage in relative location. Prior to 1492, incipient localized capitalism was broadly geographically diffused, across the coastal trading cities of Europe, Asia, and Africa (Abu-Lughod, 1991;

Blaut, 1993). Thus preconditions for capitalism were quite ubiquitous. Europe had the good fortune, however, of comparatively easy access to the Americas. This 'new world' proved readily exploitable for resources, land, gold, and silver, its plantations became a proving ground for factory labour practices, and the production of cheap sugar, coffee and cotton could be organized to cheaply clothe and energize the European working class. Rather than a Euro-centric account, attributing Europe's industrial capitalism solely to European characteristics, this analysis suggests that Europe found itself occupying a fortunate socio-spatial positionality that has enabled it to prosper for over four centuries at Asia's, Latin America's, and Africa's expense.

Geographers argue that such uneven connectivities have a significant influence on the conditions of possibility for capitalist economic development in different places, connectivities that are not inherently mutually beneficial, but tend to reinforce pre-existing power hierarchies. As in dependency and world systems theories (Amin, 1974b; Frank, 1978a, 1978b; Wallerstein, 1979; Amin et al., 1982), the impoverishment of certain people and places coevolves with globalizing capitalism, rather than being an original condition that immanent capitalist development can overcome. Dependency and world-systems theory have been criticized for over-emphasizing unequal and asymmetric connectivities, and for their pessimism about the persistence of a global periphery. They also have been criticized for their lack of attention to sub-national scales at which such processes also play out: how prosperous nations like the US have persistent, highly impoverished communities, whereas impoverished countries like Cambodia have prosperous elite neighbourhoods. These are serious shortcomings. Yet it is equally shortsighted to ignore the insight that uneven connectivities can play a critical role in shaping development possibilities.

The geographical argument that globalizing capitalism has a tendency to create and reproduce uneven geographical development, at multiple scales, due to the ways in which asymmetric connectivities shape and are shaped by place-based characteristics, forms the basis for rejecting the Rostowian teleology. If capitalism breeds underdevelopment in the periphery, then prosperity does not diffuse down the hierarchy from 'advanced' wealthy nations to their impoverished 'laggards'. It would be unwise, then, for the latter to duplicate the development strategies of the former, even if encouraged and allowed to do so.[18] In this spirit, dependency theorists argued that

---

[18] Many have noted that the wealthy countries often push poorer ones to 'do as I say, not as I did', as with parents advising their children (Chang, 2002). For example, the United States prospered on the basis of trade and infant industry protectionism from the days of Alexander Hamilton until 1945, only to then tell others to pursue free trade and market-led policies (Chapter 6).

peripheral economies should isolate themselves from globalizing capitalism's negative influences. Others have argued for socialist, communist, and state-led development.

Chakrabarty (2000: 63) argues that the kind of 'History 1' of Euro-American triumphalism, invoked by a Rostowian view of development, can and should be challenged (provincialized) by acknowledging the many alternative development trajectories that he dubs History 2 (I examine this in detail in Chapter 3). Thinking geographically about capitalism, even when invoking conventional measures of economic success and failure, likewise acknowledges the significance and potential benefits of a variety of alternative development paths. This is closer to how development is conceptualized in biology than in economics: as a set of branching paths of immanent development with no expectation that these should converge on a common teleological path (e.g. Gould, 1996).

Thinking geographically, instead of trying to enrol cultural and geographical difference into the drive for economic prosperity (commodifying it or compensating for difference with development funds), cultural difference is conceptualized as a shifting terrain of contestation over what counts as living well: a contestation with no straightforward outcome. Indeed, multivalent contestations become increasingly visible as the problems of globalizing capitalism have become particularly trenchant, at a variety of sites and scales. These alternative imaginaries and practices, located in and across civil society and political institutions and entailing various spatialities, exceed the logics and processes driving capitalism. Some of the practices that preceded globalizing capitalism persist, such as tropical subsistence livelihood systems. Others have emerged as alternatives. National scale alternatives include the state socialism that many post-colonial societies experimented with after 1950, the 'visible hand' of state capitalism in contemporary east Asia, and explicitly anti-capitalist and Islamist initiatives (Venezuela, Bolivia, Iran). Similar experiments exist at sub-regional scales (Moore, 1998; Escobar, 2008). State agencies may pursue non-capitalist agendas even as elected officials hew to neoliberal lines. Communities imagine and enact more-than-capitalist economic practices, and these may be connected together by social movements stretching across space and seeking to jump scale. Of course, different contestations reflect distinct socio-spatial positionalities and are unequally empowered, with questions remaining about their relative efficacy and capacity to realize their particular developmental imaginaries and challenge hegemonic imaginaries and practices. Nevertheless, to dismiss contestations a priori is to cede ground to the diffusionist developmental imaginary of globalizing capitalism (Rose, 2002; Featherstone, 2003; Gibson-Graham, 2006; Leitner et al., 2007b; Santos, 2008).

1.5 Conclusion

Mainstream Anglophone economists and geographers, reflecting very different disciplinary intellectual trajectories, come to very different conclusions about geography, economy, capitalism, and development. Mainstream economists have put together a powerful mathematical framework, grounded in the microfoundations of rational choice, under which capitalism offers the promise of prosperity for all and the elimination of persistent geographical differences in well-being. The only path to development is capitalist, with those who have succeeded invoked as experts who are in a position to advise others how to follow. This presumes that geography is exogenous to the economy, stresses place-based thinking about the spatialities of globalizing capitalism, and makes microfoundational assumptions about the relation between economy and society (Chapter 2). Geographical inequality is explained in terms of general laws connecting place-based causes with place-based outcomes. In this view, blockages created by place-based attributes and market imperfections can be fixed with the right actions and interventions, enabling globalizing capitalism to make good on its promise of opportunity to all.

Thinking geographically about capitalism results in a very different optic. Geography is not exogenous to the economy but co-evolves with it. Geography is not just about place: it is about the uneven connectivities that stretch between places and across scales. These uneven connectivities reflect pre-existing social and geographical inequalities, which cannot be simply assumed away (cf. Lösch, Christaller, Krugman) for the purpose of abstract theorizing: They play a vital if unpredictable role in shaping uneven geographical development. Acknowledging this means recognizing that place-based accounts are too limiting and must be supplemented by connectivity-based thinking and analysis. From a connectivity-based perspective, the economic successes and failures associated with particular places, firms, and bodies may have as much to do with their socio-spatial positionality—their uneven connectivities with other places, firms, and bodies (and scales)—as with place-based attributes.

If globalizing capitalism cannot bring prosperity to all, there can be no teleological immanent development path rationalizing a universal model of capitalist development. Nor does expertise about development necessarily reside with those who have prospered: Multiple development imaginaries and practices make sense and must be critically engaged with, not dismissed. A full appreciation of these differences between economic geography and geographical economics requires, however, that we attend to the socio-spatial ontologies mobilized by each approach: Methodological individualism meets the socio-spatial dialectic.

2

Spatialities of Commodity Production

This chapter summarizes the basic features of capitalist production from a geographical perspective—the foundations for a geographical take on globalizing capitalism. The previous chapter took up one key aspect separating geographical economics from economic geography, presuppositions about the relationship between geography and economy. But there are two others: differences in theory-language and in socio-spatial ontology. With respect to theory-language, the vast bulk of economic geographers are averse to mathematics, the default theory-language in mainstream (and thus geographical) economics, propounding in its place a variety of 'qualitative' and dialectical theory-languages. With respect to social ontology, whereas the canon of mainstream (and thus geographical) economics is methodological individualism, rational choice and micro-foundations, for economic geographers it is some variant on the socio-spatial dialectic.

I begin by elaborating on these two domains of difference, showing why ontological differences are the key, not theory language. I then examine how commodity production (foundational to globalizing capitalism) is shaped by and shapes space and time, and why the economics of production is inseparably intertwined with its politics. Third, in Chapter 3, I discuss the spatial organization of commodity production under globalizing capitalism. Fourth, I turn to the households whose income is shaped by the politics of production. Finally, I examine regulation and governance—a necessary, geographically variegated, supplement to the process of commodity production and exchange. Taken together, the socio-spatial ontology of economic geographers—the socio-spatial dialectic—reveals why narratives of globalizing capitalism as self-regulating, rational, equilibrium-oriented, and capable of bringing prosperity to all, are so deeply problematic.

2.1 Separating Paradigms: Theory-language or Socio-spatial Ontology?

Mainstream (and thus geographical) economics defines itself as a social *science*, in large part through its use of mathematics as theory-language. Reference to this theory-language cites mathematics and physics, the 'hardest' of the natural sciences, as the goal to aspire to (but see Mirowski, 1984). This has implications for how to represent the world. As Krugman (1991: 6) has put it: 'Economics tends, understandably, to follow the line of least mathematical resistance. We like to explain the world in terms of forces we know how to model, not in terms of those we don't.'[1] That line of least resistance has been constructed as the rational choice micro-foundations, suturing a particular social ontology to mathematics as theory-language, and thus to economics as science. This seems very neat, even self-evident (Mitchell, 2005), yet it is a false equation. To show this, I examine each difference in turn.

2.1.1 *The Question of Theory-language*

When mainstream economic thinking presumes that rigorous theory must be mathematical, this is bound up with an ontological philosophical position: a commitment to logical empiricism as advocated by Rudolf Carnap and Bertrand Russell. This entails a realist ontology (there is a real world out there, independent of human perceptions), an empirical epistemology (we come to know the world through our observations and experiences of it), and a mathematical/statistical methodology (explanation entails accounting for observations through mathematical logic; inferential statistics enable us to be precise about the degree of confidence that can be attached to such an explanation). Without putting too fine a point on it, this aspiration to logical empiricism makes necessary mathematics as theory-language (and econometrics as theory validation). This language (discourse) has been developed with enormous sophistication and care. For example, the culture of statistical analysis in mainstream economics tends to be far more careful than that in geography (Hendry, 2001), with some notable exceptions on both sides.

Yet logical empiricism is not the foolproof philosophy, capable of providing the value free explanation of the world, that its proponents hoped for (Sheppard, 2014b). Recognizing this, geographers have taken up post-positivist approaches to knowledge production, engaging with a variety of ontological, epistemological, and methodological commitments. If there is one unifying feature, it is scepticism about the adequacy of an empiricist

---

[1] Krugman presumes that models must be mathematical but there are many other kinds (Hesse, 1963).

epistemology or quantitative methodologies. Indeed, the bulk of Anglophone economic geographers have become dismissive of mathematics as a theory-language and quantitative measurement as the basis for validating knowledge. This has made it very difficult for geographical economists and many economic geographers to communicate constructively, since their starting points seem at odds (Martin, 1998; Amin and Thrift, 2000; Plummer and Sheppard, 2001; Sheppard, 2001a, 2006a; Peck, 2012b).

Mathematical reasoning can be consistent with post-positivist philosophies, however, and thus should not be exorcized from contemporary economic geography (Sheppard, 2001b; Essletzbichler, 2009). It can be liberated from a long-standing, unfortunate, and inaccurate association with logical empiricism that continues to plague geographers (and economists). Indeed, the arguments constituting Section 2.2 of this chapter can be formulated in the theory-language of mathematics (e.g. Sraffa, 1960; Morishima, 1973; Roemer, 1986; Sheppard and Barnes, 2015 [1990]; Duménil and Lévy, 1993; Webber and Rigby, 1996; Cockshott et al., 2009), enabling a conversation with main-stream/geographical economics—no matter how quixotic this often seems.

Rather, as I will show, the differences between mainstream economic and geographical takes on globalizing capitalism are rooted in their very different socio-spatial ontologies. When utilized within a different socio-spatial ontology, mathematical reasoning becomes consistent with very different conclusions about globalizing capitalism to those drawn in mainstream economics. Thus it is false to claim, as so many have, that the capacity of geographical economics to persuade stems from its mathematical 'rigour'. For example, mainstream (and geographical) economists are quick to dismiss Marx' analysis and value theory *tout court*, because of mathematical problems plaguing his so-called transformation problem (the question of the relation between labour values and prices of production), Yet they characteristically gloss over similar inconsistencies in their own theory of capital—the theory that underlies core claims, such as the claim that workers' wages in an open labour market approximate the marginal productivity of labor (Harcourt, 1972). How is it, then, that mathematics as theory-language remains sutured to micro-foundations as social ontology? I argue that this suturing is ideological, stemming from the taken for grantedness of economics' social ontology.

2.1.2 *Beyond the Mainstream Ontology*

As in any area of knowledge production, an economic geographic research programme entails a particular set of presumptions about the world: A socio-spatial ontology. Ontologies constitute foundational starting points for knowledge production, generating hard-core sets of beliefs about the world that hold a paradigm together, to be abandoned only as a last resort (Lakatos,

1970). In classical philosophy, different ontologies entail particular epistem-ologies (what counts as justifiable knowledge about the world, as opposed to simply beliefs) and methodologies (how such knowledge is to be acquired). By a research programme's socio-spatial ontology, I refer to how society, spatial-ity, and their inter-relations, are taken to be by its practitioners. A socio-spatial ontology shapes both what aspects of geographical reality call for explanation and what an adequate explanation might look like. Feminist and poststruc-tural philosophers have questioned this foundational approach to ontology, preferring to focus on epistemology. Setting aside the nuances of this debate, I clarify here what makes the socio-spatial ontology of geographical thinking about the political economy much more complex than that of mainstream economic thought.

Spatial aspects of these two ontological positions were examined in Chapter 1. Here, I supplement this by considering the societal components. I begin by summarizing the social theory underlying geographical economics, and the socio-spatial ontology that this entails. Notwithstanding the potential diversity of economics, I summarize here the socio-spatial ontology of the Anglophone mainstream, currently hegemonic within this discipline.[2] This constitutes the most effective and cohesive Anglophone social science para-digm of the last century, with well-defined and vigorously defended hard-core propositions. The mainstream's proponents marginalize, as 'heterodox', even deviations that seem relatively minor (at least from the perspective of others). Practitioners of such heresies find themselves largely excluded from the canonical journals and most departments. Indeed, some have concluded that the mainstream view is simply autistic with respect to such alternatives (http://www.paecon.net/HistoryPAE.htm accessed March 10, 2016). The hegem-ony of this epistemological community during the past century has been such that it has proven capable of shaping the world through the enactment of its principles, with the effect of making their plausibility that much more self-evident (Mitchell, 2005).[3]

2.1.2.1 MAINSTREAM (GEOGRAPHICAL) ECONOMICS

Mainstream economics is deemed to have laws that are ubiquitously applic-able, across space and time, amounting to what Helen Longino (2002) calls a monist account of the world. Stephen Gudeman (2001) describes this as a *universal model*:

---

[2] Tony Lawson (2003) does not believe that neoclassical economics qualifies as possessing a social ontology, but it does entail a particular, reductionist, conception of the relationship between individual behaviour and social processes (Barnes and Sheppard, 1992).

[3] The 2008 global financial crisis catalysed considerable debate within Anglophone economics about the adequacy of this paradigm, but there is little evidence that its hard-core concepts have been called into question from within the discipline.

> A universal or foundational model expresses a particular way of organizing knowledge . . . the search for certainty, whose most resilient form is essentialism or foundationalism. . . . Ontological angst is banished by positing an independent bottom level (such as the self-interested individual) from which the remaining 'facts,' 'variables,' or institutions of social life can be derived. . . . In these models, an epistemology becomes an ontology . . . some knowledge is considered . . . requiring no further justification, [providing] the foundation for the remainder. . . . Each level of economy . . . is tied to the final one (foundationalism) that is self-organized or self-sufficient (essentialism). (Gudeman, 2001: 15–16)

When combined with the expectation that theory must be expressed mathematically, the search for a universal model implies that mathematical analysis should derive unambiguous general results (theorems), which typically require extremely unrealistic simplifying assumptions for mathematical tractability.

The foundation for mainstream economics' universal model is exchange based in *micro-foundations* (Weintraub, 1979). The principal place of economic action is the market, where supply confronts demand. Any legitimate economic explanation of markets must be derivable from the rational actions of autonomous, self-interested market participants. In this view, the economy is composed of individuals with more-or-less equivalent social capacities, albeit differing in their preferences and endowments (conventionally assumed to be exogenous to the economy). Markets function as a result of these more-or-less well-informed individuals making self-interested choices to buy and sell. Under conditions of perfect competition, in which individuals are price-takers not price-makers, markets clear and profits disappear, placing the economy in a neoclassical equilibrium that is argued to function like Adam Smith's invisible hand: 'It is not from the benevolence of the butcher, the brewer, or the baker that we expect our dinner, but from their regard to their own interest. We address ourselves, not to their humanity but to their self-love' (Smith, 1776: I.ii.2).

Underlying this argument is the presumption of the *rationality* of means and ends. Individuals are presumed to make rational choices (the means), with the final outcome—ends—also rational (i.e. guided by the market, individuals realize the best outcome possible under the circumstances). There have been many criticisms of the assumptions required to guarantee that the ends (market equilibrium) have these characteristics—assumptions about rationality, perfect competition, and a Walrasian auctioneer (Ormerod, 1994; Fulbrook, 2004; Keen, 2011; Weeks, 2012). With respect to rationality, behavioural economics finally has been able to influence the mainstream, which now acknowledges that real people do not make such rational decisions (Simon, 1956; Tversky and Kahneman, 1986; Camerer, Loewenstein, and Rabin, 2003;

McFadden, 2013). With respect to the Walrasian auctioneer, John Weeks (2013) puts it as follows:

> Nothing remotely resembling a Walrasian market exists in any exchange economy, yet Walrasian markets are taken as the basis of neoclassical competitive theory.... [T]his theater of the absurd is treated as the norm, and what actually occurs as a deviation from that norm, 'false trading', that must be justified.... One has entered a quasi-religious realm, in which the observed world is false, and the world of the imagination is true. (Weeks, 2013: 20, 25)

Even as they have come to acknowledge such criticisms, mainstream economists retain their faith in the rationality and efficiency of market equilibrium outcomes: 'One of the most fundamental... ideas in economics' (Stiglitz and Walsh, 2006: 39). For example, an influential response to the behavioural research among mainstream economists has been to assert 'libertarian paternalism' (Thaler and Sunstein, 2003). If ways of altering incentive structures can be developed to ensure that individuals nevertheless make what the laws of economics determine to be the correct choice, a rational end state can nevertheless be realized. Rationality, at least of the ends, is to be defended at all costs.

Fourth, although by no means universally, the economy is constructed as if it were *vertical*: firms purchase inputs in the form of production factors, convert these into an output (via a production function), and sell this to consuming households. This abstracts from the heterogeneity and interdependent nature of commodity production: The different technologies used between and within each sub-sector of the economy, and how they are inter-related as firms in one sector sell their output as an input to firms in another sector. The study of this relational aspect—its input–output structure—has a very long history in economic thought (Quesnay, 1753–58; Leontief, 1928), receiving particular attention also from location theorists and regional scientists (Isard, 1951). Yet it tends to be set aside as an unnecessary complication by mainstream economists. Taking this relational aspect seriously, however, profoundly affects the conclusions that can be drawn about globalizing capitalism.

Fifth, it is presumed that the economic is *separable* from other aspects of socio-nature, at least for the purposes of analysis. This varies from simply treating nature and culture, etc., as exogenous to the economy (e.g. preferences and 'first' nature are simply given) to the belief that the laws of mainstream economics are foundational for all domains of human action, including our relationship with the more-than-human world (consider, for example, the current popularity of carbon markets as the presumed means to achieve ecological sustainability), and are applicable even in the biological world—equating economic competition with Darwinian selection (Becker, 1973, 1974; Fine and Milonakis, 2009).

From this, it is concluded that capitalism can be treated as if the entire economy approximates a market equilibrium—the *general equilibrium* approach (Walras, 1874; Debreu, 1959). For a long time, proofs of the existence of equilibrium were taken to be sufficient to consider equilibrium as an empirically plausible state of affairs. More recently, particularly after the emergence of dynamical systems theory, economists have come to acknowledge the necessity of demonstrating that any such equilibrium is also stable with respect to perturbations from it. When necessary, additional assumptions have been attached to the theory to guarantee convergence to equilibrium. The most popular of these, behind the 'new' macroeconomics, is rational expectations: The presumption that the expectations of economic actors align with the rational outcome of general economic equilibrium. In this view, actors move the economy toward equilibrium because they know the equilibrium state and act accordingly (Chapter 4). For some, non-equilibrium dynamics are simply not defined (Hoover, 1988) because the question of how agents behave out-of-equilibrium does not constitute a meaningful research topic. A variant on this, from mainstream economists who engage with the possibility of disequilibrium dynamics (cf. Anderson, Arrow, and Pines, 1988; Arthur, Durlauf, and Lane, 1997), is to presume that actors have the mental capacity of Turing machines—an idealized model for mathematical calculation. Markose (2005), for example, asserts that competition will force actors to acquire this decision-making capacity. These examples indicate the lengths mainstream economists are willing to go, in order to defend their hard-core presumption that equilibrium analysis adequately represents reality.

Geographical economists adopt much of this ontology, albeit noting how (exogenous) geographical space complicates the nature of equilibrium. As discussed in Chapter 1, Ottaviano and Thisse (2004) derive the 'spatial impossibility theorem' that market equilibrium in a capitalist space economy cannot satisfy the conditions of neoclassical perfect competition. Under conditions of monopolistic competition, Krugman shows that several equilibria exist, analysing their local stability to determine which are plausibly observable. Geographical economists have shown little interest in tracing disequilibrium dynamics, which is unfortunate. For Krugman's model, Christopher Fowler shows that it is unlikely that seemingly rational actions taken far from equilibrium will drive the space economy toward spatial equilibrium (Fowler, 2007, 2011). Finally, a number of studies acknowledge that geographical differentiation can undermine the welfare claims associated with market equilibria (Brakman et al., 2009; Sheppard, 2012).

To summarize, the core of mainstream/geographical economics is a social ontology presuming a universal theory, methodological individualism with equally empowered actors, the rationality of choice and outcome, a vertical, non-relational economy, and the separability of economy from other aspects of socionature, resulting in competitive market equilibria. Geography is acknowledged to complicate the derivation of equilibrium and its welfare implications, but is exogenous to the economy. In terms of spatiality, as analysed in Chapter 1, the emphasis is on quasi-autonomous bodies and territorial economies, with the different scales linked hierarchically and rooted in the scale of the body; interdependencies between the different units constituting a particular scale are presumed to be mutually beneficial under free market capitalism. This universal model, rational and deductive in its logic and self-sufficient, also implies the existence of ubiquitous 'best' practice solutions (such as structural adjustment).

2.1.2.2 ECONOMIC GEOGRAPHY

As it has evolved, and notwithstanding its previous engagement with location theory, economic geography's ontological framework departs from just about every one of these principles, in part because of its different view of economy and geography. Economic geographers approach the evolving economic land-scape as a 'going concern', characterized by complex dynamic interdepend-encies between agents and the socionatural structures that shape spatial economic systems. At any moment in time, interdependencies between agents are constrained by social and spatial structure, but over time structure and agency are mutually constituted: A socio-spatial dialectic.

This philosophical argument is fleshed out by demonstrating how the spa-tialities of capitalism compound its inherent uncertainty, unintended conse-quences, and contradictions. The spatially extensive nature of production and consumption enhances the challenges capitalists face in realizing profit expect-ations. Individual firms, even when acting rationally, should not follow the dictums of neoclassical economics, and price competition is destabilizing. Within a multi-sectoral economy, both the production of accessibility and technical change enhance the possibilities of unintended consequences and emergent, unpredictable dynamics. Even if capitalist economic equilibrium were achievable, the case for the existence of stable equilibria is profoundly compromised by the politics of production.[4] The following section grounds these claims.

2.2 The Spacetimes of Commodity Production

When it comes to understanding the functioning of the capitalist space economy, geographers typically begin with places of commodity production

---

[4] Capitalism's spatialities also complicate classical Marxian analyses of class conflict (Section 2.2.3).

rather than those of market exchange. By contrast, mainstream economics reduces production to a quasi-exchange, whereby goods demanded (purchased inputs) are transformed into goods supplied (produced commodities) by means of a production function. Further, places of production are socio-political spaces, not simply a technical relation. Transitioning from the labour market to the place of production, 'the money-owner now strides in front as capitalist; the possessor of labor-power follows as his laborer. The one with an air of importance, smirking, intent on business; the other, timid and holding back, like one who is bringing his own hide to market and has nothing to expect but—a hiding' (Marx, 1967 [1867]: 176). Technology cannot be reduced, then, to the ratio of labour to capital, the machinery used, or the size of the production facility. Labour relations, governed by these unequal politics of the workplace, and the micropolitics of work are equally influential in shaping productivity (through the pace of production, the length of the working week or fringe benefits, shirking, etc.).

Thus commodity production occurs in places where individuals with different socio-spatial positionalities encounter one another—with consequences that reflect their unequally empowered positionalities. Notwithstanding rhetoric about possessive individualism, economic actors already are differentiated into broad social groups. Beyond the economic classes identified in classical political economy (owners of labour, capital and land/resources, earning respectively wages, profit/interest, and rent), are differentiations in terms of gender, race, sexuality, and geographic location. Such groupings are by no means given, and individuals are not permanently assigned to them (notwithstanding declining class mobility since the 1980s, particularly in the United States—where occupational mobility closely depends on where you live; Chatty et al., 2014). They are internally heterogeneous social constructs, intersecting with one another, whose nature and persistence evolve relationally as these variegated socio-spatial positionalities are re-enacted. Due to inherited power structures, some of these groupings (capitalists, landowners, heterosexual men, whites, residents of Europe, North America, and Japan) are more influential and prosperous than others (workers, non-whites, women, GLBT, and residents of former colonies and dependencies). Indeed, under globalizing capitalism the broad topology of such differently empowered socio-spatial positionalities has remained remarkably consistent worldwide.

As a consequence, individuals—whose interests, perspectives, and preferences are shaped by socio-spatial positionality—are unequally empowered. Further, as behavioural economics also acknowledges, cognitive capacities and knowledge is necessarily imperfect—all the more so in a geographically extended and differentiated world. Finally, it makes sense to engage in collective action, to the extent that shared socio-spatial positionality aligns those identifying with a particular collectivity and its interests in particular locations and times. In short, individuals' actions shape, but also are shaped by, the social-spatial structures and positionalities in which they find themselves. As Marx quipped, they make a geographically differentiated world, but not one of their own choosing (Plummer and Sheppard, 2006).

2.2.1 Producing Commodities: Time, Space, and the Relational Economy

The process of commodity production necessarily extends across time (unlike the instantaneous transformation of the neoclassical production function) but also across space, a spatio-temporality that must be taken seriously. As political economy always has recognized, there is necessarily a time lag: capital is advanced ahead of production to purchase inputs (even if labour is often paid only after the work has been done), in the expectation of realizing a profit once the commodity has been manufactured, distributed to markets, and sold. Only after this can those advancing capital realize revenues from their investments, and make a profit. In Marx's (1972 [1885]) terminology:

$$M \ldots C \, (LP, MP) \ldots P \ldots C' \ldots M'$$

where M is the money capital advanced, M' is more money (to be realized at the end of the cycle), P is the production process, C is the quantity of commodities (and C' its enhancement), and LP and MP refer to the labour power and means of production utilized during the production process. The rate of profit, which must be generally positive in a going capitalist concern, is calculated per unit of time (typically per annum), and thus depends not only on the difference between revenues and costs but also on the time it takes to realize revenues (turnover time). But production also extends across space: commodities (and inputs) have to be moved from where they are produced to where they should be sold. Transcending space takes time and effort, often entailing enhanced risk because of uncertainties about how to successfully market commodities in distant markets. This challenge of overcoming spatial barriers becomes increasingly important as capitalism globalizes.

Geographers share with (classical) political economists a relational approach to understanding commodity production: firms do not just sell to households but to one another. Instead of the vertical imagery of mainstream economics, where firms typically are imagined to buy inputs and sell to households, in a relational economy firms are directly inter-related and co-dependent, within and across differentiated economic sectors (automobiles, software, and the like; cf. Figure 2.1). As for social classes and groupings, these economic sectors are heterogeneous and overlapping; social constructs that are subject to change. Through the spatial dynamics of globalizing capitalism, a distinctive mix of sectors emerges in each territorial economy—some sectors

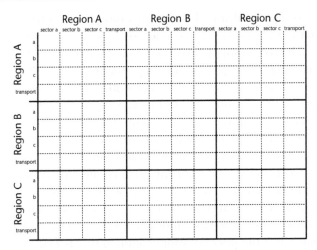

Figure 2.1 A relational (input–output) economy
Source: Author.

found everywhere, others present in just select territories—whose evolution depends also on inter-sectoral connectivities with other regions.

Each sector in a particular region is composed of a variegated population of firms, at times colluding/cooperating with one another and at times competing. They are differentiated, *inter alia*, by size, production technologies, product characteristics, business plans, capital–labour relations, routines, financial and entrepreneurial capacities, and profit rates. Within this variability, certain norms emerge against which firms' performance and profitability are judged. Firms of above average profitability relative to these norms experience windfall profits, with the potential to turn their competitive advantage into an increased market share. Less profitable firms seek to overcome this disadvantage by innovating or (more commonly) imitating more profitable firms. Failure to do so, or to acquire external subsidies, will force firms to exit the sector. Through processes of innovation, imitation, and the birth/death of firms, the distribution of firms and the aggregate regional characteristics of the sector evolve over time, following a path-dependent but by no means deterministic trajectory (Metcalfe, 1988; Webber, Sheppard, and Rigby, 1992). Evolutionary economic geography models such dynamics (Boschma and Martin, 2010), albeit with little attention to firms' co-dependence in a relational economy (Chapter 5) or to intra-firm cultural dynamics (Schoenberger, 1997).

2.2.2 Producing Space: Accessibility as Commodity

Capitalism's relationality is simultaneously spatial and inter-sectoral, each co-evolving with the other, with the spatial aspect of increasing significance under globalizing capitalism. This spatiality has profound theoretical consequences that have been largely overlooked by economists and geographers alike. In purchasing inputs to undertake production, each firm takes into account, *inter alia*, the cost of competing suppliers, costs that depend not only on the factory price but also on transport costs (and time to delivery). The interdependencies connecting sectors and regions are a collective result of these purchasing decisions. Yet transportation and communications are not simply transactions costs. They constitute the vital economic sector of transportation/communications that produces accessibility as a commodity. This commodity is consumed whenever any other commodity (or person) moves, or information flows, between places. Some aspects of this sector (infrastructure, services) operate in (and between) every region; others (transportation/ communications equipment) are produced only in selected regions. The price of accessibility, like the prices of other commodities, is endogenously determined, shaping location, purchasing, and marketing decisions. This sector thus shapes inter-regional economic interdependencies: as it evolves, it produces geographies of connectivity that themselves shape the nature and evolution of territorial economies.

Three particular aspects of the production of accessibility as a commodity are worth drawing out. First, since higher accessibility reduces turnover time, it is a collective benefit for capitalism; thus there is a deep societal incentive to raise productivity in transportation/communications (Sheppard, 1990).[5] Second, the accessibility commodity occupies a unique position within the inter-sectoral economy: it is jointly consumed with most inputs (to ensure their delivery) and all hours of labour (the journey to work, delivery of consumer goods). Third, whenever firms seek to enhance their productivity and profitability, reducing material or labour inputs per unit of output or relocating, such changes entail increased transportation requirements for some regional sectors along with decreased requirements for others, altering the price of accessibility (Sheppard and Barnes, 2015 [1990]). The effects of these changes on overall profitability are unpredictable, but vital. For example, it has been influentially argued that any cost-reducing technical change introduced by capitalists enhances the average profit rate, so long as real wages remain constant (Okishio, 1961; Roemer, 1981). Yet this is no longer guaranteed in a geographically differentiated economy; when some transportation requirements increase, individuals' cost-reducing strategies may have the unintended consequence of *lowering* overall profit rates (Sheppard and Barnes, 2015 [1990]).

---

[5] The state is heavily involved, even in squarely neoliberal economies, because of the collective nature of the benefits of enhanced accessibility; at the same time, the private sector is keen to take over this sector because of the profitability associated with control over accessibility.

This gives rise to a broader proposition: capitalism's spatiality increases the likelihood that individual capitalists' profit-enhancing strategies result in undesirable, unintended consequences. If unintended consequences are common, this raises deep questions about whether it is rational for capitalists, or workers, to pursue their self-interest. Related questions can be raised about the possibility of equilibrium. Obviously, when the pursuit of self-interest has undesirable unintended consequences then the likelihood that such actions result in a beneficial, market-clearing equilibrium is reduced.

Since commodity production takes time, static equilibrium is beside the point. The question becomes whether a dynamic equilibrium will emerge, whereby the commodities produced in one time period exactly match the (growing) demand for them in the next, enabling all produced commodities to be sold and all demands satisfied—expanded reproduction (Morishima, 1973). Dynamic equilibrium is possible in principle: for a given geography of production and technologies and a given distribution of income, it is possible to calculate prices and quantities that satisfy this situation (Marx, 1972 [1885]; Sheppard and Barnes, 2015 [1990]). Such a 'golden age' trajectory (Harrod, 1948; Robinson, 1962: 52) promises unlimited accumulation. Achieving this in practice is highly problematic, however: see Chapter 4. A great deal of faith has been placed by some in the capacity of markets to provide the necessary coordination (Hayek, 1937; Sayer, 1995), a founding parable of the neoliberal revolution. Unless this can be demonstrated for a multi-sectoral, geographically differentiated economy, however, it remains no more than an ideological article of faith.

The second challenge is that any dynamic equilibrium that does emerge is likely to be disrupted by the politics of production. It has long been established that the average profit rate and the real wage are inversely related in a multi-sectoral capitalist economy (Sraffa, 1960; Harcourt, 1972; Marx, 1972 [1867–96]; Morishima, 1973; Roemer, 1981). This can be visualized as a downward sloping wage–profit frontier for any territorial economy (Figure 2.2, Pavlik, 1990). Beyond this, Morishima established what he calls 'the fundamental Marxian theorem': the monetary profit rate is positive only if there is exploitation of workers in labour value terms.[6] Thus the maximum feasible

---

[6] Notwithstanding Marx's claim that labour values frame prices of production, his own multi-sectoral transformation problem runs into difficulties, generating debate to the present day about the logical coherence of labour values (Foley, 2000; Cockshott, 2005; Kliman, 2006; Garegnani, 2012). Yet the neoclassical theory of aggregate production functions is equally problematic (Harcourt, 1972). Neoclassical theory concludes that labour, capital, and land/resources must be compensated according to their marginal productivity, which is inversely related to a factor's relative abundance (under assumptions of diminishing returns). Thus a labour-scarce economy should adopt capital-intensive technologies. In a multi-sectoral economy, however, 'reswitching' is possible: a capital intensive technology may be the best choice when wages are *low*, as well as when they are high (Garegnani, 1966; Pasinetti, 1966; Pavlik, 1990; Sheppard and Barnes, (2015 [1990]).

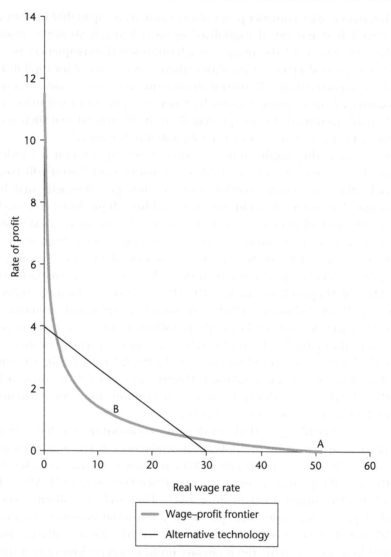

Figure 2.2 The wage–profit frontier in a capitalist economy
Source: Author, based on data from Pavlik (1990).

average real wage (A in Figure 2.2) must ensure that the average labour value of the wage goods consumed is less than the average hours of labour worked to purchase them, with the average profit rate rising as wages decrease from there. Colloquially, the surplus produced annually under capitalism is a pie to be divided between workers and capitalists (but also landlords and resource owners, see Section 3.1.1). This distribution of income is not determined by the marginal product of labour and capital (footnote 6), but reflects the relative political power of owners of capital and of labour power.

In the theory-language of mathematics, the equations determining the relationship between prices, wages, and profits in a multi-sectoral economy require that one variable must be exogenous (Harcourt, 1972; Pasinetti, 1977; Sheppard and Barnes, 2015 [1990]). Conventionally, this unknown is taken to be the wage or profit rate, set by political struggle. This shapes where a particular territorial economy finds itself along the wage–profit frontier (e.g. at B in Figure 2.2), setting the broad distribution of income between wage-earners and profit-makers. No matter where such a resolution lies, however, it is also in the collective interest of capitalists and/or workers to change it. It follows that any such dynamic equilibrium is politically unstable: a 'knife-edge' equilibrium (Solow, 1956). This broad picture carries forward into a capitalist space-economy, where it is profoundly complicated by co-evolving spatialities. Thus it is important to attend to the highly interdependent emergent geographies of value and production.[7]

2.2.3 Spatialities of Value

The above discussion of accessibility and disequilibrium abstracts from the spatial dynamics of value. On the face of it, the default measure of the value of a commodity is market price: this is what economic actors calculate and respond to. Firms seek to set prices for their outputs, at particular locations and times, that maximize their rate of profit over costs of production (Lee, 1998); realized prices reflect also demand in those markets. Non-commodity inputs to production (labour, capital, knowhow, and land) are also valued through market prices (wages, profit and interest rates, and rent). All these prices vary across space and time.

As noted above, the price of accessibility as a commodity, itself varying across space and time, shapes the geography of all commodity prices (and wages). All these prices are interdependent, but for a given geography, set of technologies, and political conditions, the inter-sectoral geography of prices that would prevail in equilibrium can be calculated (Sheppard and Barnes, 2015 [1990]). In the mainstream view, these prices are socially optimal—Adam Smith's invisible hand—reflecting the marginal utility of commodities and the marginal productivity of inputs. From a geographical perspective, however, this representation is profoundly misleading. Reswitching means that the market prices of inputs can depart dramatically from computations of their marginal productivity. The forces of supply and demand shaping realized commodity prices do not simply reflect fully informed freely arrived at rational choices, based on individuals' given (and unobservable) utility functions, but are inflected by power relations, cultural identities, etc. Finally,

---

[7] Known in economics as price/quantity dynamics.

putative equilibria are unstable. Nevertheless, these price geographies feed back to shape subsequent decisions by various economic actors: emergent price geographies shape regional economic dynamics.

The same argument applies to the pricing of inputs: it is common knowledge that rents vary across space for a variety of reasons, but so do wages and profit and interest rates. Such variation can be systematically explained under conditions of equilibrium, but their disequilibrium dynamics remain poorly understood. But, again, such produced geographical differentiation deeply matters. Take, for example, Figure 2.2, which describes a systemic conflict of interest between those whose livelihoods depend on earned wages and those living off profits. As noted, this figure abstracts from the spatial variation of wages and profits, tracking average wage and profit rates (in equilibrium). Spatially differentiated wages, and profits, characteristic of the geography of capitalism, become the basis for conflict among wage earners (workers) in different places, and among capitalists, greatly complicating, and possibly profoundly destabilizing the class politics of capitalism laid out in broad strokes by Marx (Galtung, 1971; Sadler, 2000; Sheppard and Glassman, 2011). Adding landowners and rents (and other markers of socio-spatial difference) only further complicates the political dynamics of capitalism.

Yet there remain profound questions about the adequacy of market prices as a measure of the value of commodities; indeed, Barnes (1996) questions whether value can be adequately quantified at all. Use value, the idiosyncratic measure of what an object means to a particular person in a particular place and time, cannot readily be reduced to a number. As Marx noted, exchange happens because those participating in it must have opposite assessments of the use values being exchanged: at the agreed on price, each values the other person's commodity higher than their own. Market prices are quantitative. Mainstream economics equates them with marginal utility, but this necessitates adopting a profoundly unrealistic socio-spatial ontology. Marx also developed a sophisticated framework of labour value, correcting inconsistencies in earlier versions popularized by Smith and Ricardo. Empiricist reasoning has been dismissive of labour value simply because it offers no direct signals that actors respond to (e.g. Samuelson, 1967). Yet Marx' point was precisely that appearances are deceiving: that surface measures of value elide underlying forces shaping these (exploitation, in his case). Notwithstanding Marx's transformation problem, labour values are no more inconsistent than mainstream economists' arguments about wages and marginal productivity. Further, empirical calculations of labour value closely correlate with equilibrium market prices (exchange values, in Marx's terminology), keeping open the question of the insights into capitalism (and its others) that can be gained from attention to labour value (cf. Henderson, 2013). Labour value also necessarily varies geographically, *inter alia* as a result of incorporating the labour value of accessibility into calculations of the labour value of all commodities, raising questions about the validity of claims made on the basis of Marx's aspatial value theory (Sheppard, 2004).

Since economic geography exceeds purely economic relations, this raises further questions about the adequacy of market prices as the measure of value, and possible alternatives. Consider, for example, nature–economy relations. Here, even mainstream ecological economists argue that market prices are inadequate, advocating for 'full cost' pricing to take into account the environmental costs of commodity production. Yet this presumes that the more-than-human world can and should be commodified, and that—with a corrected pricing mechanism—capitalist markets can enact an ecologically sustainable 'green' capitalism. There are considerable grounds to be sceptical of such claims, and for exploring such alternatives as energy-based theories of value (Georgescu-Roegen, 1971; Costanza, 1980).

2.3 Conclusion

Whether or not mathematics is your theory-language of choice, thinking geographically invokes a very different socio-spatial ontology for understanding globalizing capitalism than mainstream (geographical) economics, coming to very different conclusions about its possibilities. Instead of reductive methodological individualism (and territorialism), geographical thinking implies a socio-spatial dialectic. Its starting point is the spaces of commodity production, not those of the market and consumption. Differently positioned actors encounter one another within these spaces, as capitalist owners hire workers whose only commodity on offer is their labour power. Yet capitalist owners face two challenges as they seek to realize an adequate profit on the capital they advance: Overcoming existing spatio-temporal barriers to production, circulation, and exchange, and managing the political *contretemps* of the production process.

A vital, largely overlooked, aspect of commodity production is how accessibility itself is produced as a commodity. The production of accessibility shapes the connectivities between places of production and consumption, produced connectivities that in turn feed back to alter the conditions of possibility for commodity production in uneven ways. Beyond this, the production of accessibility as a commodity disrupts pre-existing accounts of capitalism. Its complex dynamics undermine the likelihood that rational choice can rule, because it increases the likelihood that the seemingly self-interested choices of individual actors result in unintended consequences—quite different from those envisioned when strategic choices were made. These dynamics also undermine accounts of the politics of production that reduce it to a class conflict: the different socio-spatial positionalities of capitalists and workers—even setting aside other aspects of their social positionality—create complex political geographies in which class differences may be subsumed by geographical differences.

In light of this, it may seem puzzling that the socio-spatial ontology of mainstream (geographical) economics remains so influential notwithstanding its profoundly unrealistic starting point. Some would link that influence to its deployment of mathematics as theory-language, asserting a certain construction of science, but that argument is flat-out wrong. It seems reasonable to conclude, then, that the answer lies in the realm of discourse, representation, and ideology. From its inception, the mainstream ontology of mainstream economics has pitted itself against Marxian analysis (see Preface). Its invocation of perfect competition reassures those bodies and places benefiting most from globalizing capitalism that these gains reflect their diligence and creativity—rationalizing capitalism as the manifestation of Smith's hidden hand and as productive of opportunity for all, everywhere—with the failures of others, elsewhere, attributed to their inadequacies. Given that the prosperous are in a position to circulate the most influential discourses, through the actions of ministries, universities, international organizations, think tanks, etc., it is not surprising that this hagiographic account has become taken for granted.

As discussed in Chapter 1, this account relies heavily on place-based imaginaries of cause and effect. Having established the logical point that the production of accessibility—connectivity—is a key aspect of how really existing capitalist economies evolve, and taking up the argument from Chapter 1 that attention to uneven and asymmetric connectivity opens up the possibility of very different accounts of inequality under globalizing capitalism, I turn now to detailing how the logics laid out here shape capitalism's uneven geographies.

3

The Uneven Geographies of Globalizing Capitalism

In this chapter, I apply the logics of spatialized commodity production, laid out in Chapter 2, to the core processes of capitalism (or any economic system): production, consumption and the distribution of the net surplus. In so doing, I seek to account for why globalizing capitalism—no matter what the relation between the market and the state—is generative of socio-spatial inequality.

3.1 Geographies of Production

I begin with the spatially distributed actions of capitalists. Whereas initial theorizations of the geography of commodity production, heavily influenced by German location theorists and American neoclassical economics, focused on accounting for equilibrium location patterns of firms on an isotropic plain, reinvented by Krugman (Chapter 1), geographers became increasingly dissatisfied with this approach—both for its methodological individualism and its uncritical endorsement of the goal of profit maximization (e.g. Massey, 1973). Yet classical political economy had little to say on the geographies of production (other than rent and land use). Notwithstanding Marx' scattered discussions of space, its theorists basically treated the economy as a national unit for the purpose of analysis—methodological nationalism. This lacuna persists in contemporary heterodox economics.

As geographical political economists set about making sense of emergent spatialities of commodity production, attending to the reciprocal relationship between economy, space, and time, they have tended to focus on bounded territories—industrial clusters, and urban, regional, and national economies. This very much aligns with geographical economics' place-based account of geographies of production; it falls short, I argue, of appreciating the complex spatial dynamics generative of uneven geographical development.

3.1.1 *Territory: Spatial Divisions of Labour*

One approach to understanding territorial economies has been to account for why places come to specialize in different economic activities. At the local scale, land use patterns are seen as determined by rents and the property market. The highly influential mainstream principle is the 'highest and best use' doctrine. In this view, the efficient operation of land markets, absent externalities, will ensure that the rent-maximizing activity is also the best (i.e. most profitable) use for a plot of land (Alonso, 1964; Von Thünen, 1966 [1910]). From the perspective of geographical political economy, this is far too simplistic. First, adopting the focus in this scholarship on differential land rent (cf. Ricardo, 1817; Marx, 1972 [1885]), land use patterns that maximize the average profit rate for capitalists are not identical with those that maximize average rents for land owners (Sheppard and Barnes, 2015 [1990]: chs 6 & 7). This is because rents are calculated spatially, per hectare, whereas profit rates are calculated temporally, per annum.

Beyond this, introducing land ownership complicates the politics of production (and consumption), as there is now a tripartite tradeoff envelope of profits, rents, and wages (Figure 3.1), with capitalists, workers, and land- and resource-owners struggling over the economic surplus. A point such as A in Figure 3.1 expresses nothing more than the mean profit rate, real wage, and rent across a geographically differentiated territorial economy, one outcome

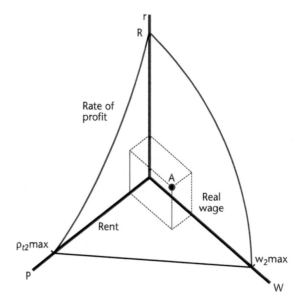

Figure 3.1 The wage–profit–rent frontier
Source: Author.

of such a struggle. Yet any such outcome is subject to destabilization as capitalists, workers, and landlords act individually and collectively, in competition and collaboration, to improve their relative position (with all the caveats about unintended consequences discussed in Chapter 2). Dynamics are complex, given not only the heterogeneous socio-spatial positionalities within each of these groups, but also the complex inter-relations between locally variable rents, wages, profits, and prices (e.g. via monopoly rent, Sheppard and Barnes, 2015 [1990]: 133–5), and aggregate outcomes (i.e. the position on the tripartite envelope).

At larger scales, where land rent is not an important differentiating factor, mainstream conventional wisdom once again proves problematic. Geographical economists utilize theories of inter-regional and international trade (Ohlin, 1933; Krugman, 1991) to explain spatial divisions of labour. In this view, given comparative advantages can be identified for each region, determining patterns of specialization that are optimal for individual capitalists, that region, and the inter-regional economy, creating the necessary microfoundational justification for such a spatial division of labour as a desirable equilibrium outcome. These neat principles—underwriting the free trade doctrine—do not readily work in a multi-sectoral capitalist space economy. For example, the Hecksher–Ohlin rule that labour abundant regions should specialize in labour-intensive economic activities, is disrupted by the possibility of reswitching (Chapter 7).

Rejecting such static equilibrium approaches, geographical political economy seeks to understand how spatial divisions of labour emerge through political, cultural, and economic processes, whereby current specializations reflect the evolution of place-based characteristics, their intersection with broader processes, and the connectivities between territories. As Doreen Massey (1984) has put it, regional specialization:

> can be seen as the product of the combination of 'layers', of the successive imposition over the years of new rounds of investment....The very fact that a region may, through the variety of its economic activities, be embedded in a multitude of spatial structures, each entailing different organization of dominance and subordination, serves to emphasise that it is not regions which interrelate, but the social relations of production which take place over space.... [S]hifts in the dominant spatial division of labour may produce a complete change in the very geographical pattern of spatial differentiation.... Regions themselves are products of these processes. (Massey, 1984: 117–18, 122, 123)

Spatial divisions of labour also have other dimensions than the kind of commodity a region specializes in. There are spatial divisions between different kinds of labour, for example manual vs. cognitive (Hymer, 1972; Dicken, 1992); and with respect to how labour is gendered (Massey, 1994). Again,

49

these divisions are not determined by place-based characteristics (endowments), but emerge from how the differently scaled and networked actions of corporations, state agencies, and workers, as well as broader-scale political economic shifts, intersect with territory.

3.1.2 *Place: 'New' Industrial Districts*

Invoking a spatial division of labour entails, of course, the problematic simplification that regions can be treated as spatially homogeneous. Yet production facilities cluster within sub-areas of any such region, reflecting the profit-maximizing intents of their capitalist owners and the broader politics of production. One somewhat facile way to determine such intra-regional patterns would be simply to down-scale the theory, subdividing into smaller regions and repeating the exercise. Alternatively, it is possible to calculate which allocation of production facilities to plots of land within a region, each producing a given kind of good with a particular technology, would maximize mean profit rates—those that are optimal from capitalists' perspectives (Sheppard and Barnes, 1986; Sheppard and Barnes, 2015 [1990]). But there is no reason to believe that individual profit-maximizing strategies would result in this pattern, and any such equilibrium would be continually subject to disruption as a result of the shifting politics of production and related technological changes. As firms cluster within the region, prices of production will vary from one firm to another in the same sector, reflecting their relative location and production technologies. There is little reason to believe that the resulting prices must be consistent with those utilized to calculate comparative advantage, and every reason to believe that more than one economic sector will emerge as profitable within any given region. In short, neither bottom up methodological individualism nor top-down methodological territorialism suffices: geographies of production are shaped by how individual actions, broader spatial structures, and the shifting politics of production dialectically co-evolve.[1]

A prime example of this kind of dialectical complexity was highlighted in the research into industrial districts and city-regions that emerged in the 1980s (Chapter 1). Seeking to account for why spatial agglomerations can prosper in face of the centrifugal tendencies of globalizing capital, three sets of factors were advanced: transactions costs, tacit knowledge, and the sociocultural context. The first derived from the new institutional economics,

---

[1] Also important here are shifting relationships with the more-than-human world. As captured in Sraffa's terminology of 'the production of commodities by means of commodities', the vast majority of this kind of economic analysis neglects the biophysical world. I take this up in Chapter 8.

where the organization of production and exchange is theorized as a rational choice between decentralized market transactions, corporate hierarchies or networks, on the basis of which market structure minimizes the transactions costs of doing business (Coase, 1937; Williamson, 1985). Allen Scott (1988b) drew on this to explain the emergence of 'new industrial spaces' after the end of the Fordist/Keynesian period of nation-state led development, arguing that the combination of more flexible production technologies (making small batch production more efficient), more demanding consumers (seeking more choice and higher quality), and less rigid labour markets reduced the transactions costs for inter-firm networks relative to large corporations and pure market exchange, encouraging the formation of dynamic spatial clusters of inter-related firms. He saw these developments as reinforcing, again, the increasing returns to agglomeration under which clusters of firms had emerged during the nineteenth century (Marshall, 1890; Young, 1928). Tacit knowledge refers to the exchange of uncodifiable information between participants in a cluster. Such 'buzz' can enhance profitability, has strong cultural and performative elements, and is enhanced by face-to-face communication, favouring agglomeration (Polanyi, 1966; Leyshon and Thrift, 1997; Storper and Venables, 2003). The broader socio-cultural milieu, constituted in the place where firms have clustered, is seen as capable of reinforcing, or blocking, economic dynamism, depending on its assemblage of cultural and governance norms (cf. Signorini, 1994).

Taken together, these overlapping and interdependent factors constitute a complex set of relational assets, whose presence or absence in a place is argued to facilitate or inhibit local competitiveness and economic dynamism (Storper, 1997; Scott and Storper, 2003; Scott, 2006a). More controversially, it was asserted that spaces with the right mix of such assets constituted the locales for a possible post-Fordist 'second industrial divide', where manufacturing would also create high quality and well paid work (Piore and Sabel, 1986; Amin, 1989; McDowell, 1991).[2] One such potential asset that has recently received considerable attention, but also criticism, is the so-called 'creative class', which cities worldwide are developing strategies to attract or locally develop (Florida, 2002; Peck, 2005). This approach also has been generalized to the concept of global city-regions, a worldwide set of megalopolitan agglomerations argued to prosper through a generative combination of such assets. Scott (2006b) argues that these are the emergent nodes around which a new global geography of production is precipitating. The logic of the

---

[2] Remarkably, as attention turned to why certain places are successful, economic geographers turned away from their previous obsession with failure, crisis, and regional restructuring: instead of complementing an understanding of crisis with one of growth, the former was abandoned in favour of the latter (Werner, 2016).

relational assets argument is place-based, however. It seeks to account for economic growth on the basis of emergent local attributes, without attending to the role of a locale's positionality within globalizing capitalism. Further, notwithstanding the wealth of studies arguing that success is correlated with the presence of asset class X, unsuccessful places have not been systematically analysed to confirm the absence of X there, a selection bias favouring the relational assets thesis.

3.1.3 *Connectivity and Positionality: Global Pipelines and Production Networks*

Notwithstanding the emphasis in industrial districts theory on the relational nature of local assets, one vital aspect of relationality was neglected—the relationalities that stretch beyond but nevertheless affect places. Ann Markusen hinted at this, arguing that 'sticky places in slippery spaces' were not simply Marshallian locally-created phenomena, but also emerge through the trans-local strategies of corporations and the state (Markusen, 1996). A subsequent literature finds that 'buzz' is not simply local, but flows through 'global pipelines' (Oinas, 2002; Bathelt and Glückler, 2003). This reflects a broader argument within socio-spatial theory that the nature and economic potential of places also depends on the emergent connections of people and events therein with other places and scales (Agnew, 1987; Massey, 1991; 2005). This broader context is not simply an undifferentiated, 'flat' geography, but has its own centres and peripheries.

Particularly in this neoliberal era of globalizing capitalism, geographies of production are increasingly networked across space. These include the multi-facility networks created and organized by trans-local corporations, whose intra-corporate transactions account for about a third of global trade. Yet there is more to networking than intra-corporate transactions. In what Richard Baldwin (2006) has dubbed 'the great unbundling', commodity production is increasingly functionally and geographically disintegrated. Global commodity chains and production networks are assemblages of corporate branch plants, franchises, original equipment manufacturers, and sub-contractors (Hopkins and Wallerstein, 1994; Gereffi, 1996; Kaplinsky, 2000; Dicken et al., 2001; Coe et al., 2004; Hess and Yeung, 2006). Indeed, Yeung (2012) argues that such corporate networks are an emergent characteristic of Asian capitalism, where territorial economies are particularly affected by exogeneity (i.e. extra-territorial processes). Networks span geographical space without covering it (Leitner, 2004), in ways that may have little to do with geographical proximity (the physical distance between places), making for complex geographies. These networks also are maintained, and shaped, by the emergent but geo-graphically uneven production of accessibility: Logistics networks moving physical objects through material space, and geo-technological communica-tions networks facilitating the movement of information and finance (the Internet, intra-nets, GPS, RFID codes, etc.).

Geographical research has by now established the vital importance of such connectivities in shaping: (i) the fortunes of the various enterprises that they connect together; (ii) the location, technical change, production, and market-ing decisions taken by their owners and managers; and (iii) the places where these activities gather. These are profoundly relational processes: the various nodes (places, firms, actors) depend vitally on their connectivity and position-ality within such networks (Coe and Yeung, 2015). Thinking geographically, places, firms, scales, and connectivities co-evolve.

As discussed in Chapter 1, Anglophone geographers have tended to stress the emergent, flexible, and flattened nature of networks, particularly under the influence of actor-network theory (Latour, 2005; Murdoch, 2005). Yet the bulk of really existing networks already exhibit socio-spatial structure, through which centrally located nodes exert influence over peripheral ones (Dicken et al., 2001). Such intra-network power structures also are not simply an unpredictable emergent feature of flat actor-networks. While occasionally dramatically reshaped, pre-existing power hierarchies act to reproduce them-selves. This is true within the social space of networks, but also translates into marked regularities in geographic space. Even the telecommunications net-works that Castells (1996) envisioned as catalysing an all-embracing space of flows reinforce socio-spatial differentiation (Figure 1.1).

3.2 Uneven Geographies of Consumption

As noted in Chapter 2, a relational approach to the economy reminds us that the consumption of commodities has a strong inter-industrial component—the consumption by firms of other firms' capital goods. Bearing this in mind, I focus here on the more conventional aspect of consumption by households: Consumer goods or 'final demand'. Capital goods consumption is part of the geography of production outlined above. Households come in various sizes, structures and compositions, varying across space and time. In mainstream economic thinking, however, this societal complexity is reduced to individ-uals, presumed to make rational choices about consumption in light of given income levels and preferences. In this mainstream spirit, understanding con-sumption means studying markets for consumer goods: the location of retail-ers, consumers' behaviour, and spatial price gradients. Beginning with central place theory, this body of research moved to a more general consideration of the inherently monopolistic nature of spatial competition, of pricing strat-egies, and of spatial price equilibria (Lösch, 1954 [1940]; Denike and Parr,

1970; Curry and Sheppard, 1982; Norman, 1986; Nagurney, 1987; Mulligan and Fik, 1989; Mulligan, 1995; Plummer, 1996). Yet even within this relatively narrow domain, with consumption reduced to individuals' price-based choices still emphasized in geographical economics, it turns out that the spatiality of commodity production undermines conventional economic wisdom. In a spatially differentiated market, it is rational for retailers to maximize their rate of profit on capital advanced—the measure of profitability favoured in post-Keynesian and Marxian thinking—rather than maximizing total profits as is presumed in conventional microeconomic theory (Sheppard, Haining, and Plummer, 1992; Lee, 1998). Further, reinforcing the spatial impossibility theorem (Chapter 2), the spatial dynamics of competition need not converge on spatial price equilibria (Sheppard and Curry, 1982): such equilibria are at best locally stable, and individual retailers may find it in their interest to disrupt them, taking advantage of spatial price wars (Plummer, Sheppard, and Haining, 2012).[3]

Other economic geographers have examined aspects of market structure, such as the impact of corporate big box stores on retailing, and their capacity to drive small retailers out of business and dramatically reshape geographies of consumption—the where, when, and price of goods sold (Coe and Wrigley, 2009), and the emergence of market structures (Birkin, Clarke, and Clarke, 2002).

But what do we mean by consumer *markets*? In mainstream/geographical economics, markets are conceptualized as having given characteristics, the context within which consumers and producers make their choices. Perfect competition is presented as the ideal; this is where Adam Smith's invisible hand prevails, realizing mainstream economics' social ontology. Yet perfect competition is impossible in a spatially differentiated economy. Monopolistic competition is its closest approximation (and the focus of geographical economics), but other market structures—for example monopsonistic competition, oligopoly, and monopoly—are also possible. The question of how a market structure emerges in the first place is rarely asked in this tradition, although (as noted above) 'new' institutional economists hypothesize that firms rationally choose between corporate hierarchies, markets, and networks, on the basis of minimizing their transaction costs (Williamson, 1985).

By contrast, geographers find approaches developed in economic sociology more compatible with their sense of how capitalism works. This includes attention to how information networks unequally shape participants' ability to take advantage of markets ('the strength of weak ties'), and more generally

---

[3] In the language of mainstream economics, these need not be Nash equilibria.

how markets are always embedded within societal contexts (Granovetter, 1973, 1985; White, 1988; Polanyi, 2001 [1944]; Grabher, 2006). But they are particularly interested in the dynamics of how markets are constructed (Callon, 1986, 1998; Mackenzie, Muniesa, and Siu, 2008; Çaliskan and Callon, 2010). Rather than a exogenous menu of given market structures, markets are regarded as emergent features whose evolution and nature are shaped by theoretical predispositions, ideology, interests, technologies, and geographies (Rose, 1999; Aune, 2001; Mackenzie et al., 2008; Mackenzie, 2009; Mirowski and Plehwe, 2009; Peck, 2010a). For example, perfectly competitive markets are not a given feature of the world, but come into existence if participants believe in their desirability and/or actively create them (cf. Garcia-Perpet, 2007). Similarly, the technologies used to trade securities in financial markets (and the economic theories driving them) produce financial markets in their image (Mackenzie and Millo, 2003). More abstractly, economic theory can construct the economy in a certain way, reflecting influential presumptions about how an economy should be—only then to point to those constructed features as empirical support for the theory (Mitchell, 2005). For example, the neoliberal revolution since the late 1970s has dramatically moved the goalposts in terms of the influence of discursive norms about the effectiveness, appropriate scope, and societal benefits of market-based competition (Fine and Milonakis, 2009). As Keynes (1936) memorably put it:

> Practical men who believe themselves to be quite exempt from any intellectual influence, are usually the slaves of some defunct economist. Madmen in authority, who hear voices in the air, are distilling their frenzy from some academic scribbler of a few years back.[4] (Keynes, 1936: 170)

Thinking geographically about marketization under globalizing capitalism supplements the sociological literature in two ways. First, marketization is examined through the lens of a socio-spatial dialectic—how these processes reflect but also shape the spatiality of exchange. For example, Berndt and Boeckler (2009) examine how the construction of international agricultural markets depends on complex processes of 'b/ordering': the mulitfaceted maintenance and dissolving of geographical and economic borders (including those around waste and the body, Gidwani, 2012; Parry, 2012). Second, is attention to the more-than-human processes bound up in marketization. Marketization depends in part on the affordances of non-human objects (machines, technologies, databases), on the physical properties of the objects being traded, and

---

[4] Of course, there is a geography to this production and performance of economic belief (and its elevation to knowledge); mainstream economic thinking emerges from the global north often with the vision of making it ubiquitous, e.g. the free trade doctrine (Chapter 6).

on biophysical processes shaping both production and exchange. It also depends on the cultural politics of consumption.

3.2.1 *The Cultural Politics of Consumption*

Strategizing about how to come to terms with the circumstances they find themselves in, consumers should not be reduced to rational actors choosing between differently priced alternatives. There is a cultural politics to consumption—the politics of life itself, once households lose or abandon the means to produce their own commodities. First, preferences are never given. They are an emergent feature of the spatio-temporal context within which potential consumers reside. Societal norms about how to live properly and what it means to live well vary across space and time and structure consumers' wants and desires. Second, consumption is rarely an individual choice: Acts of consumption reflect collective, cultural processes, bound up with cultural identity and difference and with societal and political norms. They are shaped directly and indirectly by the social networks individuals belong to, identify with, and aspire to join; consumption simultaneously performs individual identity, hails collective identities that potential consumers associate with, and shapes the kind of subject that s/he aspires to. Second, acquiring basic needs (food, water, and shelter) comes prior to the opportunity to express preferences and desire. To equate the consumption of necessities with preferences and desire is a logical error. Yet basic needs are also not given by, say, biology: They evolve, vary geographically, and reflect changing technological possibilities and cultural norms. Finally, choices are always constrained. A basic 'law of economics' is that demand falls as price increases. But to what extent is this because of the price substitution effects (directing demand to other cheaper goods) and income effects (reduced spending power) highlighted in mainstream theory, and to what extent is it due to how unaffordability and inaccessibility increasingly constrain choice (Sheppard, 1980)?[5] Revealed preference analysis excludes this last possibility by fiat.

Economic and cultural geographers have paid much attention to these aspects, under the label of cultural political economy. In terms of consumption as a cultural performance, they have examined the relationship between retailers' actions (marketing and branding strategies, store location, and design), acts of consumption, and subjectivity/identity. They have paid particular attention to social difference—gender, class, race, age, sexuality, etc.—as both shaping

---

[5] Preferences are the great unobservable of mainstream economics—as foundational as, and less tangible than, labour values in Marxist economics. It is commonplace to infer 'revealed' preferences from individuals' observed choices, but such inference presumes that observed individuals are in fact making unconstrained choices. This is functionalist reasoning, a circular logic whereby the presumed outcome (choice) becomes the explanation (choice-making).

and shaped by retailers' and consumers' actions (Jackson and Holbrook, 1995; Cook and Woodyear, 2012; Mansvelt, 2012). Questions of place, space, scale, and mobility are central to geographical analysis of consumption. Consider, for example, retailers' advertising and branding strategies (Pike, 2011), actions that demonstrably shape consumers' desires by manipulating their identification with and access to consumer goods. These range from invoking place, landscape, and mobility in representations of retailers and their products, to geodemographic marketing (the use of georeferenced databases to target consumers on the basis of their presumed identity and location, Goss, 1995; Harris, Sleight, and Webber, 2005), to digital harvesting of consumers' information for commercial purposes, e-commerce, and location-based services (Zook, 2012).

More avowedly political acts also shape geographies of consumption and production. One example is middle class consumer activism, around such issues as real ale, local and organic food, green production, fair trade, and sweatshop production (Clarke et al., 2007), which has significantly altered production geographies. Notwithstanding controversies about whether intended impacts have been realized, about inadequacies in labelling and monitoring, and about corporate strategies that take advantage of these emergent markets, consumer activism has promoted small-scale production and localized markets, and improved labour relations and less environmentally deleterious production at distant locations (those connected into the networks instigated by such activism). A second example is the governance of consumption. In this historical phase of globalizing capitalism consumption dominates the gross domestic product of the world's wealthiest economies, implying that actions by the state and non-state institutions to promote consumption and elevate consumer confidence have become important to territorial economic policy-making. President George W. Bush's nationwide call on US residents to consume after the 9/11 attacks of 2001, seeking to redress their negative economic impacts and reinforce national identity, is just a particularly trenchant example of a suite of multifaceted, little noticed quotidian practices seeking to elevate 'consumer confidence'. Such politics can be conceptualized in terms of consumer citizenship: residents of a territory asserting their rights as consumers, and being called to accept their responsibility to consume (Soper and Trentmann, 2008).

Geographical scholarship on the cultural politics of consumption challenges mainstream (geographical) economic approaches by demonstrating how cultural and economic processes coevolve, instead of treating culture as exogenous. Yet this research has also tended to focus on the relatively prosperous bodies and spaces of globalizing capitalism—those who have the means to choose. For the abodes and spaces of the 'precariat', a persistent and arguably increasing byproduct of globalizing capitalism (Standing, 2011), consumption is dominated by necessities, with a politics of necessity and desperation as much as of identity and choice. Our understanding of these aspects remains impoverished.

3.3 The Politics of Production

In Chapter 1, I pointed out that commodity production is an inherently political process, a key aspect that is excluded from the mainstream ontology. This politics plays out in two principal domains: work and governance. Together, these shape the distribution of the global economic surplus across bodies and places.

3.3.1 *Geographies of Labour*

A characteristic feature of capitalism is that the work of commodity production depends on a labour market, through which labour's supply and demand are mediated. Geographers have invested much effort in understanding how the geographies of labour depend on much more than supply and demand (Peck, forthcoming). The limited spatial mobility of labour poses immediate spatial bounds on the extent of labour markets, creating spatial segmentation. This segmentation maps fairly neatly, as commuter sheds, onto the extended functional urban areas where non-agricultural employment agglomerates. Of course, further segregation occurs within a commuter shed, along occupational and spatial lines. Within such spatially segmented markets, employment possibilities, and wages, depend on how the functioning of the labour market marries supply with demand, and on the economic prospects of the firms in that region. Technological change also shapes working conditions; shifts from Fordist mass production toward flexible specialization in certain places such as the Third Italy is associated with a flexibilization of labour (Christopherson and Storper, 1989; Wood, 1992). Within any segmented labour market, cultural and political processes also shape economic outcomes. Labour markets are governed by cultural norms shaping who is hired for what kinds of work, conditions of work, and consumption bundles (McDowell, 1991; Massey, 1994). Workers' identities are also constituted in and beyond the workplace (McDowell, 1997, 2003; Wright, 2001, 2006; Werner, 2012a). In terms of politics, local states will intervene with (de)regulatory and governance strategies designed to promote the local economy, often framed as 'improving the business climate' (Peck, 1996).

Yet what happens within territorial labour markets does not just depend on place-based factors. Broader scale processes shape local dynamics—processes involving scale and connectivity. Four kinds of such forces can be identified. First, firms may threaten to relocate production elsewhere because of high labour costs (wages, salaries, fringe benefits, training and education costs), putting pressure on a locality to rein labour costs in. Alternatively, low labour costs may be part of a strategy of seeking to attract inward investment (Harvey, 1989b; Leitner, 1990). Second, shifts in broader scale political discourses and governance norms shape local labour markets. In particular, the rolling out of neoliberal norms has placed enormous pressure on nations, regions, and municipalities to deregulate labour markets and reduce the power of organized labour. Thus Altha Cravey (1998) describes how structural adjustment in Mexico (a form of neoliberalization) dramatically transformed regional labour markets and the gendering of the workforce, as momentum shifted from the masculine, unionized import-substituting industries around Mexico City and Monterrey, to the feminized, low wage Maquiladora export processing zones along the US border. Clearly these first two processes have been mutually reinforcing: the worldwide harmonization of neoliberal policies underwrites the enhanced mobility of production facilities, which reinforces pressure for deregulation. Such broader developments have catalysed local pro-growth coalitions, in which the private and public sector, civil society, and selected labour unions (often in construction) ally to enhance local competitiveness (Logan and Molotch, 1987). Third, often working against such alliances, are pro-worker initiatives: organized labour cooperating across localities to seek better local working conditions or at least stem the tide of deregulation, and other inter-place networking such as the living wage and immigrant rights movements (Wills, 1996; Luce, 2004).

Fourth, is labour migration. Mainstream analysis depicts this as the response to supply–demand imbalances, as individuals seek to optimize the returns to their labour by moving between markets. The ruling presumption is that such imbalances disappear, migrants increase their wages and salaries, and inter-regional inequalities dissipate (Borts and Stein, 1964; Siebert, 1969; World Bank, 2009). Things are very different in practice, however. Migration is highly selective—younger and more pro-active residents are far more likely to migrate, depriving regions of outmigration of their most valuable residents whose relocation benefits destination regions. Labour migration is also far more than a process of individual utility maximization: Chain and circular migration, highly concentrated clusters of inmigrants, complex household livelihood strategies, gender oppression, and environmental degradation as push factors, etc., vastly complicate the process. Migration also co-evolves with political, cultural, and biophysical processes (cf. Chapter 8). Political factors also shape who benefits, and where: wealthy countries raise barriers to migration from the post-colony, except for those wealthy enough to purchase citizenship. Migration is closely bound up with identity formation, and racism, xenophobia, and other forms of discrimination undermine migrants' success and happiness. Processes of climate and environmental change alter the costs, benefits, and trajectories of migration (e.g. people abandoning degraded or flooded environments), but migration also alters human–environment relations in places of origin and destination, and movement itself has environmental consequences.

3.3.2 *Labour Geographies*

Economic geographers also study the ways in which workers/employees shape the economic geographical landscape: For all their power and influence, capitalists are not the only economic actors invested with agency (Mitchell, 1996; Herod, 2001; Mann, 2007). This entails understanding how the inevitable political struggles over profits vs. wages (and rents) play out across various inter-related scales, ranging from places of production to regional- and national-scale organizing movements and labour markets, to global struggles. At the local scale, as Marx pointed out, the spatial agglomeration of workers within a place of production (whether factory, farm, fast food franchise, or financial services firm) enhances the possibility of collective action. Common working conditions help create a collective identity as workers: grievances and achievements are shared, and readily communicated. The farmers' daughters hired into the New England textile firms in the first half of the eighteenth century became among the first US workers to go on strike. This action was motivated by the spatial strategies of textile capitalists, who had built mills in neighbouring towns and threatened to relocate work there unless the women agreed to lower wages. The collective action was successful enough that the women were replaced by waves of immigrant workers (initially from Canada, then Europe)—only for them also eventually to organize and strike. This culminated in a wholesale relocation of less skilled textile operations to the Piedmont region of the southeastern US: a large-scale geographical reshaping of the US national economic landscape that is replicated at global scales today.

Unions, as they emerged, also perforce developed geographical strategies. Within the US, early strikes exhibited strong spatial clustering (Earle, 1982) as organizing followed the shifting geography of manufacturing. Yet unions also learned that successful campaigns involved scale jumping (taking local struggles to the national or international scale) and networking (connecting labour struggles in different places), through mechanisms as varied as linking local unionizing to national organizations and flying pickets—taking the protest rapidly from one facility to the next. Such collective action became increasingly difficult as globalizing capitalism neoliberalized. Indeed, the shift from Fordism to neoliberalism was triggered in part by the very success of unionization in Europe, North America, and Australia/New Zealand. This was compounded by the emergent geographies of globalizing capitalism. The rapid regional restructuring that occurred in 'old' (unionized) industrial regions in the 1970s as Fordism ran out of steam, undermining union power there, was catalysed by the relocation of commodity production to non-unionized, lower wage, less regulated regions and countries (Fröbel, Heinrichs, and Kreye, 1980; Peet, 1987; Amin, 1989). With unions characteristically organized at the national scale, such developments undermined workers' capacity for collective action.

Although the reshaping of the economic landscape triggered by workers' agency has often had the unintended consequence of turning short-term local gains into longer-term regional losses, as plants close and investment switches to less hostile places or more profitable opportunities, labour organizing continues to have its own successes. For example, the closely coordinated nature of contemporary global production networks is vulnerable to collective action: disruption at one node can imperil the entire production line. In addition, unions have found ways to tap into moral debates about child and sweatshop labour, through consumer boycotts and reputational damage to brand names, triggering the international monitoring of working conditions. They also are adapting to the changing geography of labour—organizing in hotels and restaurants, among undocumented migrant workers, etc. (Wills, 1996; Herod, 1998b; Hale and Wills, 2005; Herod and Aguiar, 2006).

The uneven geographies of globalizing capitalism substantially complicate the nature and consequences of labour's agency, however, beyond the spatial struggles between workers and capitalists (Martin, Sunley, and Wills, 1994). First, pre-existing uneven geographical development can pit different groups of workers (and capitalists) against one another. Workers relatively favoured by the current situation, a 'labour aristocracy' (Bettelheim, 1972), may see their interests as more closely aligned with those of local capitalists and the state than with workers in other places (and sectors), working against the interests of such workers and undermining class identity (Galtung, 1971; Hudson and Sadler, 1986; Herod, 1998a). These uneven geographies immensely complicate Marx's 'workers vs. capitalists' narrative (Sheppard and Barnes, 2015 [1990]; Gibson-Graham, Resnick, and Wolff, 2000; Sadler, 2000; Sheppard and Glassman, 2011). Issues of culture and gender also intersect in complex ways with place and labour's agency. Already existing cultural relations in place will affect the emergence there of collective (class) identity, and vice versa. The effectiveness of workplace actions also will depend on the domestic sphere, and vice versa: Domestic partners (usually women) are active on the picket line, and success or failure can shape household dynamics. Finally, territorial political processes shape the nature of union organizing and its relationship to capital and the state. At the local scale, historical dynamics shape the conditions of possibility for collective action (for example, right to work states in the US create a hostile legal environment for plant-based union organizing). At the national scale, capitalist regulatory regimes range from market-oriented models, where unions are seen as an anathema, to corporatist regimes where they are incorporated into national economic planning. It is to these politics that I now turn.

3.3.3 *Geographies of Governance and Regulation*

The conception of capitalism developed here explains why capitalist markets are not the self-regulating institutions, enabling a socially beneficial and harmonious equilibrium outcome, that Adam Smith's invisible hand parable suggests. Given this incapacity, states play a formative role in shaping capitalism, one that varies across space, time, and scale (Polanyi, 2001 [1944]; Brenner et al., 2003; Jessop and Sum, 2006). On the one hand, states seek to manage incipient and emergent spatio-temporal capitalist contradictions and crises that emerge as a result of the conflicting interests between the owners of labour power, capital, land, and resources. (Of course, conflicting interests do not automatically result in political contestation; shared positionality must be complemented by shared identity.) In this vein, democratic governments find themselves having to mediate the interests of those seen as responsible for guaranteeing economic growth and prosperity (owners of capital and resources), and those who supposedly re-elect them (owners of labour power). Offe (1984) conceptualized this as states being caught between the conflicting imperatives of accumulation and legitimation, but there is more to states than this, of course, and more to governance than states.

First, states are also the arenas where cultural and identity politics play out at the national scale, in ways that greatly complicate the class politics emphasized in Marxian state theory. This is much more than attending to the interests of landowners. Second, states also have come to acknowledge the significance of a third, more-than-human imperative of socio-ecological sustainability: The 'second contradiction of capitalism' (O'Connor, 1991; While, Jonas, and Gibbs, 2010). Third, states exhibit a certain degree of autonomy from the economy: They do not simply mediate others' conflicting interests but accrue the power to shape these, and thereby capitalism. Fourth, states are complex and heterogeneous assemblages of politics, the law, and bureaucracy that cannot be conceptualized as a unitary actor responding to well defined imperatives. States are complex organisms, with multiple and often conflicting mandates and roles. Much of their everyday power resides in an alphabet soup of state agencies, sometimes in synch but often at odds with one another, but also with the politicians who represent the public face of the state, and the legal provisions and mandates they are supposed to implement.

Finally, states are geographically complex and heterogeneous. On the face of it, nation-states are national territorial entities, exerting defined powers over citizens of a clearly demarcated nation-state. There is agreement about what constitutes national sovereignty, a European conception formalized in the 1648 Treaty of Westphalia, although the domestic organization of these powers depends on national constitutions. Yet it is a mistake to conceptualize states as sovereign rational actors, each with their own territory to govern, as in the realist school of international relations theory. John Agnew has dubbed such thinking the territorial trap; Brenner calls it methodological nationalism (Agnew, 1994; Brenner, 2004). States also are multi-scalar territorial enterprises, with hierarchies of sub-national states accorded constitutionally defined powers over sub-national territories. State-like institutions can also be constructed above the scale of the nation-state (the European Union). Further, as discussed in Chapter 1, these various scales and their inter-relations are social constructs that are subject to revision (cf. Swyngedouw, 1997b; Brenner, 1999).

Yet even this multi-scalar extension of the national territorial state model fails to adequately capture the spatialities of government. On the one hand, territorial states at every scale seek to extend their influence beyond their boundaries, through extra-territorial geopolitical and geoeconomic strategies (e.g. Smith, 2004; Phelps, 2007; Agnew, 2009). On the other hand, extra-territorial connectivities shape the actions of territorial state institutions, as in debates about how states should govern extra-territorial actors acting and residing in their territories (immigrants, inward direct investment, supra-national institutions).

These geographies are further complicated by the many ways that governance exceeds states, undertaken also by non-state actors. Governance, conceptualized as the creation of conditions for ordered rule and collective action (Stoker, 1998), is exerted *inter alia* by supra-national institutions (the UN, Bretton Woods institutions, the WTO, etc.), by non-government organizations, by corporations, and by non-state political entities (social movements, paramilitary networks, etc.). The power exerted by such non-state actors is not rooted in a territorial mandate, in the first instance, even though the actions of supra-national institutions are shaped, unevenly, by their member-states, and corporate identities often reflect their geographical origin. Indeed, in this neoliberalizing phase of globalizing capitalism their power comes from transcending the geographical reach of states through the construction of trans-national networks.

Notwithstanding such complexities, geographical political economists have put much of their effort, until recently, into making sense of the shifting and variegated nature of multi-scalar territorial state governance (e.g. Storper, 1997; Brenner, 2004). Since capitalist dynamics, *inter alia*, entail an ongoing political contestation over the surplus produced by the economy, how does this play out in different territorial contexts? Seeking to understand how Keynesianism ruled for as long as it did in the west, took different forms in different countries, was substituted for by developmental states in Asia and

Latin America, only to enter a terminal crisis in the late 1970s, geographers turned to regulation theory for answers (Aglietta, 1979; Dunford, 1990; Jessop, 1990).

Regulation theorists argue that nation-states face options as to how to organize the necessary relationship between the public and private sectors under capitalism, by combining a regime of accumulation (how commodity production is undertaken) with a mode of social regulation (how the state regulates the market to manage the national balance between supply and demand) into a regulatory ensemble (Lipietz, 1986). The ensemble governing a territorial economy varies over time, since no ensemble can persist forever; sooner or later it finds itself struggling with emergent crises of capitalism that it is no longer able to manage. This triggers a chaotic phase of experimentation until an ensemble emerges with the capacity to resolve or displace the current crisis, which then becomes the basis for the next historical phase (Lipietz, 1986). This is clearly not an equilibrium-oriented conception, whereby the ensemble is chosen for its superior properties; this conceptualization amounts to a complex, dynamic evolutionary system, out of equilibrium and with periodic crises that can become bifurcation points, with path-dependence and unexpected shifts in trajectory. In this view, Fordism/Keynesianism was a stable ensemble in the West until the mid-1970s, whereby national-scale regulation of the economy was the norm. It then entered a period of crisis reflecting both internal contradictions (the rising power of organized labour relative to national capitalists, reducing profitability), and external destabilization (the relocation of production to lower-cost locations outside these states). After a period of crisis, neoliberalization emerged as the new ensemble: A socio-economic shift from Keynesian demand management to 'supply-side economics', but also a scalar geographical shift (Chapter 1). With deregulation and privatization and the opening of national borders to economic flows, national-scale regulation of the economy diminished (by no means disappearing), with supra-national regulation and sub-national economic clusters (industrial districts, etc.) becoming increasingly important.

Yet these ensembles also exhibit geographical variation, with different national contexts formulating different versions of Keynesianism (Brenner, 2004) and neoliberalism (Peck, 2010a), also outside the first world economies whose shifting norms set the terms of reference by which other countries are judged (Lipietz, 1987; Webber and Rigby, 1996; Glassman and Samatar, 1997; Yeung, 2014). They may also vary across scale, between local and nation-states, depending also on national rules governing central-state relations (Tickell and Peck, 1992; Painter, 1997).

For the past fifteen years, geographical political economy has applied this approach to making sense of how, beginning in the 1980s, globalizing capitalism suddenly, unexpectedly, and ubiquitously shifted from state-led development (Keynesian, developmental, and socialist states) to neoliberalization. This includes analyses of the nature and diffusion of neoliberal governance, debates about how neoliberalism came to replace seemingly impregnable state-led modes of regulation, why the anti-state rhetoric of neoliberalism does not accord with the centrality of certain state roles within neoliberal ensembles, the persistence of activities contesting neoliberalism, and why neoliberalism 'in the wild' is persistently geographically variegated—never converging on a pure, ideal-typical neoliberal model (Rose, 1996, 1999; Larner, 2000; Brenner and Theodore, 2002; Peck and Tickell, 2002; Harvey, 2006, 2007; England and Ward, 2007; Leitner, Peck, and Sheppard, 2007a; Hart, 2008; Brenner, Peck, and Theodore, 2010; Peck, 2010a, 2010b; Peck, Theodore, and Brenner, 2012). Eschewing equilibrium-oriented thinking, the focus is on processes of change rather than states of the world. Some, concluding that these changes continue largely unchecked even after the 2008 global crisis, stress the ubiquity of neoliberalization, notwithstanding variegated trajectories and outcomes (Brenner et al., 2010; Peck, 2010a). Others, concerned that this conceptualization reduces the world to variants of neoliberalism thereby leaving no space for imagining alternatives, emphasize contestation and the significance of smaller-scale alternative practices, under the radar now but forming a rich ecosystem of experiments to draw on as neoliberalism reaches its spatio-temporal limits (Gibson-Graham, 2006; Leitner et al., 2007b; Gibson-Graham, Cameron, and Healy, 2013).

This geographical approach avoids the simplified categorizations of sociologists and political scientists who study 'varieties of capitalism', an approach that seeks to classify national political economies in terms of their closeness to two ideal-typical poles—free market (US/UK) capitalism and coordinated (German/Japanese) capitalism—presuming that these first world exemplars suffice to capture the range of possibilities available to all nations. But it is also important to move beyond a national territorial imaginary. Theorizing scale, geographers study how supra-national scale processes, institutions, norms, and policies (e.g. Structural Adjustment Programs, post-Soviet 'shock therapy', the EU single market, WTO regulation of 'free' trade) helped propagate neoliberalization to most nation-states. They also examine how, within nation-states, such principles have been downloaded to local states, cities, and even neighbourhoods, as well as how local-scale actions shape larger scales. Theorizing networks and connectivities, they study 'policy mobilities': how neoliberal principles, for example, became 'best practice' policies that take flight, rapidly moving between localities and mutating en route (Peck, 2009; Peck and Theodore, 2010). Important debates remain, particularly about whether neoliberalism has become ubiquitous, whether political economic accounts suffice, and whether and how neoliberalization is contested (Barnett, 2005; Leitner et al., 2007b; Ong, 2007; Barnett et al., 2008). There is an active interest in the spatialities of social movements contesting neoliberalization, although the impact of such contestations on economy–state relations remains understudied (Featherstone, 2008, 2012; Leitner et al., 2008; Routledge and Cumbers, 2009; Sparke, 2013). Yet the broad contours of the uneven geographies of this shift from nation-state regulation to neoliberal governance are now quite well understood.

3.4 Conclusion

With respect to geographies of commodity production, since the 1980s both geographical economists and economic geographers have stressed the importance of territory and place, including their inter-scalar relations. This tends to reinforce place-based accounts of growth and decline, wealth and poverty, even as globalizing capitalism entails ever-increasing uneven and asymmetric connectivities. Global production networks now receive considerable attention, reflecting the dominance of unbundled trans-national production. Notwithstanding the emergent characteristics of all complex networks, there is a persistent structure to production networks that positions some places, firms, and economic sectors as central and powerful, shaping events elsewhere, and others as peripheral and marginal. From this perspective, explanations of economic success and failure cannot be reduced to the characteristics of places, firms, and bodies; connectivity-based explanations deserve at least as much attention. Turning to consumption, an emergent area of research, work examining bodies, places, and consumption underlines how consumption is a cultural political process, shaped also by geographical differentiated processes of marketization—the discourses, technologies, and geographies through which markets take form.

These economic processes are bound up with the politics of production. Capitalism is far from the harmonious, self-governing phenomenon stressed by its proponents. Households provide the labour necessary for commodity production, even if this is not their primary purpose (Chapter 8). Again, we observe complex geographies and uneven connectivities: Labour markets must be organized over space and time, connected through such processes as wage rate differences, and the migration of households and firms. Yet workers (supported by households and communities) are also political agents, whose strategies to enhance their share of the net surplus created by commodity production involve connectivities of labour organizing, shaping those of commodity production.

In terms of governance and regulation, marked differences have been observed in state–market relations over time but also over space—geographically variegated and historically differentiated capitalism. There is an ongoing process of experimentation with governance models, seeking to align the contradictions of globalizing capitalism with the political interests of territories. Again, connectivities reflect and shape these variegations. Hegemonic nation-states, and global institutions marching to the same drummer, seek to impose ubiquitous global governance norms, through the downscaling of global discourses and the transfer of norms between places via policy mobilities. These impositions encounter resistance and counter-mobilities—both from states with the power to resist, and from grassroots more-than-capitalist practices.

This attention to the uneven geographies of globalizing capitalism entails the presumption that temporality also matters—equilibrium is the exception rather than the rule. Yet economic geographers have been less interested in conceptualizing spatio-temporality than spatiality, an unfortunate lacuna. The two following chapters take up this challenge.

4

Capitalist Dynamics: Continuity, or Crisis?

Globalizing capitalism is far from the harmonious, static equilibrium-oriented economic representation that has been bequeathed to society by mainstream economic theorists. As noted in Chapter 2, the bulk of equilibrium-oriented accounts of a capitalist space economy evacuate time altogether from accounts of capitalism, focusing on the conditions of possibility for static spatial equilibrium.[1] There exists an enormous, contradictory literature on the dynamics of capitalism, offering very different accounts of its ability to redress potential contradictions. In this chapter, I review these accounts before turning, in Chapter 5, to the question of spatio-temporality. In Section 4.1, I examine how mainstream economic theorists seek to establish conditions of dynamic (spatial) equilibrium stretching infinitely into the future, or examine cyclical behaviour with respect to putative equilibrium cycles. Here, temporality is linear and ahistorical, the emphasis being on continuity and the possibility of smooth capitalist development along a 'golden' growth path. Marxian and post-Keynesian political economists take temporality more seriously, emphasizing the crisis-ridden nature of capitalism. Neither literature, however, contemplates the possibility that the uneven geographies of globalizing capitalism might complicate capitalist dynamics.

4.1 Atemporal Capitalist Dynamics

4.1.1 *Dynamic (Spatial) Equilibrium*

Dynamic economic equilibrium describes a growth path along which the conditions of static equilibrium are reproduced: a path of untrammelled accumulation. Marx' theory of extended reproduction was exactly this kind

---

[1] The multiple equilibria identified by geographical economists imply that there is a path dependence to capitalist dynamics, which Krugman (1996) misleadingly dubs self-organization. Here, temporality is reduced to initial conditions.

of model of putative dynamic equilibrium—albeit as a thought experiment, not a claim about the nature of capitalism (Marx, 1972 [1885]; Morishima, 1973). He (like Ricardo) believed that capitalism would eventually stagnate (Section 4.2). Twentieth-century economists were more optimistic, laying out conditions under which capitalism could continue indefinitely. Drawing from Keynes, Evsey Domar and Roy Harrod argued that this would be possible if savings in any given year equal investment and are a constant proportion of national income (Domar, 1946; Harrod, 1948). Such a capitalist economy would have what Harrod dubbed a warranted growth rate, dependent on productivity and the savings rate, that enables dynamic equilibrium. Markets clear across time, with everything produced now being consumed later; but production technologies were assumed to be unchanging. Kaldor (1957) proposed a technical progress modification, whereby the productivity of labour grows with the capital–labour ratio.

Robert Solow (1956) pioneered a neoclassical exogenous model of growth in which technological composition (the ratio of labour to capital) was an outcome of profit maximizing behaviour by capitalists, determined by an aggregate production function. The Cobb–Douglas production function he used does not countenance increasing returns to production (unlike Harrod), so he introduced technical change in the form of an externally defined time parameter governing the rate of growth. Here, capitalism's warranted growth rate depends on both the speed of technical change and the population growth rate, profits are zero (net revenues are reinvested in growth), and individual agents optimize returns. Paul Romer (1990) influentially extended this, catalysing a family of endogenous growth models in which increasing knowhow ('human capital') generates increasing returns (unlike the diminishing returns and perfect competition of neoclassical theory) and non-zero profits. Romer's model is restricted to dynamic equilibrium paths that can be derived from microfoundations, assuming 'well behaved' utility and production functions.[2] The only controversial question, at least for some mainstream economists, is whether state intervention is necessary to achieve the socially optimal growth path.

Whereas Marx' thought experiment embraced a multi-sectoral macro-economy, the Harrod–Domar and the Solow–Romer approaches ignore this complexity. For neoclassical growth theory in particular, ignoring this poses two deep problems. First, there is no independent means of measuring the quantity of capital—one of the variables in the production function—without knowing the rate of profit (the price of capital). But the profit rate itself depends on the quantity of capital, creating an irresoluble paradox (Robinson, 1953–54). Further, as discussed in Chapter 2, aggregate production

---

[2] 'Well behaved' is almost synonymous with assuming production functions that are not plagued by the reswitching challenge to neoclassical theory (see Chapter 2, cf. Burmeister, 1980).

functions are not adequate for describing the relationship between the quantity and price of production factors—diminishing marginal returns to a production factor are not guaranteed. Building on these critiques, political economists examined the prospect of dynamical equilibrium for a multi-sectoral economy. Generalizing Marx, Michio Morishima (1973) outlined the very strict conditions under which dynamical equilibrium is possible for a multi-sectoral economy: a unique combination of relative output levels across sectors that is consistent with dynamical equilibrium. This avoids the two problems noted here (in a multi-sectoral economy capital is broken down into its physical components), and can be extended to the space-economy (Sheppard and Barnes, 2015 [1990]), but again assumes that production technologies are unchanging. Pasinetti (1981) adds a constant rate of technical change in each sector (all inputs declining at the same rate, per unit of output), a constant rate of growth of demand for each consumer good, and population growth, deriving complex conditions under which dynamical equilibrium is possible. In all such conceptions of dynamic equilibrium, time is reversible and not historical: the models can be run forward or backward in time, as they have no emergent properties.

A lingering but vital question is whether such dynamic equilibria are stable—can they be arrived at from an economy initially in disequilibrium? How do agents identify and move toward the dynamic equilibrium that mainstream economists represent as capitalism's optimal outcome? One trick, long popular in macroeconomics, is rational expectations: Simply assume that individual economic agents can construct complete knowledge about the future (Muth, 1961; Sargent and Wallace, 1975; Pesaran, 1987), and/ or know where the equilibrium lies. Concluding that it is in their interest for the economy to be in equilibrium, knowledgeable agents will act to ensure that equilibrium is achieved. The extreme dynamical complexity of capitalism would seem to invalidate the possibility of rational expectations. Yet Markose, for example, argues that this does not pose a challenge for agents, advancing 'theoretical reasons that market agents can be assumed to have full computational capabilities of Turing machines and why in no small measure the non-computable environment that necessitates the inductive methods of inference and problem solving . . . are endogenously generated by the activity of such agents' (Markose, 2005: F165). A second highly influential rationalization of equilibrium is the efficient markets hypothesis: assuming that prices are dynamically random, that is, each price change is independent of the past, actual market prices are presumed to incorporate all the information necessary for agents to realize equilibrium (Fama, 1970, 1991). '[A]ny and all information about prices is reflected in the prices, and new information is instantaneously reflected in the prices, and all agents operating in a market are not only fully rational but are also in command of complete information about the market and about other investors and their strategies . . . : you cannot beat the market' (Rickles, 2007: 956–7).

The rational expectations and efficient markets hypotheses have been profoundly undermined by the 2008 financial crisis. If Federal Reserve 'guru' Alan Greenspan and the vast majority of economists, professionally trained to understand the economy, failed to predict this crisis, it is profoundly implausible to assume that the average economic agent knows the future. The efficient markets hypothesis, the theoretical basis for the neoliberal supposition that financial instruments and institutions function best when deregulated, is 'marred only by being quite wrong' (Shalizi, 2002: 391).

Even political economic theories face similar problems of realizing convergence to dynamical equilibrium. With respect to individual agents, Duménil and Lévy (1987, 1991) examine the 'cross-dual' dynamic interdependence of quantities of commodities and their prices, asking whether convergence happens. They find that convergence requires the unrealistic, quasi-rational expectations assumption that actors already know the equilibrium conditions and act with respect to these. More broadly, even if the economy were to find itself in dynamical equilibrium, this would be destabilized by the politics of production (Chapter 2).

Interestingly, the doyens of the competing economic discourses shaping twentieth-century economic policy during growth and crisis—Keynes and Fordism on the one hand, and Hayek and neoliberalism on the other—shared a deep suspicion of such equilibrium-based mathematical reasoning. Keynes and Hayek both believed that agents have to deal with the radical uncertainty of an unknowable future (cf. Knight, 1921), but nevertheless were confident in the resilience of capitalism in the face of uncertainty. Their disagreement was about how to ensure resilience (Keynes, 1936; Hayek, 1937; Butos and Kopl, 1997). Keynes averred that uncertainty causes agents to hoard money (as many private sector institutions have done since 2008), requiring the state to intervene to create work and stimulate demand in a crisis. During the Great Depression, Roosevelt's Fordist New Deal did exactly this; Krugman advocates for this as the alternative to austerity politics today. Hayek argued that competitive markets are the only way to finesse uncertainty, a position formalized in Fama's efficient markets hypothesis and used to justify austerity.

These various mainstream perspectives on capitalist economic dynamics, notwithstanding differences, share the mainstream ideology that capitalism is the least worst mode of production. This drives what counts as a legitimate theory: theories of how capitalism works, rather than why it does not, become plausible (and politically attractive to prospering bodies and places). The strong version of this is to believe in the plausibility of micro-foundations-based dynamic equilibrium; the weaker version is that crisis happens, but is not fatal to capitalism's promise.

4.1.2 *Theorizing Capitalist Cycles*

The proposition that the dynamics of capitalism are cyclic dates back to the nineteenth century, not only to Marx' notion of periodic capitalist crisis (Section 4.1.1), but also to such mainstream theorists as Juglar and Jevons (for a brief survey, see Medio, 2008). Briefly, cycles of widely varying period-icity have been proposed, from 3–4 year Kitchin cycles in business inventories, to business (Juglar) cycles of 8–10 years, Kuznets demographic swings (13–15 years), Kondratieff/Schumpeter cycles of ~50 years, and world historical cycles (Arrighi, 2010). Theories of economic cycles can be aligned into two clusters: mainstream and political economic.

Mainstream theorists represent cycles as up- and down-swings of constant periodicity around economic equilibrium, driven by such factors as time lags in or imperfect information, shifts in tastes, energy prices, terms of trade or taxes, the lumpiness of fixed capital, immigration waves, and clusters of innov-ations that the economy must adjust to (e.g. Schumpeter, 1939; Freeman, Clark, and Soete, 1982). Business and Kondratieff cycles have received particu-lar attention, generating controversies concerning their causes and existence. Mainstream explanations have been offered in the spirit of both Austrian economics (Hayek)—stressing the responsiveness of entrepreneurs and mar-ket mechanisms to disequilibria caused by uncertainty, and New Classical (rational expectations) economics—stressing the persistent effects of random shocks that generate cyclical behaviour notwithstanding general equilibrium, complete information and rational action (van Zijp, 1993). As Medio (2008) puts it:

> [T]here has recently been a revival of what we would call the 'static prejudice' in economics, whose most explicit expression is perhaps 'equilibrium business cycle theory'. In a nutshell, this theory describes the working of the economy by means of a model whose deterministic part is characterized by a unique, stable equilibrium. A stochastic part is added to it which depends on imperfect information of economic agents, whose decisions are therefore mistaken. (Medio, 2008)

For example, monetary theories of the business cycle stress agents' incomplete and asymmetric information, generating fluctuations around equilibrium (Helwig, 2008), and Francois and Lloyd-Ellis (2003) model cycles with respect to equilibrium based on delays in capitalists' decisions to implement research and development.

Within political economy, theorists stress that cycles are not defined with respect to economic equilibrium and often display imperfect periodicity. Kalecki (1968) emphasizes capitalists' investment decisions as driving the business cycle. Minsky (1993), theorizes the endemic nature of financial crises due to the over-expansion of credit in boom times (2008 has been described as a 'Minsky moment'). Others highlight under-consumption triggering a downturn, due either to income inequality (Hobson, 1922) or to capitalists' overoptimistic 'animal spirits' in boom periods (Keynes, 1936). Goodwin (1967) theorized completely endogenous capitalist cycles due to the interaction of capital accumulation with labour market dynamics—a regular cycle that circles around but never approaches a hypothetical unstable equilibrium. Mandel (1995), in the spirit of Marx, emphasized capitalist long waves with a regular twenty-five-year upswing, terminated by falling profit rates, and a downswing of uncertain periodicity driven back upward by political processes. Arrighi (2010) proposed four world-historical capitalist cycles since the fourteenth century, each ending in a flurry of financial speculation, successively centred on Genoa, Amsterdam, the UK, and the US (interpreting the financialization culminating in the 2008 crisis as the putative end of the US phase of global capitalist hegemony, with the centre shifting to China).

4.2 Theorizing Capitalist Crisis

Whereas mainstream economics' faith in the self-regulating capacity of markets and the pervasiveness of equilibrium placed the question of capitalist crisis more-or-less off limits, the opposite is the case for post-Marxian political economy: the old joke is that Marxist theorists of capitalism have predicted eight of the last three crises. In the aftermath of globalizing capitalism's signal 2008 financial and economic crisis, interest in crisis theory has been dramatically reinvigorated. Was this a temporary displacement from equilibrium, of unusual amplitude: a 'perfect storm' of market imperfections and irrational behaviour? Was it the next downturn in long-run Kondratieff or Kuznets cycles, after that of 1929? Or is it evidence for the inherent, possibly fatal, likelihood of crises within globalizing capitalism? Rejecting the first of these interpretations, a family relationship can be noted between some theories of capitalist cycles (e.g. those of Mandel, Kandratieff, or Goodwin) and those of capitalist crisis. Crisis theory concerns itself with two kinds of potential crisis: endemic crises that periodically plague capitalism (also the domain of cycles theorists), and the possibility of an existential crisis, fatal to the reproduction of capitalism.

One clear difference between crisis theories and those discussed in Section 4.1, however, is how temporality is conceptualized. Whereas theories of capitalist cycles presume temporal regularity, with capitalist fluctuations governed by cycles of given frequency and amplitude, crisis theory conceptualizes temporality as historical and evolutionary. Future crises, even when driven by the same processes, are an emergent outcome that is contingent on the nature and resolution of previous crises.

As for mainstream theories of capitalist dynamics, the ongoing, ever-fraught debates about the nature and causes of endemic capitalist crisis can be traced back at least to the nineteenth century. Thus contemporary interpretations of the 2008 crisis rework the question of whether capitalist crisis is caused by under-consumption, over-accumulation, disproportionality, or the tendency of the rate of profit to fall (TRPF).[3] Theories of *under-consumption* predate Marx (Mandeville, 1795; Malthus, 1820; Sismondi, 1827), and are based on the notion that labour is not paid the full value added of the commodities produced. It follows that household demand cannot match the supply of commodities, implying that sooner or later some produced commodities (consumer goods) will remain unsold, and profits unrealized. Marx himself argued, drawing on his calculations about expanded reproduction (1971; Marx, 1972 [1885]), that underconsumption theory should be rejected as it entails an overly narrow conception of capitalism. It does not account for the significant sales to other firms—capital goods—purchased with the profits not otherwise paid to workers. Dynamical equilibrium is always possible in principle—but not necessarily in practice (Marx was equally critical of Say's Law—that supply always creates it own demand—implying that over-accumulation is impossible.)

Over-accumulation has received a lot more traction. Friedrich Engels (1962 [1878]) initiated this line of argument, identifying a crisis-ridden 'anarchy of production' in capitalism:

> [T]he ever increasing perfectibility of modern machinery is, by the anarchy of social production, turned into a compulsory law that forces the individual indus- trial capitalist always to... increase its productive force.... The enormous expan- sive force of modern industry... appears to us now as a necessity for expansion, both qualitative and quantitative, that laughs at all resistance. Such resistance is offered by consumption, by sales, by the markets for the products of modern industry. But the capacity for extension... of the markets is primarily governed by quite different laws.... The extension of the markets cannot keep pace with the extension of production. The collision becomes inevitable, and as this cannot produce any real solution so long as it does not break in pieces the capitalist mode of production. (Engels, 1962 [1878]: 379)

Hilferding (1981 [1910]) elaborated on this theme. 'For Hilferding, over- investment is a result of capitalist misjudgment. The deficiencies of the capit- alist system have been reduced to the subjective irrationality of capitalists.... Hilferding identifies the deficiencies of capitalism at the level of the relations between capitalists, and not at the level of the class relation' (Clarke, 1994: 48). Others have contributed to this line of debate, albeit sometimes confusing

---

[3] I am indebted, here, to Simon Clarke's (1994) comprehensive analysis of these theories.

over-accumulation with under-consumption (Kautsky, 1901–2, 1910 [1892]; Sweezy, 1942; Luxemburg, 1951 [1913]; Baran and Sweezy, 1966).

Analysing the 2008 crisis, John Bellamy Foster and Harry Magdoff adopt Sweezy's position: '[A] realistic assessment of recent economic history is best conducted through a framework that focuses on the interrelationship between the stagnation tendency of monopoly capital and the forces that to some extent counter it' (Foster and Magdoff, 2009: 19). Harvey argues: 'The problem this time is more like the 1930s: underconsumption, or a lack of effective demand in the market' (Harvey and Wachsmuth, 2012: 270). Anwar Shaikh (2010) stresses over-accumulation:

> [A] new boom began in the 1980s in all the major capitalist countries, spurred by a sharp drop in interest rates which greatly raised the net return on capital.... Falling interest rates ... lubricated the spread of capital across the globe, promoted a huge rise in consumer debt, and fuelled international bubbles in finance and real estate.... At the same time, in countries such as the US and the UK there was an unprecedented rise in the exploitation of labour, manifested in the slowdown of real wages relative to productivity. All limits seemed suspended, all laws of motion abolished. And then it came crashing down. (Shaikh, 2010: 45)

Disproportionality stresses how production expands more rapidly than demand in some sectors, whereas the opposite is the case in others, creating imbalances that depart from any trajectory of dynamic equilibrium. As Michael von Tugan-Baranovsky argued: 'If ... the directors of production had complete knowledge of the demand and the power to direct labour and capital from one branch of production to another, then, however low consumption might be, the supply of commodities could never outstrip the demand' (Tugan-Baranowsky, 1901 [1894]: 33). Hilferding extended this to finance capital, critiquing under-consumption in the process: 'underconsumption ... has no sense in economics except to indicate that society is consuming less than it has produced. It is impossible, however, to conceive of how this can happen if production is carried on in the right proportions' (Hilferding, 1981 [1910]: 241). He argued that finance capital contributes to disproportionality by making possible the purchase of massive amounts of capital equipment that, as sunk capital, reduces capital mobility and enhances the potential for disproportionality crises.[4]

---

[4] There remain questions, of course, about whether there are adjustment mechanisms within globalizing capitalism that would mitigate disproportionality problems. Eduard Bernstein (1902) argued that the growth of a labour aristocracy, extending the domestic market, cartels, joint stock companies, and an emergent credit system, as well as the opening of foreign markets through imperialism, would mitigate such crisis tendencies. Hilferding's finance capital analysis also points to what contemporary theorists would call market imperfections as a cause of disproportionality. Indeed, catalysed by Hayek, proponents of globalizing capitalism point to markets as the best mechanism for mitigating disproportionality—although the complexities and hurdles associated with spatio-temporally extensive market-oriented adjustment mechanisms in a multi-sectoral economy are characteristically overlooked.

Robert Brenner (2009) explains the 2008 crisis in disproportionality terms, as the consequence of long-term overinvestment in the fixed capital sector due to inter-capitalist competition between the US, Germany, and Japan.

> The fundamental source of today's crisis is the steadily declining vitality of the advanced capitalist economies over three decades.... The long term weakening of capital accumulation and of aggregate demand has been rooted in a profound system-wide decline and failure to recover of the rate of return on capital, resulting largely—though not only—from a persistent tendency to over-capacity ... in global manufacturing industries.[5] (Brenner, 2009: 2)

The tendency of the rate of profit to fall (TRPF) stresses an argument central to Marx' own analysis of capitalist instability: technical change tends to be labour-saving, but profits depend on the rate of surplus value (i.e. the proportion of the value created by workers during the working day that is withheld by capitalists as potential profit). Since labour-saving technological change reduces the hours of labour per unit of capital invested, if the rate of surplus value remains constant then profits per unit of capital advanced must fall. The TRPF only gained momentum as a theory of crisis relatively recently, as an explanation of the 1970s crisis of Fordism/Keynesianism in the West: 'By the early 1970s there was widespread agreement amongst Western Marxists that the fall in the rate of profit was the cause of the crisis and not its consequence' (Clarke, 1994: 63). Some saw this as a result of the politics of production: Unionized Fordist workforces had succeeded (with state support) in raising real wages, thus reducing profit rates (Glyn and Sutcliffe, 1972). 'Fundamentalists' stress Marx' own argument about technological change, 'objective' tendencies of capitalist production that push toward ever more capital intensive production methods, rather than the 'subjective' conditions of class struggle (Mattick, 1969; Yaffe, 1973). This was complemented by critiques of Okishio's (1961) mathematical refutation of Marx's theory of the TRPF (e.g. Shaikh, 1978; Rigby, 1990). With the advent of empirical quantification of both labour values and profit rates, there has been an ongoing debate about whether or not average profit rates have been falling (Webber and Rigby, 1996), that has carried over into debates about whether the TRPF caused the 2008 crisis (Harman, 2009; Kliman, 2009; Smith, 2010)—debates that remain plagued by disagreement over how to measure the rate of profit.[6]

The seemingly interminable, internecine, either/or debates about which of these four factors is the correct explanation of a given capitalist crisis are

[5] Brenner, like many Marxist economic theorists, feels the need to invoke certain aspects of a putative Marxian equilibrium. His argument, for example, heavily depends on the presumption of reconvergence to an 'established rate of profit' (2009: 25. See also 2009: 29, 33).

[6] http://thenextrecession.wordpress.com/2011/11/20/measuring-the-us-rate-of-profit-up-or-down/ accessed March 8, 2016.

unproductive: in fact, the conditions of possibility for capitalist crisis are over-determined. There are many ways in which profit realization can become problematic—triggering smaller and larger moments of crisis—and equally many ways in which capitalism pushes beyond such emergent barriers to capital accumulation (Lebowitz, 2005). The broader point, discussed in Chapter 2, is that the self-interested actions of capitalists, seeking to enhance profitability, can have the unintended consequence of lowering average profit rates. Harvey (1982b), advancing an argument for how spatiality intersects with the possibility of capitalist crisis, generalizes the notion of TRPF to any situation where such counter-intended consequences ensue. As we have seen, in a spatially extensive capitalist economy producing the accessibility commodity, the likelihood of such unintended consequences increases.

David Harvey (1982b) theorizes the possibility of crisis in terms of three 'cuts'. His first cut, like Marx's, emphasizes that cyclical dynamics of over-accumulation and counter-intended consequences are endemic to capitalism, triggering economic restructuring and an economic bust. Firms close and machinery and equipment are abandoned, triggering a devalorization of fixed capital that eventually writes off enough of the previous over-accumulation for production to initiate a new cycle of boom and bust. His second cut emphasizes challenges of temporality, and the role of finance in enabling temporal fixes. Large-scale production requires investment in capital-intensive fixed capital, requiring large sums of money to be raised now, to pay for equipment that may not realize profits on that investment for years (if at all). He notes that finance institutions and the credit system are essential institutions for dealing with this problem—for assembling the resources necessary for large purchases, managing the variable and sometimes long time lags between investment and payoffs. Finance markets ease the flow of capital from less to more profitable areas of the economy, smoothing out cycles of over-accumulation and devaluation, and fictitious capital multiplies investors' options and flexibility. In all these ways, the financial credit system offers the promise of a temporal fix to capitalism's crises by advancing money now that will only be realized later. Yet he also argues that such fixes are at best temporary—they cannot overcome the dynamical crises associated with over-accumulation. Harvey's third cut is geographical, what he calls the spatial fix—a theme conspicuous by its absence from the vast majority of the crisis theory literature.

4.3 What about Spatiality?

The theorists of capitalist dynamics discussed in Sections 4.1 and 4.2 have little to say about space. Even when temporality is conceptualized historically, space and time are essentially Newtonian: reduced to a coordinate system with respect to which economic growth is computed, in which time is orthogonal to (independent of) space.

The dominant implicit spatial imaginary is methodological territorialism (nationalism). For theories of dynamic equilibrium, a set of characteristics defines the (national) economy—quantities of production factors, technology, and rates of change—that determine its warranted growth rate and trajectory. This implies a teleological developmental imaginary. National economies with identical properties would follow the same path, implying that slower growing economies should acquire the same place-based attributes as more prosperous/faster growing economies. The multi-sectoral version can be extended to incorporate multiple territorial economies with distinct characteristics, incorporating also connectivities between them, but dynamical equilibrium requires that this geographical differentiation is unchanging. This makes globalizing capitalism inconsistent with dynamic equilibrium, because globalizing capitalism is bound up with geographical change.

Theorists of capitalist cycles, mainstream or 'heterodox', also typically resort to methodological territorialism. Seeking to show that cycles could be consistent with rational expectations, Lucas and Prescott (1974) experimented with 'island' models of spatially separated markets that workers search among seeking a higher wage. Arrighi's (2010) world-historical framework describes phases, during which a particular place becomes the hegemonic core. The shift between phases, he argues is marked by geographical shifts in the location of the hegemonic core, the increased geographical size of that core, and an area of influence of enhanced geographical scope.

Economic geographical research on cycles, open to questions of spatio-temporality, has been at best intermittent. Examples include the diffusion of unemployment cycles between urban labour markets (Bassett and Haggett, 1971; Bartels, Booleman, and Peters, 1978), the spatio-temporal convergence of real estate investment cycles (Leitner, 1994), Markusen's (1985) theory of profit cycles within economic sectors and their implications for uneven regional development, and Harvey's reiteration of Thomas' discussion of the seemingly interdependent dynamics of economic cycles on the two sides of the Atlantic (Thomas, 1972; Harvey, 1982b).[7]

Political economic crisis theory has also long shared this geographical blindspot. Territorial economies are treated as bounded, separate units of analysis (consider Brenner's comparison of the US, Germany, and Japan, or Webber and Rigby's analysis of East Asian national economies), each collapsed onto the head of a pin—a pincushion model of globalizing capitalism. Geographical contributions to crisis theory certainly exceed this imaginary, although

---

[7] Brian Berry's (1991) *Long-Wave Rhythms in Economic Development and Political Behavior* does not unpack the geographical heterogeneity of cycles.

arguably not to the degree that they should. Consider Harvey's third cut, the spatial fix, which has four variants. First, the land market helps reconfigure the built environment and make it more flexible, by directing investments in land to 'highest and best' uses. In this view, land markets mediate space in the same way that finance markets mediate time. Second, the global diffusion of capitalism mitigates accumulation problems at home by creating new markets for investment abroad (cf. Bernstein). Third, spatial barriers to profit realization, the geographical separation of places of production from those of consumption, increasing the time lag between investment and the realization of profits, can be mitigated by communications technologies that accelerate the movement of commodities and capital. This is what Harvey (1985), quoting Marx, terms 'the annihilation of space by time' (an imaginary according to which time eventually trumps space). Fourth, territorial governance structures emerge that facilitate local capital accumulation.

The spatialities of crisis tendencies in capitalism have been elaborated by others. Neil Smith (1984) highlights processes of geographical differentiation and equalization, and related 'see-saw' movements of capital between regions, as well as the emergence of urban rent gaps—where the promise of higher returns trigger reinvestment in, say, abandoned downtown areas (e.g. gentrification). Some have emphasized decline (regional economic restructuring), others aspects of growth—the emergence of 'new industrial spaces' (Massey and Meeghan, 1982; Scott, 1988; Storper and Walker, 1989). Others emphasize how these issues play out across, reshaping, geographical scales (Brenner, 1997; Swyngedouw, 1997b; Cox, 2013), and connectivities (Sheppard, 1990; Dicken et al., 2001). I take up spatio-temporality in Chapter 5. For present purposes, however, the key issue is how spatiality matters.

A socio-spatiotemporal dialectic clearly is at work in this literature: Spatio-temporality is continually (re)produced, with emergent spatio-temporalities shaping the dynamics of globalizing capitalism. The question, however, is whether and to what degree these dynamics are shaped by emergent spatio-temporalities. Harvey has given this more thought than most, profoundly shaping others' conceptions, and is quite clear: Temporal and spatial fixes (note their separate treatment) can displace and alleviate crises, affecting the spatial dynamics of capitalism: 'Without uneven geographical development capital would surely have stagnated, succumbed to its sclerotic, monopolistic and autocratic tendencies and totally lost legitimacy as the dynamic engine of a society that has pretensions to being civilized' (Harvey, 2014: 161). Yet such fixes cannot ultimately trump deeper crisis-inducing processes of over-accumulation and counter-intended consequences (Harvey's TFRP). In this interpretation, uneven geographical development is a 'moving' contradiction of capital, but not what he terms a foundational contradiction. In other words, spatio-temporality does not alter the deep crisis tendencies of capitalism. His arguments are grounded in the problematic claim, however, that Marxian value theory remains unaffected by the spatialities of capital accumulation. This is not the case, raising questions about whether his first-cut over-accumulation crisis is as inevitable as he claims (Sheppard, 2004).

4.4 Conclusion

Those theorizing capitalist dynamics have developed the broadest possible spectrum of representations. Proponents of capitalism develop theories—dynamic equilibrium, endogenous growth, and cycles with respect to equilibrium—that represent capitalism as a smooth, harmonious, and progressive economic system (consistent with their arguments about static equilibria). Capitalism's critics emphasize what they see as inherent tendencies toward periodic or even existential crisis. By and large, notwithstanding strong disagreements, the bulk of those theorizing capitalist dynamics implicitly agree on one thing: Capitalism's spatiality does not trouble their core theoretical arguments, even though it can be an important empirical wrinkle.

Geographers have sought to draw out the spatial implications of capitalist dynamics, ranging from lead and lag regions for economic cycles, to Smith's see-saw model and Harvey's spatial fix. Yet even here, only certain aspects of spatiality are at play—those stressing territory and the annihilation of space by time. Even David Harvey comes close to this position. In previous chapters, I have argued that the implications of taking spatiality seriously are quite fundamental. The following chapter returns to this theme by engaging closely with spatio-temporality.[8]

---

[8] Note also that this entire discussion does not address how the disequilibrium dynamics of capitalism depend on how economic and more-than-economic processes co-evolve (Chapter 8). As in Sraffa's aesthetic representation, it reduces capitalism to the production of commodities by means of commodities; Harvey (2014) also self-consciously limits himself to capital rather than capitalism, on the grounds that foundational contradictions exist within the economic processes themselves. But is not just that things are fluid, with the context changing. Vitally, these are interdependent dynamics: changes in non- or tangentially economic processes affect more purely economic processes, as well as vice versa.

5

Globalizing Capitalism's Spatio-temporalities

Globalizing capitalism is plagued with internal conflicts and contradictions, an emergent socio-spatial process that is characteristically out of equilibrium, whose dynamics also cannot be reduced to economic mechanisms. In this chapter, I explore its spatio-temporalities.

To date, economic geographers have taken up this question within two subfields that too often, unfortunately, are represented as opposed to one another: evolutionary economic geography and geographical political economy. Evolutionary economic geography emphasizes disequilibrium dynamics and emergent spatial characteristics, but presumes a fixed geographical backcloth. It tends to deploy a hierarchical scalar imaginary that presents larger scale geographies as the context within which firms act. It also neglects the politics of production and its implications for capitalist dynamics (Section 5.1). Geographical political economy takes spatio-temporality more seriously (Section 5.2). However, it has leaned toward emphasizing the 'annihilation of space by time', reducing spatiality to place. Uneven and asymmetric connectivities (e.g. inter-regional trade, global production networks, migration) foster dynamical complexity, creating disequilibrating tendencies that are further complicated by the politics of production.

This generates spatio-temporalities that are characteristic of complex dynamical systems more generally: evolutionary, path-dependent, and subject to the possibility of internal deconstruction as well as external disruption (Arthur et al., 1997; Rosser Jr, 2000; DeLanda, 2006). This implies that globalizing capitalism is characterized by a high degree of uncertainty about current and future states of affairs; notwithstanding a great deal of persistence, its trajectories can take highly unpredictable turns. Conceptually, extending the socio-spatial dialectic into the temporal domain reveals fascinating parallels between dialectics, complex dynamics, and assemblages (Sheppard, 2008). Time and space are not external, Newtonian coordinates, with respect to which events can be located. For complex dynamical systems, spatio-temporality has emergent properties constituted through the persistent non-local interactions connecting system elements (Prigogine, 1996). Emergent spatio-temporalities in turn shape globalizing capitalism's trajectories of change, in ways that are more fundamental than Harvey acknowledges.

Section 5.3 examines the implications of this analysis for development possibilities under globalizing capitalism. The geographical imaginaries legitimizing a diffusionist stage-ist account—methodological territorialism and the claim that connectivities are mutually beneficial—are neither theoretically nor empirically persuasive. The ongoing presence of uneven, asymmetric connectivities, co-evolving with globalizing capitalism, implies that disadvantaged places and people should be exploring alternative economic possibilities to those of globalizing capitalism.

5.1 Evolutionary Economic Geography

Evolutionary Economic Geography (EEG) has been described as one of the most rapidly growing areas of research in the Anglophone social sciences since 2000 (Boschma and Martin, 2010). As developed by its most influential proponents, EEG is a spatialized spinoff from the stream of neo-Schumpeterian evolutionary microeconomics developed by Nelson and Winter (1982). Yet EEG is not simply derivative of evolutionary economics: Its proponents repeatedly demonstrate that spatializing evolutionary economics is a distinctly non-trivial extension, bringing new insights to aspatial evolutionary economics. Yet it does replicate Nelson and Winter's focus on firms as the agents of change and on generalized Darwinism. Firms' successes or failures depend on Darwinian competition with one another within a broader environment that shapes the conditions of success.

There has been considerable debate, also among its proponents, about whether taking evolutionary processes seriously in economic geography should be reduced to this Darwinian imaginary. Other evolutionary models have been mooted, including complex adaptive systems and path dependence (Martin and Sunley, 2006, 2007). More generally, it has been pointed out that other theoretical traditions—geographical political economy, institutional economic geography, and relational approaches—also prioritize such evolutionary properties as historical time, emergence, path dependence, and nonlinear dynamics (Grabher, 2009; MacKinnon et al., 2009; Hassink, Klaerding, and Marques, 2014; Martin and Sunley, 2014). EEG is dominated, however, by the application of Darwinian evolutionary theory from biology—grounding evolutionary outcomes in theories of species competition and survival.[1]

---

[1] As in mainstream economics' self-referential parallels with the mathematics of (nineteenth-century) theoretical physics (Mirowski, 1984), analogies with biology function to reinforce the

5.1.1 *Generalized Darwinism and Evolutionary Economic Geography*

Evolutionary Economic Geography brings Darwinian notions of variety, inheritance, retention, and selection to the analysis of the spatial dynamics of firms and industries. Generalized Darwinism 'asserts that the core principles of evolution provide a general theoretical framework for understanding evolutionary change in complex population systems (from physical to social systems), but that the meaning of those principles and the way that they operate is specific to each domain' (Essletzbichler and Rigby, 2010: 43–44). Rejecting the ideal-typical, representative agent of mainstream microeconomics, the analytical entry point is that variety arises from micro-behaviours within diverse populations of firms, directed by inherited durable, quasi-genetic routines—the equivalent of genes in Biology—emerging from inter-firm competition (Boschma and Frenken, 2006).

EEG explains the spatial evolution and concentration of industries in terms of how the locations of firm entry, exit, and spinoffs shape the distribution of organizational routines within a certain territorial population of firms. Spatial differentiation is conceptualized as 'the outcome of a selection process operating on heterogeneous firms and their location choices' (Boschma and Frenken, 2006: 293). Evolution is largely a local affair: localized search and knowledge spillovers, spinoff firms, and labour mobility are conceptualized as prime vehicles for routine replication (Boschma and Wenting, 2007; Essletzbichler and Rigby, 2007; Boschma and Frenken, 2011). At any time, the incumbent firms in a locality are deemed a potential source for subsequent spinoffs and knowledge spillovers, as well as being attractors for (re)locating firms. More successful firms are deemed 'fitter', producing more successful spinoffs than their rivals and accounting for the formation and persistence of clusters (Boschma and Frenken, 2006, 2011).

'[T]he primary dynamic in the economy' (Boschma and Frenken, 2006: 285) is Schumpeterian competition between firms seeking to gain supra-normal profits 'through innovation or through early adoption of a new product or process' (Nelson and Winter 1982: 203). Change is predicated on the 'creative destruction' of novelty (innovations, and new firms, industries, and networks), and thereby of variety in firm characteristics. Routines that increase firm fitness or profitability have a greater chance of survival, reproduce more

---

discipline's status as a science: biological laws function to naturalize economic competition as similarly guaranteeing evolutionarily superior outcomes (nature red in tooth and claw). Thus it is worth reflecting on the fact that Darwin's own thinking about competition and selection was in fact influenced by Adam Smith's political economy as he sought to theorize how order can emerge without conscious design (Sober, 2006). It is also worth recalling how such analogies were used by Herbert Spencer and his followers of social Darwinism to justify racism and eugenics (Peet, 1985).

quickly, and are transferred locally to other firms. Selection is thus a result of market competition, with path-dependent first mover advantages for firms and regions. Boschma and Frenken (2006) summarize this succinctly:

> As long as firms show routinized behavior, market competition acts as a selection device causing 'smart' fit routines to diffuse and 'stupid' unfit routines to disappear. In particular, differential profits leading to differential growth rates render fitter routines to become more dominant in an industry. (Boschma and Frenken, 2006: 278)

EEG scholars prioritize the 'unbounded' capacity of human agency, serendipity, and subsequent path dependent growth, capable of obviating pre-existing regional (dis)advantages (Boschma and Lambooy, 1999), over the role of preexisting territorial structures, historical legacies or the selection environment. 'If institutions play a role, it will be more often in an endogenous manner as entrepreneurial firms, consumers and government officials engage in collective action to establish new institutions' (Boschma and Frenken, 2009: 5). A key concept is related and unrelated variety in a region. Related variety implies that novelty is regionally path dependent: prior regional specializations in technologically related industries generate new industries by recombining existing routines: 'branching' (Iammarino, 2005; Boschma and Frenken, 2011). Unrelated variety highlights the inherent uncertainty associated with innovation, and the possibility that new industries emerge from a diversified, rather than regionally specialized, industrial structure, keeping windows of locational opportunity open to some extent for all regions (ter Wal and Boschma, 2011).

Generalized Darwinist EEG, like micro-foundations more generally, presumes that firms and their routines are reasonably autonomous from the constraints of territorial institutions and structures. The more-or-less accidental creation of new routines, and their path- and place-dependent replication at firm and regional scales, is seen as the major determinant of geographically uneven economic development (Boschma and Frenken, 2006). Proponents acknowledge that regional institutions also are relevant enabling and constraining contexts, shaping the fitness of routines and thereby region-specific technologies and trajectories of technical change (Rigby and Essletzbichler, 2006), yet they prefer to set aside the 'imprecise' institutional brush in order to focus on firm behaviour (Boschma and Frenken, 2006, 2009). Thus detailed analysis of territorial environments and institutions is rare within EEG. Firms co-evolve with the regions they inhabit, with regional institutions and other characteristics shaped by and shaping intra-regional firm population dynamics. This shapes the competitiveness of a region's population of firms, as well as the attractiveness (i.e. competitiveness) of that region as destinations for mobile firms.

5.1.2 *EEG's Socio-spatial Ontology*

Summarizing, EEG stresses the out-of-equilibrium evolution of regional populations of firms in co-evolution (in some accounts) with relevant characteristics of those regions. History matters, but the socio-spatial ontology is limited largely to bottom-up multi-scalar dynamics. Firms are conceptualized as individual, autonomous agents: inter-firm and inter-sectoral interdependencies are neglected, as is the possibility that individual plants are components of larger space-transcending corporate structures shaping local possibilities. This entails a particular 'layered ontology' (Hassink et al., 2014: 4) of hierarchical scaling, dubbed hierarchy theory in ecology (Wu, 2007): In this imaginary, fast-moving processes, operating at finer geographical scales (firms), drive change at the next larger scale (regions); by contrast, slow-moving processes at larger geographical scales constrain processes at lower (firm) scales. In EEG, regions themselves are largely understood in methodological territorial terms: as quasi-autonomous bounded spatial units (Boschma and Frenken, 2006, 2009). When costs of inter-regional interaction are high, regions can be analysed independently of one another; when these are low, regions are conceptualized as merging into larger aggregate geographical containers for firm-level dynamics (figs 2.2, 2.3 in Essletzbichler and Rigby, 2010). This is a bottom-up ontology: a multi-scalar territorial spatiality, driven by firm-level behaviour. Its micro-foundational imaginary is perhaps why Boschma and Frenken acknowledge a family resemblance to neoclassical economics (Boschma and Frenken, 2006; Martin and Sunley, 2014).

An important theoretical question remains, however: if EEG self-consciously relies on biological theory for inspiration and analogies, why restrict this to Darwinian evolutionary theory? Summarizing two competing theoretical schools, evolutionary developmental biology and developmental systems theory, each seeking to link the dynamics of the evolution of species with those of the development of organisms, Martin and Sunley (2014) argue that attending to these enables:

> [a] move to a more systemic and holistic understanding of spatial economic evolution, one that considers not just industrial evolutionary dynamics but also the wider economic, institutional, and sociopolitical structures produced by and constitutive of uneven geographical development.... We ... envisage an ontology based on a multilevel abstraction, but of nested, interacting and co-evolving spatial–economic developmental systems, rather than simply units defined by rules or routines. (Martin and Sunley, 2014: 721)

Richard Norgaard (1994: 84) offers a related critique of Generalized Darwinism's bottom-up ontology: 'With more emphasis on coevolutionary processes, the directionality of evolution is no longer determined by a steady advance toward perfect fitness with an unchanging environment. Species are no longer thought to get better and better at anything. And...changes in the [broader] environment are important explanatory variables in evolutionary history.'

Taken together Norgaard and Martin and Sunley point to a major limitation in generalized Darwinism—its neglect of how firms and other species also shape their broader environment. Attention to this—to bottom-up as well as top-down inter-scalar causal relations, opens the analysis to questions that are much bigger than those of firms' fitness—questions of how broader socio-spatial structures emerge.

5.2 The Emergent Dynamics of Globalizing Capitalism

Put abstractly, the spatial dynamics of globalizing capitalism exhibit features characteristically associated with non-linear complexity: equilibrium is a contingent rather than a necessary outcome, spatio-temporality is an emergent feature, and small disruptions can be profoundly disruptive. There is persistence, but also emergence and unexpected twists and turns. This is true even if we abstract from the complexities of the politics of production, and all the more so once we incorporate more-than-economic processes: politics, power, culture, and materiality.

5.2.1 *Time–Space Compression: Is Place the Key?*

As argued in Chapter 2, much of the contemporary thinking about how spatio-temporality matters in globalizing capitalism focuses on places. The reasoning is quite straightforward: globalizing capitalism is producing a shrinking world in which differences in relative location are of diminishing importance (Kirsch, 1995). Under this geographical imaginary, the explanatory logic becomes place-based: the features of places and regions make the difference between success and failure.

In its 2009 *World Development Report: Reshaping Economic Geography*, the World Bank advocated what it calls space-neutral policies: presuming (with Rostow) that all countries, regions, and cities are on a common developmental path, and (with Kuznets) that capitalist economic development naturally goes through phases of increasing and then decreasing socio-spatial inequality, the World Bank's '3-D' scheme sees spatial intervention as the last resort (Kuznets, 1955; Rostow, 1960; Williamson, 1965; World Bank, 2009). Critiquing this 'one size fits all' approach to capitalist economic development, those advocating regional policies for the European Union have recently argued that regional and national context matter, and that policies should be 'place-based': differentiated according to geographical context, particularly a place's institutional capacities and local expertise

(Barca, 2009; Barca, McCann, and Rodriguez-Pose, 2012: 5): 'globalization has made space and place more rather than less important. The unique aspects of a locality and the ability to create and strengthen a comparative advantage are at the heart of economic development and success.'

Notwithstanding its focus on uneven geographical development and regional restructuring, the same imaginary has dominated geographical political economy. Harvey repeatedly invokes Marx's notion of the annihilation of space by time and the more general notion of space–time compression—which he coined to express how our globalizing world can be 'characterized by speed-up in the pace of life, while so overcoming spatial barriers that the world sometimes seems to collapse inwards upon us' (Harvey, 1989a: 242). With spatial barriers disappearing, place-based attributes become the key to geographical differences in economic growth. In this view, places succeed or fail by developing distinguishing characteristics that give them a competitive advantage, for example through local entrepreneurialism (Harvey, 1989a, 1989b; Leitner, 1990; Hall and Hubbard, 1998).

Time–space compression, according to which time trumps space, has been an influential notion in human geography and geographical political economy since the 1990s (Sheppard, 2002).[2] Beyond the industrial districts literature (Chapter 3), examples include spaces of flows, cultures of mobility and the mobility turn, the tyranny of distance giving way to that of real time, and global flowmations (Thrift, 1994; Virilio, 1995; Castells, 1996; Luke and Ó Tuathail, 1998). Some are reluctant to cede the field entirely to temporality: Harvey (1996) stresses how space is continually restructured and produced under capitalism, Thrift (1994: 221) notes that mobility 'takes up both space and time', and Castells (1996: 465) insists that the 'space of flows' determines a 'timeless' time: 'Space shapes time in our society, thus reversing a historical trend'. Yet methodological territorialism prevails in contemporary discussions, even those emphasizing scale and networks. As argued in Chapter 3, scalar thinking emphasizes the inter-relations between territorial units across different scales, and the most influential conceptualizations of networking emphasize flattened and malleable networks, with flat ontologies receiving recent attention (Marston, Woodward, and Jones III, 2007). In these analyses, places (or, for flat ontologies, sites) are the spatiality that matters. As in Evolutionary Economic Geography, uneven, asymmetric connectivities receive little attention.

---

[2] This is also the case for geographical economics.

5.2.2 *Relational Dynamics: Making the Case for Connectivity*

The presumption that a shrinking world is producing a flattened world—the world of Lösch and Krugman—is misleading. Consider, for example, the huge efforts that financial services firms go to, investing in improved connectivities, building spatially separated exchanges, and undertaking micro-locational strategies, in order to save just a few micro-seconds relative to their competitors (Lewis, 2014; Zook and Grote, 2014). Thus it is worthwhile to examine how emergent spatial connectivities shape capitalist dynamics.

The spatial dynamics of even the most simplified multi-sectoral, multi-regional capitalist economy are complex. Consider the case of a two-sector (wage and capital goods), two-region economy in which, in each time period, capitalists make their best guess profit-rate maximizing decisions about how much capital to invest in commodity production (Figure 5.1: Bergmann, Sheppard, and Plummer, 2009). There is no presumption that economic actors would already be aware of equilibrium: they make their best guesses based on what they know at the time when they must act. This is a fully globalized world, in which transport costs are zero but goods are traded between regions on the basis of price differentials. Wages are fixed and the politics of production are ignored, as is the possibility of technological change. Computing the dynamics of this system, there are conditions under which it converges to

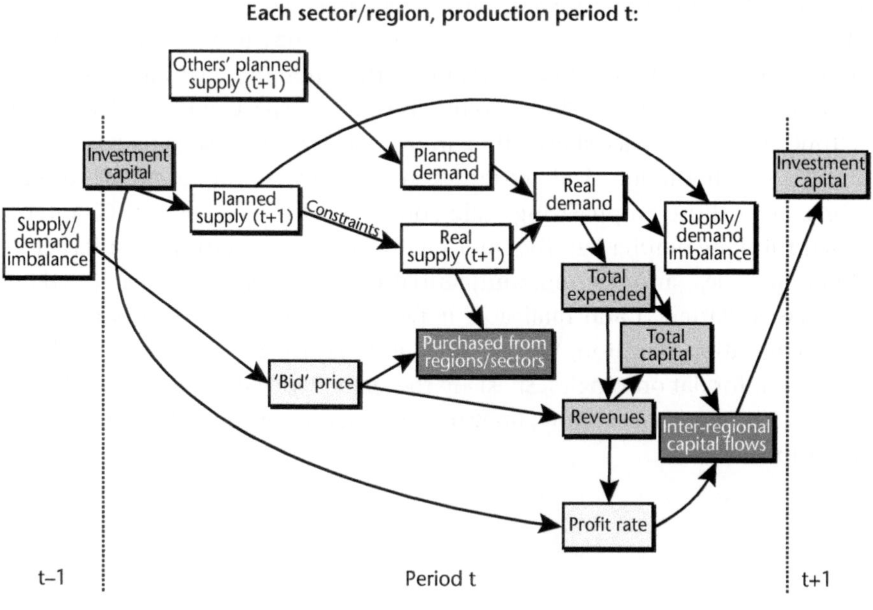

Figure 5.1 Out-of-equilibrium commodity production dynamics
Source: Drawn by Luke Bergmann, author. Used by permission.

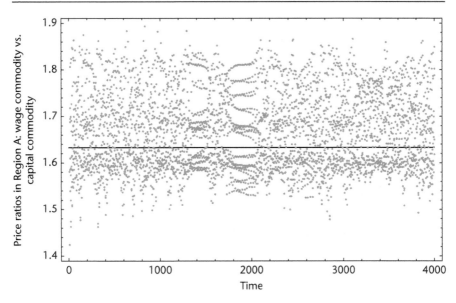

Figure 5.2 Inter-regional disequilibrium dynamics: quasi-chaotic behaviour of price ratios in region A

Source: Bergmann et al. (2009), Figure 3.

long run dynamical equilibrium, also in the absence of prior knowledge about equilibrium. But the more responsive agents are to the consequences of past actions, the more likely the system is to exhibit dynamical complexity or even chaotic behaviour (Figure 5.2). Indeed, regional collapse is possible (Figure 5.3). Thus even under this simplified scenario there is no guarantee that geographically differentiated capitalist production and exchange are governed by self-regulating markets.

Since we know that incorporating the production of accessibility consistently complicates economic geographical theory (Chapter 2), undermining the rationality of economic actions, it is reasonable to presume that incorporating transportation and communications into the analysis, essential to globalizing capitalism, will further complicate these spatial dynamics. On the other hand, in mainstream models of capitalism, technical change can smooth out capitalist dynamics. To consider these possibilities, Bergmann (2012) extends this framework to include the transportation sector, as well as the possibility of technical change in each sector and region. The real wage is presumed to be fixed (no politics of production). Firms in each sector and region choose stochastically from sets of possible technologies, defined as combinations of wage, capital, and transportation inputs from each region, per unit of output. These technologies emerge from experimentations by firms

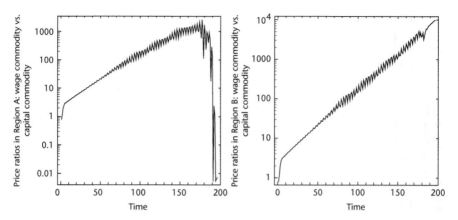

Figure 5.3 Inter-regional disequilibrium dynamics: collapse of capital goods sector in region A

Source: Bergmann et al. (2009), Figure 4.

seeking to raise their profit rate above the social average.[3] Possible dynamics are indeed complex. Regions and firms may end up in dynamical equilibrium, either specializing in what is revealed as regions' comparative advantage, or exhibiting balanced development along identical trajectories in both regions. But these are just two of what turn out to be many emergent possible spatio-temporal trajectories: others include regional collapse, divergence, and divergence followed by reconvergence.

5.2.3 *Incorporating the Politics of Production*

As discussed in Chapter 2, the politics of production, playing out across multiple scales, are an unavoidable and destabilizing aspect of the spatial dynamics of globalizing capitalism. EEG recognizes the role of firms and the actually existing diversity of regional populations of firms. Yet 'an excessive focus on firm-level routines is likely to obscure how the unequal distribution of economic resources through space is also a result of power dynamics' (Hassink et al., 2014: 5). These power dynamics, operating within, between, and across scales ranging from the enterprise to the globe, both reflect and (re)constitute the uneven socio-spatial positionalities of various participants.

---

[3] This extends the approach taken in Evolutionary Economic Geography, to incorporate inter-firm and inter-regional trade, and to consider how changes in the broader environment—triggered by firms' actions—affect firm survival. As Norgaard (1994) argues, accounting for such dialectical relations between organisms and their environment vastly complicates Darwinian narratives seeking to explain survival 'of the fittest' as solely dependent on organisms' genetic and other characteristics.

At the enterprise scale, EEG stresses firms' problem-solving capacity as innovators, under the presumption that their members will cooperate. For example, while recognizing the necessity for firms to regulate potential internal conflicts of interest, Nelson and Winter (1982: 112) argue 'fear of breaking the truce is, in general, a powerful force tending to hold organizations on the path of relatively inflexible routine (sic)'. This abstracts from the politics of production, however, from the unevenly empowered struggles between a firm's members over the distribution of the profits. Commons, a forerunner of evolutionary economics, argues that conflict and disorder is pervasive, implying that the overriding challenge of evolutionary theory is to explain how order and harmony emerge from intra-firm conflicts, rather than presuming harmony (1934: 57–8). By definition, capitalist firms are plagued by contentious, unequally empowered attempts to capture a share of profits (Bowman and Toms, 2010). These are an integral part of firms' routines and competitiveness strategies, which should be conceptualized as intra-organizationally conflictual (Massey, 1984: ch. 8; McDowell, 1997; Hudson, 1999; Sheppard, 2000). EEG's problem-solving view inadequately portrays such intra-firm struggles, neglecting also how organization and organizational routines are a locus of conflict and governance (Dow, 1993; Coriat and Dosi, 1998; MacKinnon et al., 2009).

Within a regional population of firms, inter-firm rivalry also has a significant political/power aspect, again neglected in EEG. Generalized Darwinism's focus on the positive-sum game of value-adding innovation ignores the darker side of Schumpeterian 'creative destruction' (Baumol, 1990; Baumol and Litan, 2007; Foster, 2011)—and endeavours to capture value from one another (Bowman and Ambrosini, 2009). Firms frequently survive by reducing the fitness of their competitors rather than increasing their own fitness, with the implication that innovating firms commonly fail to realize value from their investments (Teece, 1986). Potential monopoly rents are frequently captured by powerful incumbents, redistributing value among unequally positioned firms (Levy, 2008; MacKinnon, 2012).

Labour geographies further complexify the politics of production, connecting intra-firm struggles to regional and national politics. Struggles within firms are shaped by the presence of, strategies utilized by, and constraints on labour organizing. Labor organizing is regulated by—but also contests—regional and national institutions and legal structures. It reflects the influence and alliances of economic classes, which themselves are geographically inflected. For example, organized labour in prosperous regions may work in alliance with capitalists in order to foster local growth machines, at the expense of the interests of workers in less prosperous regions (Galtung, 1971; Hudson and Sadler, 1986; Logan and Molotch, 1987; Herod, 1997).

The politics of production also involves regulation and governance, of course. On the one hand, firms and workers appeal to local, regional, national, and supra-national state, legal, and para-statal institutions and agencies, lobbying against discrimination and for special treatment. In response, the decisions of these agencies, and the actions of those charged with implementing such decisions, intentionally and unintentionally alter the conditions of possibility for capitalists and workers. These conditions are geographically (and economically and socially) differentiated, reshaping the spatial dynamics of globalizing capitalism. It would be naïve to assert that the politics of production necessarily disrupts or destabilizes these dynamics, but it certainly enhances their complexity.

5.3 Provincializing our Understanding of Globalizing Capitalism

The inescapable conclusion of this analysis of the dynamics of globalizing capitalism is that these are complex, characteristically out-of-equilibrium dynamics, reflective *inter alia* of economic and political contradictions. As noted in Chapter 1, this raises vital questions about the implications of globalizing capitalism for the conditions of possibility for well-being in different parts of the world. Do the dynamics of capitalist development diffuse from the North Atlantic to the rest of the world, putting all countries onto the same, teleological developmental trajectory, for good or ill (Rostow, 1960; Warren, 1980; Blaut, 1987)? Or does capitalist development in this core undermine the conditions of its possibility in peripheral regions, triggering and necessitating different development trajectories elsewhere (Wallerstein, 2004; Arrighi, 2010)? This has become a major issue of inter-disciplinary debate.

From the diffusionist perspective, those leading the charge toward capitalist development can (and should) help lagging countries catch up, in the name of eventual prosperity for all: big-d Development in the spirit of globalizing capitalism (Hart, 2002). Critics allege, however, that diffusionist thinking, equated with the Eurocentrist assertion that the North Atlantic history of economic development is/should be everyone's history (Blaut, 2000; Chakrabarty, 2000), is as disempowering as it is inadequate. It disempowers, because it confines the agency of economic history, at least since 1492, squarely to Europe (and its white settler colonies). As Dipesh Chakrabarty (2000) notes:

> insofar as the academic discourse of history ... is concerned, 'Europe' remains the sovereign, theoretical subject of all histories, including the ones we call 'Indian,' 'Chinese,' 'Kenyan,' and so on. There is a peculiar way in which all these other histories tend to become variations on a master narrative that could be called 'the history of Europe.' (Chakrabarty, 2000: 27)

The corollary is that such countries, deemed 'late adopters', are castigated for their laxity and inadequacies, represented as needing help from their elders. If the diffusionist view constituted a complete and adequate account of the spatial dynamics of capitalist development, then such Eurocentrism and castigation would be inescapable. Yet the complex spatial dynamics summarized in Section 5.2 suggest otherwise: Capitalist development in core regions, nations, cities, and intra-urban districts may well undermine the possibility for peripheral spaces to develop in the same way.

Chakrabarty dubs the diffusionist account History 1, and offers a critique that has become a core argument motivating post-colonial theory.[4] Drawing on Marx, he argues that the hegemonic power of the History 1 narrative of globalizing capitalism erases alternative potentially productive trajectories:

> Marx opposes to History 1 another kind of past that we will call History 2. Elements of History 2, Marx says, are also 'antecedents' of capital, in that capital 'encounters them as antecedents,' but—and here follows the critical distinction I want to highlight—'not as antecedents established by itself, not as forms of its own life-process.' (Marx, 1971: 899, quoted in Chakrabarty, 2000: 63)

Locating the trajectories of History 2 outside Europe, in the post-colony, and revalidating these, he seeks to provincialize the supposed universality of the European narrative.

Notwithstanding the spatial terminology running through his analysis (Europe, the post-colony, provincialization), Chakrabarty (a historian) has nothing to say about *spatio*-temporality. Yet it is possible to revise his analysis, laying out the conditions of possibility for Spatial History 1 and Spatial History 2. The former is consistent with two spatial imaginaries: methodological nationalism, and mutually beneficial connectivities. The latter, the necessary (if habitually erased) and entangled co-existence of alternative trajectories of change, follows from recognizing that globalizing capitalism entails uneven and asymmetric connectivities that tend to reinforce trajectories of uneven geographical development.

Consider, first, the geographical imaginary I have dubbed methodological territorialism. As discussed in Chapter 1, reducing the spatiality of capitalism to quasi-autonomous spatial units (bodies, cities, regions or nations), for the

---

[4] The feature of post-colonial theory that I focus on here is its geographical remit: its attempt to theorize the distinctive political and economic characteristics of that region of the world constituting the post-colony (a region whose boundaries are very much subject to debate, but references people and places with a shared a history of dependence on some colonial power). Definitions of post-colonial theory often emphasize culture, discourse, and representation (e.g. Said, 1978, 1994; Zein-Elabdin and Charusheela, 2004), and the situated nature of knowledge production (Pollard, McEwan, and Hughes, 2011). Culture, representation, and situated knowledge are central themes in critical economic geography, irrespective of whether analysis focuses on the post-colony (aka the 'global south', cf. Sheppard and Nagar, 2004).

purpose of theorization and analysis, naturalizes place-based explanations: differentiated place-based attributes are hypothesized to explain geographical differences in economic performance. Irrespective of the causal factors asserted, there is a common logic. Like regression analysis, common relationships are assumed to hold everywhere, setting up a norm with respect to which exceptions can be identified, praised, or criticized. As discussed earlier, such theoretical accounts cut across the theoretical spectrum, ranging from climate or governance as the key to the wealth and poverty of nations (Sachs, 2000; Rodrik et al., 2004; Collier, 2007; Acemoglu and Robinson, 2012), to relational assets that enable clusters of firms to prosper (Amin and Thrift, 1994; Porter, 1995; Storper, 1997), to variegated political economic accounts of the role of urban entrepreneurialism, class, regulatory regimes, or worker activism in place (Harvey, 1989b; Ward, 1997; Florida, 2002; Brenner, 2006; Glaeser, 2011; Storper, 2013).

Strangely, this imaginary can also be found among post-colonial theorizations of the conditions separating the North Atlantic metropole from the spaces of the post-colony. Although the constitutive force is relational—the impact of colonialism—colonialism's connectivities are very much in the background in discussions of the differences consequent on colonialism. Chakrabarty's formulation is framed around two distinct kinds of history (Europe vs. non-Europe), with the latter argued to be the product of such distinct features in the post-colony as the subaltern and the importance of religion.[5] Partha Chatterjee (2001) emphasizes the pervasive presence of political society in the post-colony. Kalyan Sanyal (2014) highlights the predominance of a need economy and surplus populations, requiring a distinctive developmental strategy. In each case, even though the authors trace these distinctive features to the uneven global relations constituted through colonialism, contemporary analysis is territorial. It divides the world into the binary of two different kinds of regions, one the product of a European/North Atlantic trajectory and the other reflecting the distinctive features of the post-colony—features whose distinctiveness challenges the capacity of theories developed for the North Atlantic to function effectively in the 'south' (cf. Connell, 2007; Comaroff and Comaroff, 2011). Internal critiques do not escape this. Thus Vivek Chibber (2013) argues that the differences identified by Chakrabarty, Chatterjee, and Ranajit Guha are illusions that do not stand up to careful scrutiny, a consequence of over-simplified caricatures of the two regions. In his view, this vitiates any need for a distinctive post-colonial theory. Gidwani and Wainwright (2014) acknowledge the regional characteristics highlighted by Sanyal (93 per cent of India's workforce is

---

[5] Recent attention to post-secularism in the North Atlantic realm questions this latter distinction.

engaged in informalized employment), even as they argue that his post-colonial Marxism is not necessary to account for these.

The second geographical imaginary consistent with diffusionist and stageist accounts of development is the claim that connectivities are mutually beneficial. This imaginary is central to mainstream (geographical) economic theory. On the one hand, the unrestricted mobility of production factors (labour, capital, know-how) from places of excess supply to those of excess demand is supposed to balance out pre-existing differences in factor endowments, equalizing development possibilities everywhere. On the other, unrestricted ('free') trade in commodities enables every place to identify and invest in its comparative advantage, producing, and exporting products that take advantage of this. This enables every territory to benefit from free trade, irrespective of pre-existing geographical differences in resource and factor endowments.

The geographical imaginaries of methodological territorialism and mutually beneficial connectivities each reinforce a diffusionist account of globalizing capitalism and economic development—Spatial History 1. Yet much of what we know about the spatio-temporality of globalizing capitalism suggests that these scenarios are neither theoretically defensible nor empirically plausible. As I have argued throughout, uneven, asymmetric connectivities are an important shaping factor of uneven geographical development—Spatial History 2. If globalizing capitalism is unable to deliver on its promise of opportunities for all, then locations in the post-colony, but also across the complex fractal geographies of a 'global' South (Sheppard and Nagar, 2004; Sheppard, 2014a), cannot be blamed for their precarity, on the grounds that they failed to clamber up the ladder extended by prosperous societies. This default diagnosis, characteristically emanating from North Atlantic and global institutions (e.g. the World Bank), belies reality. Rather, uneven and asymmetric connectivities can mean that prosperous bodies and places have been kicking the ladder away (Chang, 2002). When globalizing capitalism fails, precarious bodies and places would do well to consider defying such well-meaning, follow-the-leader advice: other more-than- or non-capitalist economic processes are not only worthy of consideration, but also may be the only way forward.

5.4 Conclusion

In the approach developed here, space and time are inherently co-implicated and emergent properties of globalizing capitalism: Historical geography *matters*. Agents neither have Turing machine-like decision-making skills (fully informed, perfectly rational) nor are they already aware of potential equilibrium outcomes (rational expectations). While it is possible that dynamic equilibria can contingently emerge from the best-laid plans of locally informed actors seeking to enhance their positionality, complex out-of-equilibrium capitalist spatial dynamics are equally likely. Capitalism is internally unstable, characteristically out-of-equilibrium, for reasons that extend beyond class differences and conflicts. The characteristics of places shape their conditions of possibility, but uneven, asymmetric connectivities play an equally important role. Even restricting analysis to economic processes, connectivities co-evolve with the uneven geographies of capitalism as a result of the production of accessibility and the socio-spatial dialectic. These are further complicated by the politics of production, as well as by capitalism's 'fictitious' commodities: more-than-capitalist practices and imaginaries, the more-than-human world and finance (Chapter 8).

A salient conclusion of this analysis is that stageist accounts of global economic development (Spatial History 1, to riff on Chakrabarty) are implausible and unsustainable. The contradictory, complex and (in certain space-times) chaotic and crisis-ridden dynamics of globalizing capitalism imply that alternatives to capitalist economic processes may be necessary for those bodies and places experiencing persistently deleterious encounters with big-d Development (Spatial History 2).

By definition, crisis is an unexpected deflection from normality; those setting the norms (the global North) thus have the capacity to shape who gets to frame what counts as crisis and the reasons behind it (Werner, 2016). Global crises coagulating in the post-colony or the periphery (the 1980s third world debt crisis, the 1997 Asian financial crisis, the 2015 Greek crisis) readily can be, and are, dismissed on the basis of place-based arguments of economic or governance failure in 'backward' places. Another way of looking at such crises (stretching back to colonialism and slavery), however, is that they are conditions of possibility for ongoing prosperity in the 'global' North (whose institutions are consistently rescued in such crises). The 2007 crisis—dubbed global even though many parts of the post-colony, as well as Canada and Australia, barely felt a ripple—has the capacity to disrupt this narrative of peripheral inadequacy, because misrule was located literally in the heartland of capitalism (Wall Street, the City of London). That it has not had this effect—that the poor, the periphery, debt, and state regulation again are blamed for the crisis, whereas financial institutions are bailed out as 'too big to fail'—does not make the narrative true (Mirowski, 2013; http://krugman.blogs.nytimes.com). But it underlines the difficulty of imagining and realizing alternatives, and of reframing where blame may actually lie.

To drive these arguments home, in the next two chapters, I turn to the question of global commodity trade: the economic connectivity most commonly believed to be mutually beneficial under globalizing capitalism.

6

The Free Trade Doctrine—A Critique

Comparative advantage is the best example of an economic principle that is undeniably true but not obvious to intelligent people

(Samuelson, 1969)

In a word, the free trade system hastens the social revolution. It is in this revolutionary sense alone, gentlemen, that I vote in favor of free trade

(Marx, 1848)

In order to interrogate the role of connectivities under globalizing capitalism the case of international trade is a worthy starting point (notwithstanding economic geographers' broad neglect of the subject). More than any global flow, the international trade of commodities has been asserted to be mutually beneficial for all participating nations ever since European capitalism gained global reach in the early nineteenth century. Global trade, long a vital economic connection between places, is regarded by mainstream economics as mutually beneficial, relatively symmetric, and benign, at least in principle—an example of the connectivities variant of Spatial History 1 discussed in Chapter 5. This assertion, also the predominant view among policymakers worldwide, is what I call the free trade doctrine. Interrogating this doctrine thus offers a critical case through which to assess the capacity of globalizing capitalism to bring wealth and development to all.

The free trade doctrine is the clam that unrestricted international trade can be mutually beneficial for all participating countries that appropriately identify what they should specialize in and export. Since the mid-eighteenth century, practically every self-styled economist or political economist of global repute has found it important to examine this claim. Samuelson's view (see the epigraph above) has trumped Marx's, as is evident in geographical economics. As discussed in Chapter 1, Baldwin utilizes Krugman's theory of geography, trade, and development to conclude that a historical downward trend in transportation costs accounts for both the historical polarization in economic well-being between North and South, and its current putative (re)convergence. In Baldwin's narrative, high transport costs prior to the seventeenth and eighteenth centuries prevented global divisions of labour. Between 1846 and 1914, 'globalization 1' lowered transportation costs to the point where a geographical specialization of manufacturing, in the first world, was the stable global equilibrium outcome: 'as history would have it, the North won at the South's expense' (Baldwin, 2006: 13).[1] After a 'counter-globalization' interregnum between 1929 and 1945, 'globalization 2' has further lowered communications costs to the point where a geographical specialization of manufacturing is no longer the equilibrium outcome. He argues that this explains current (re)industrialization in the global South, which he takes as evidence of convergence toward a new global equilibrium. The 2009 World Development Report makes essentially the same argument, that all territories follow a common Kuznetsian path of economic development whereby socio-spatial inequality initially increases under capitalism, only to reconverge toward socio-spatial equity as development proceeds (Kuznets, 1955; World Bank, 2009).

In this chapter, I critically assess this doctrine, mobilizing the idea of entanglement. I use entanglement to covey the idea that international trade is bound up with all kinds of other processes and mechanisms. The narrow socio-spatial ontology invoked by mainstream trade theorists, through their restrictive assumptions, seeks to cut through this Gordian knot to the essence of trade. I question the status and validity of the doctrine they derive. I begin by discussing the role of trade within globalizing capitalism, showing how the free trade doctrine stems from disentangling a particular way of thinking about global trade from the multifaceted processes that dialectically co-evolve with it (Section 6.1). I then critically assess the economic theories developed on the basis of this disentanglement to rationalize the free trade doctrine since Ricardo, including the extensive recent attention to geography in mainstream trade theory, analysing the blinkered socio-spatial ontology that makes these claims possible (Section 6.2). I then turn to really existing trade discourses and practices (Section 6.3). To illustrate the limitations of trade economists' place-based perspective on comparative advantage, I review the broader historical processes creating the inequalities that European-centred capitalism inherited when Britain declared itself a free trade nation in 1846 (inaugurating Baldwin's globalization 1). I examine how the free trade doctrine came to be constructed as a global norm through British colonialism, and how other

---

[1] Other economists acknowledge that colonialism played a role in this polarization, but primarily as a place-based narrative of how Europe imposed poor governance on the colonies (Acemoglu et al., 2002).

capitalist nations responded: What now is dismissed as 'protectionism' was key to the prosperity of second generation industrializing nations (Germany, the US, Japan). Finally, I examine how contemporary trade relations, embedded within post-colonial global divisions of labour, call into question the free trade doctrine. I show how socio-spatial positionality shaped when and where the doctrine becomes an acceptable and plausible discourse, but also who wins/loses when 'free' trade is practised.

6.1 The Entanglements of Commodity Trade

The movement of commodities across space connects the world together in incredibly complex ways. If we could visualize and animate these flows, they would flicker across the landscape, inter-connecting bodies, firms, markets, neighbourhoods, cities, regions, and countries, in ways that reflect, reproduce, and transform both economic connectivities and their place-based imprints. The genius of mainstream trade theory (and economics) has been its willingness to cut this Gordian knot, disentangling trade from its relational determinants. This involves a heroic feat of simplification, much lauded in mainstream economics in the name of scientific parsimony (Occam's razor), which also has the effect of legitimating the free trade doctrine. Figure 6.1, from *The New Introduction to Geographical Economics* (Brakman et al., 2009), visualizes this disentangled representation of trade. Given the intimate relationship between visualization and economic theory (Buck-Morss, 1995), and the political implications of this particular disentanglement, I seek to bring light onto what this mainstream representation makes invisible by summarizing some salient entanglements of trade that are conspicuous by their absence from this figure. I return to these in more detail in Chapter 7.

First, are the entanglements of economy: the complex ways in which various economic activities are interlaced through commodity trade. François Quesnay envisioned this as the *tableau économique* in 1759, an idea central to Marx's puzzling about how capitalism can create value and reproduce itself in volume three of *Das Kapital*. Wassily Leontief formalized these as an input–output table, given spatial expression by Walter Isard (Quesnay, 1753–58; Leontief, 1928; Isard, 1951; Marx, 1972 [1885]). This conception of the production of commodities by means of commodities has caused all manners of headaches for neoclassical (and Marxian) theories of growth, distribution, and value (cf. Sraffa, 1960; Harcourt, 1972; Sheppard and Barnes, 2015 [1990]; Barnes, 1996). Second, are the entanglements of spatiality. In Figure 6.1 the complex spatialities of commodity trade are reduced to international flows, aggregated by national economy and sector and tracked empirically through

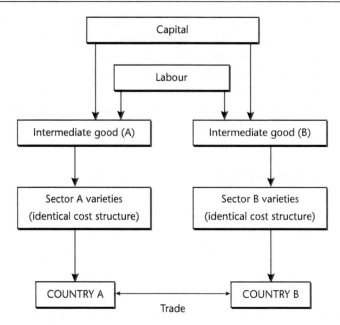

Figure 6.1 Disentangling global trade
Source: Brakman et al. (2009), figure 9.8, p. 374. Reproduced by permission.

'state-istics' (Taylor, 1996).[2] Very often, this is further reduced to a theory of just two point-like countries of equivalent status (methodological nationalism), with no transport costs. Sub-national inter-regional trade has received occasional attention, but almost always as a minor sub-theme within international trade.

Third, is trade's entanglements with other global flows and connectivities. Commodity trade co-evolves with foreign direct investment, global production networks, international finance markets, migration, and movements of information and knowledge—all largely excluded from international trade theory. Fourth, is entanglements with the political. One widely discussed aspect is governance: the horizontal connectivities of international trade are co-implicated with complex multi-scalar territorial governance structures: local initiatives to advance global competitiveness, national attempts to influence cross-border flows, and public and private global governance regimes (The Bretton Woods institutions, the WTO, Trade-Related Aspects of Intellectual Property Rights agreements, corporate governance networks, etc.).

Fifth, are entanglements with more-than-capitalist exchange. An elementary example is how the production and exchange of commodities for profit is always accompanied by other modalities of production and exchange

---

[2] This is changing as large firm-level databases become available (Ottaviano, 2010).

(e.g. Gibson-Graham, 2006; Gudeman, 2008). These range from Local Exchange Trading Systems (LETS), to global fair trade and international barter (US $12 billion in 2015, http://www.irta.com/about/the-barter-and-trade-industry/ accessed March 10, 2016; local barter boomed during the post-2008 world economic crisis). Sixth, a hallmark of economic geography has been establishing the many ways in which economic processes are entangled with the more-than-economic: with culture, affect, care, discourse, power, and more-than-human materialities (see also Chapter 8).[3] Holding these entanglements in mind, what vision of trade has emerged from cutting this Gordian knot?

6.2 Mainstream Trade Theory

Mainstream trade theory is voluminous, but exhibits a rather monolithic trajectory since Adam Smith and David Ricardo (cf. Wong, 1995). This trajectory can be signposted with five broad stages of theorizing. First, Smith argued that free trade is always desirable as it extends the market (Smith, 1776). Between two nations, trade would be mutually beneficial if each had an absolute cost advantage in a different product. This was not good news for England, however, where wages and prices were higher than many other nations—and Smith was an ardent proponent of state action to enhance England's terms of trade (such as its Navigation Acts, requiring that British ships be used for moving goods throughout its Empire). Second, David Ricardo's theory of comparative advantage finessed this problem, creating the orientation point for all subsequent theory. With given national differences in production technologies, and no international migration, it is advantageous for two nations to trade as long as each specializes in a commodity that they are relatively more efficient at producing, by comparison to the other—comparative advantage. This made the potential of mutual gains from trade much more generally applicable: every nation was seen as having something it could produce relatively efficiently, as a result of its particular endowments, with potential gains from trade thus available to all irrespective of cost differences. Ricardo's theory served as much to propagate Lockean liberalism as it did to establish the free trade doctrine. This doctrine had already become a core liberal principle by the end of the eighteenth century (cf. Sheppard, 2005). Ricardo's famous stylized empirical example, trade between England and Portugal, also falsified the historical record of a trading relationship that consistently enriched England and impoverished Portugal (Sideri, 1970; Peet, 2009). Yet Samuelson (1969) regards Ricardo's theory as the most influential argument in mainstream economics.

[3] In contemporary socio-spatial theory, the term materialities references the physical properties of objects and of the technologies applied to them (including those of digital technologies), opening the question of more-than-human agency—their causal influence over human imaginaries and practices.

Third, in the 1930s Heckscher and Ohlin founded the 'modern' theory of international trade (formalized by Samuelson), incorporating Ricardo into the emergent paradigm of neoclassical economics (Heckscher, 1919; Ohlin, 1933). Here, comparative advantage is determined by a nation's relative abundance of production factors rather than production costs. Assuming the validity of aggregate neoclassical production functions, when a production factor is abundant in a nation, its lower marginal productivity makes it cheaper relative to other production factors. Specializing in activities that draw heavily on the locally abundant factor will thus realize national comparative advantage. For example, nations with abundant labour should specialize in and export labour-intensive products, whereas those with abundant capital should specialize in capital-intensive products. Since any profit-maximizing capitalist would presumably seek to use more of what is cheaper, this also had the compelling implication that the rational choices of individual capitalists both match the national interest and conform to comparative advantage. Thus free domestic and free international trade complement one another.

Fourth, the 1990s 'new' theory of international trade developed a further modification, seeking to account for what was dubbed 'intra-industry' trade. This referred to reciprocal trade in manufactures amongst industrialized capitalist countries, which economists finally felt compelled to address. Based on recently developed theories of monopolistic competition (Dixit and Stiglitz, 1977), this approach sought to account for where, across two countries, industrial clusters would emerge (Helpman, 1990; Krugman, 1990; Grossman and Helpman, 1991). Fifth, is the 'new new trade theory' that has emerged since 2000. Focusing on trade as a choice of firms rather than an action of countries (i.e. on microfoundations), firms are heterogeneous and do not participate equally in trade. Nevertheless, the doctrine still holds in general equilibrium '[t]he endogenous emergence of these non-neutral productivity gains magnifies *ex ante* comparative advantage and provides a new source of welfare gains from trade' (Bernard, Redding, and Schott, 2007: 60).

Within mainstream theory, each stage of theorization is presented as a revolutionary advance on the previous one. Yet they are sutured together by their capacity to reproduce and reconfirm a set of Lakatosian hard-core propositions that rationalize the free trade doctrine (Lakatos, 1970; McGovern, 1994: see Table 6.1). As is well known, these propositions rely on a series of heroic assumptions that, *inter alia*, disentangle trade from everything else. Quasi-perfect competition drives profits to zero (net of fixed costs): 'assumptions of free entry and exit by firms that are ex ante identical, are infinitesimal in scale, and compete non-strategically' (Neary, 2009: 2). Representative economic agents act rationally, on the basis of perfect information. The international economy is in equilibrium: Trade balances, markets clear, and all production factors are fully employed. Geography is practically non-existent:

Table 6.1. Hard-core propositions of mainstream trade theory

Proposition 1	Trade patterns are determined by differences in comparative production cost ratios between countries
Proposition 1a	Intra-industry trade is explained by the differentiation of products across countries and consumers' preference for variety
Proposition 2	Where there are different relative prices across countries, there will be gains from trade in exchanging goods at intermediate price ratios
Proposition 2a	Even in the absence of comparative cost differences, there may still be gains from intra-industry trade, in terms of consumer choice, if traded goods are differentiated, or if economies of scale stimulated by international trade generate comparative cost differences
Proposition 3	Free trade (with appropriate compensation) increases the welfare of all trading partners

typically, there are two countries of equal size and influence, with no internal spatial differentiation, and transportation costs associated with trade are ignored. Under such assumptions, it can be deduced that appropriate specialization and trade enhances aggregate international output, and that each country can be better off (i.e. obtain more commodities for the same effort) through trade than in autarchy.

The implausibility of these assumptions has provided much grist for criticism. Beyond this, empirical tests have not been kind to the theory. Leontief's paradox (the US, with the world's highest capital–labour ratio, exports commodities whose capital–labour ratio is *lower* than that of its imports) remains a stubborn thorn in the eye of trade theorists, as it is the opposite of what the 'modern' theory predicts (Leontief, 1956). Confirmation of the Prebisch–Singer hypothesis, that primary commodity exporters face historically declining terms of south–north trade in exchange with manufacturing commodity exporters, undermines the 'win–win' predictions of the free trade doctrine. Finally, the failure of global differences in the returns to labour and capital (wages and profit rates) to dissipate undermines another central prediction of the 'modern' theory: factor price equalization (Samuelson, 1948). Such empirical negations, while utilizing positivist standards for truthfulness adhered to by mainstream economics, have had to withstand repeated challenges within economics. They have not been refuted, but the theory stubbornly survives (Helpman, 1999; Subasat, 2003; Ocampo and Parra, 2006).

Theoretical critiques of the mainstream theory also have been prominent at times. In *Against the Tide*, Douglas Irwin painstakingly recounts these debates: infant industry arguments, the terms of trade, increasing returns, high wages, welfare considerations, and strategic trade policy (Irwin, 1996). Although each of these counter-arguments is logically valid, it is nevertheless dismissed (by free trade proponents when they were proposed, and by Irwin in his assessment) as not crucially undermining the free trade doctrine. In short, they are presented as the exceptions that nonetheless prove the rule.

6.2.1 *Adding 'Geography'*

Recently, the 'new' trade theory has paid increasing attention to geography, with the effect of adding nuance and improving empirical performance. Krugman linked imperfect competition with transportation costs and labour migration to explain intra-industry trade (Krugman, 1991). Typically, transportation costs are treated as an 'iceberg': a deduction that melts productivity away as goods are transported. With such transportation costs, and by integrating the Ricardian, 'new' and 'modern' theories into a single two country model, the standard results of Ricardo and Heckscher–Ohlin are replicated (Brakman et al., 2009: chapter 9).

Yet the iceberg specification is profoundly unrealistic: it implies that freight rates do not fall with distance (Fingleton and McCann, 2007). Geographical economists thus experiment with a variety of other transport cost specifications, and different geographies. They have treated transport costs as a fixed charge rather than an iceberg (Cukrowski and Fischer, 2000; Tharakan and Thisse, 2002; Ottaviano and Thisse, 2004). They have explored 'density dependent' transport costs, where the freight rate falls as the amount shipped increases, also embedding two (equally accessible) regions within two countries trading with one another (Behrens et al., 2003). They have examined spatial differentiation within a country, dividing it into regions that trade with a spatially undifferentiated second country (Courant and Deardorff, 1992; Krugman and Livas Elizondo, 1996; Paluzie, 2001; Mansuri, 2003; Crozet and Koenig-Soubeyran, 2004; Hanink and Cromley, 2005). In *A Spatial Theory of Trade*, Rossi-Hansberg (2005) reinvents a much earlier geographical research programme on location, specialization, and trade across continuous space (Curry, 1970, 1989; Beckmann and Puu, 1985). They have explored uneven international geographies, the clustering of countries into continental world regions and preferential trade areas, and differences in national endowments (Rauch, 1999; Villar, 1999; Cukrowski and Fischer, 2000; Venables and Limão, 2002; Davis and Weinstein, 2003). Occasionally, they recognize that trade is entangled with foreign direct investment, dubbed 'oligopolistic general equilibrium' (Markusen, 2002; Neary, 2009). Such geographical complexities lead to a variety of conditions under which the derived general equilibrium deviates from the free trade doctrine, including scenarios where regions and countries lose as a result of trade. '[T]here is a sense in which the new developments in mainstream trade and growth theory have eliminated the centre of trade theory. There are no core propositions that can be embraced without strong qualifications' (Darity Jr and Davis, 2005: 164).

One geographical issue receiving particular attention has been the question of how mainstream trade theory can be reconciled with the empirically compelling gravity model. Long ago, Ron Johnston (1976) showed that the gravity model, whereby trade correlates positively with the size of the national economy but negatively with distance, provides a good empirical fit to international trade statistics. Without noticing Johnston, economists have reinvented this wheel, elevating transport costs from a readily ignored minor complication, to the cause of the 'six major puzzles in international macroeconomics' (Obstfeld and Rogoff, 2000). Since formulations consistent with the gravity model provide a much better fit with empirical trade data than those that neglect distance, this has become a powerful *ex post* strategy for reinforcing the empirical status of mainstream theories—and thereby the free trade doctrine. The fewer the exceptions, the stronger the rule. Theorists have duplicated early 1970s strategies, offering a rational choice theoretic foundation to gravity models of human spatial interaction that is consistent with the gravity model (cf. Domencich and McFadden, 1975; but see Sheppard, 1978, 1980). Thus Jacks, Meissner, and Novy (2009: 2) are able to conclude that 'all micro-founded trade models produce a gravity equation of bilateral trade. Ricardian, "modern" and "new" theories of trade, alike, have been reconfigured to make them consistent with the gravity formulation' (see also Deardorff, 1998; Eaton and Kortum, 2002; Chaney, 2008; Melitz and Ottaviano, 2008).

As with spatial interaction theory three decades ago, heterogeneity becomes the key to forcing the square peg of a microfoundational equilibrium theory into the round hole of the gravity formulation. Heterogeneity of preferences and firms within a particular territory rationalizes why apparently identical agents would undertake spatially heterogeneous actions, in terms of where they buy from and/or ship to, as predicted by the gravity model. Not only this; virtually all of the puzzles that spatial scientists addressed in the 1970s with respect to the gravity model vex trade economists today—how to specify the distance friction effect, how to handle 'zero' intra-territorial distance, how to incorporate direct and indirect connectivities, why the distance coefficient varies so much from study to study (Anderson, 1979; Anderson and van Wincoop, 2004; Bosker and Garretsen, 2007; Disdier and Head, 2008). These unacknowledged parallels send a shiver down this recovering spatial scientist's spine. Yet trade economists also ignore two central issues in the earlier geographic literature: The difficulty of accurately estimating distance coefficients in the presence of spatial autocorrelation (i.e. when economies of similar size are proximate to one another; Curry, 1972; Griffith, 2007), and the use of entropy maximization to estimate trade models (Senior, 1979).

6.2.2 *The Socio-spatial Ontology of Mainstream Trade Theory*

While repetitive of the ontology of spatial science, mainstream trade theorists' attention to geography has moved this body of scholarship some way beyond the two country, two characteristics, two commodities disentanglement that

Ricardo brilliantly pioneered, to challenge aspects of the free trade doctrine. Nevertheless, the socio-spatial ontology underlying this framework drastically simplifies the spatial and other entanglements stressed by geographers, limiting the degree to which mainstream propositions are challenged. I detail some of this in Chapter 1 but some salient aspects are worth reiterating (Plummer and Sheppard, 2006; Sheppard, 2011a):

1. *The economy, only.* Processes of commodity production, market exchange, and accumulation are treated in isolation from the more-than capitalist and more-than economic processes with which they are co-implicated. Economic interdependence (the first entanglement of Section 6.2) is generally neglected.

2. *Methodological territorialism.* Two scales of actors are envisaged, each as contained spaces: autonomous, equally empowered individuals with given resources and preferences, and autonomous equally empowered (national) territories with given endowments. The body is the determinant scale: economics' obsession with microfoundations implies that national-scale phenomena are determined by bodily-scale rational actions. This eliminates relationality and unequal power relations, conceptualizing countries as subject to identical laws, conditional on contextual differences in place-based characteristics, aligning them onto a teleological capitalist development trajectory (catalysed by trade).

3. *Exogenous geography.* All geographical features, place-based characteristics and distance metrics, are exogenous: 'Geography is as exogenous a determinant as an economist can ever hope to get' (Rodrik et al., 2004: 134).

4. *A flat world.* It is usually presumed that each country is equally positioned within the global system; that no cores and peripheries exist. (Recent research has introduced unequal, exogenous geographies, but as a variation on the flat world ontology, rather than as an alternative starting point for theorization.)

5. *Limited temporality.* With the economy presumed to approximate general economic equilibrium, time is not only separated from space, but collapsed to a fixed point. It is assumed that the economy is self-regulating (close to a stable equilibrium), and that any losers from trade can be fully compensated by those who gain (Stolper and Samuelson, 1941). There is no space for history: how endowments come into existence (e.g. as England deindustrialized Asia in the eighteenth century), or how countries fared under the free trade doctrine (Sideri, 1970).[4]

---

[4] Garretsen and Martin (2010) examine the implications of (4) and (5) for both geographical economics and economic geography.

Theory construction always requires simplification, of course, but the question is whether the essence arrived at is robust to relaxing these assumptions. In this case, I argue that it is not.

6.3 The Free Trade Doctrine in Light of Globalizing Capitalism

All ubiquitous knowledge claims have distinct geohistorical origins, whose interrogation can help identify potential limitations to those claims (including claims to ubiquity), and this is certainly the case for the free trade doctrine. The doctrine gained global salience during both of the globalization eras identified by Baldwin, propagated by particular economic interests and discourses located within the economic hegemon of that era (the UK and the US respectively). Britain declared itself a free trade nation in 1846 (Trentmann, 2008), as did the US at the Bretton Woods conference on 1944 (culminating in the founding of the World Trade Organization in 1995). Thus any empirical assessment of the free trade doctrine should attend to these eras. In the highly abbreviated discussion possible in this context, for each era I examine whether the free trade doctrine, with its focus on place-based conditions of comparative advantage, suffices to account for the relationship between globalizing capitalism and uneven geographical development.

6.3.1 *Britain as Free Trade Nation*

By 1846, when Britain formally adopted free trade principles, in addition to being the core of the world's largest colonial system—the empire on which the sun never set—it had become the centre for European manufacturing (particularly cotton textiles). From the perspective of Ricardo (1817), whose book was thirty years old by now, and who sat in the Parliament where free trade became the law of the land, it made eminent sense that Britain's comparative advantage would lie in manufacturing, whereas that of India would be in raw cotton. In this view, trading Indian cotton for British textiles and clothing was economically rational and should be beneficial for both parties. Indeed Richard Cobden, organic intellectual leader of the pro-free trade Anti-Corn Law League, argued passionately for replacing colonial oppression with free trade (Cobden, 1846). Other European nations initially followed suit. Yet really existing connectivities, combined with the unequal benefits of specializing in manufactures rather than raw materials, belie this analysis (and not only in the case of England and Portugal).

Corn Laws had been passed by the UK Parliament in 1815 to regulate the price of wheat in Britain, which had fallen by half after Napoleon's defeat ended the blockade against wheat imports from the European continent. This made grain farming highly profitable, and bread prices—a staple for urban workers—rose significantly. The Anti-Corn Law League (ACLL) was formed in Manchester in 1838 to fight for repeal. The free trade doctrine made sense in the place and time where it emerged: early nineteenth-century Britain. Lockean liberalism dominated public discourse, and beliefs gained currency by aligning themselves with this. This was a time when British urban industrial capital was challenging the hegemony of rural landowning rentier capital, and organized labour was struggling for social influence under the Chartists. Manchester's economic trajectory was aligned with free trade interests: a city whose economic future lay in manufacturing and trade, heavily dependent on markets in Europe, North America, and the Empire. This was fertile ground for free trade, but it had to be improved, sown, and tended before the idea could sprout and be harvested as knowledge. At this point, the liberal faction of Manchester's elite had gained the upper hand, securing a municipal charter under Cobden's leadership that gave Manchester more autonomous political status (Kidd, 2002). 'Manchester men' demonstrated that political action can bring change. Cobden, a cotton textile capitalist (partner in a calico printing factory), successfully led the ACLL, working with the Chartists and convincing conservative Prime Minister Robert Peel, at the expense of his Conservative majority and his own political career, to manufacture a coalition that repealed the Corn Laws in 1846.

In fact, Corn Law repeal was a final act of trade liberalization. Other trade restrictions, notably bans on the export of machinery and the emigration of skilled workers, had already been lifted by the early 1830s—before the founding of the ACLL (Polanyi, 2001 [1944]). Cobden made the case on moral and rational grounds. Corn Law repeal would give workers more purchasing power ('a bigger loaf') and free trade is essential to peace between nations, 'uniting us in the bonds of eternal peace' (Cobden 1846, 6). It was essential to appeal to rationality in this Enlightenment age, and Cobden regularly lectured on political economy as justifying the free trade doctrine (Hinde, 1987). He emphasized Adam Smith's principle that trade extends the market, deliberately neglecting Ricardo's recently published theory of comparative advantage (Ricardo, 1817). Ricardo's argument was unpopular with working classes that the ACLL sought to ally with (Semmel, 1970; Winch, 1996). Cobden's collaborators had much more pragmatic concerns; by allowing cheaper foreign wheat imports, Corn Law repeal had the potential to lower the money wage in Manchester factories, thereby boosting profits and Manchester's global competitiveness.

While it has become conventional to assert that the free trade doctrine is derived from Ricardo's theory of comparative advantage, substantial evidence suggests that causality runs the other way. English political economy had long supported the principle of free trade. '[R]oughly up to 1600, Free Trade as a program meant developing the staple system and fettering or even breaking up merchants' companies. After 1600 it meant forcing the doors of those companies to make it possible for every trader to enter them' (Schumpeter, 1954: 324 fn. 3). The doctrine diffused rapidly from the North Atlantic realm, with laissez faire, during the eighteenth century. '[F]ree trade was increasingly considered as part of the autonomy of the individual, which was held to imply a "natural right" to trade as he pleased. . . . It was practically always associated with positive economic effects' (Schumpeter, 1954: 371). Ricardo's frequent correspondent and loyal supporter, John Ramsey McCulloch, described the methodology of British political economy as follows: 'Observations are scarcely ever made or particulars noted for their own sake . . . it is, in the peculiar phraseology of this science, the effectual demand of the theorist that regulates the production of the facts or raw materials, which he is afterwards to work into a system' (McCulloch, 1824: 29).

Opinions differ about the degree to which the ACLL exerted agency over Peel's decision to repeal the Corn Laws, but there is little doubt about its influence in representing repeal as the symbolic origin of free trade. Repeal of the Corn Laws thus marked the moment when the regional interests of Manchester jumped scale to become the national interest. It symbolized England's commitment to the free trade doctrine—the spatio-temporal moment when free trade shifted from a discourse to a world-changing performance. The period of general prosperity in England that followed 1846 in turn gave free trade proponents a powerful empirical justification, even though the degree to which free trade contributed to that prosperity is uncertain: England's commitment to zero tariffs lasted sixty-eight years (Bairoch, 1993).

Yet it is highly misleading to attribute Britain's prosperity to countries rationally specializing, on the basis of natural, place-based attributes defining comparative advantage, and trading to their mutual benefit. England's colonial positionality had already enabled it to destroy the well-developed cotton textile industry it had discovered in India, an industrial sector whose productivity and quality far exceeded European manufacturing at that time. In short, Britain took advantage of its asymmetric and uneven colonial connectivities with the south Asia subcontinent, pursuing mercantilist policies that undermined the profitability of cotton textile production in India, relocated that industry to Britain, and used its power over global trade routes to undermine cotton textile production in continental Europe. Marx alluded to this case in his critique of globalizing capitalism, but others have documented it exhaustively since (e.g. Ray, 2011; Beckert, 2014). In short, comparative advantage was not some exogenous place-based attribute, but was itself manufactured by Britain, to its advantage. The industrial revolution experienced in Britain and Europe, while certainly accelerated by local entrepreneurial inventiveness, co-evolved with deindustrialization in south and east Asia

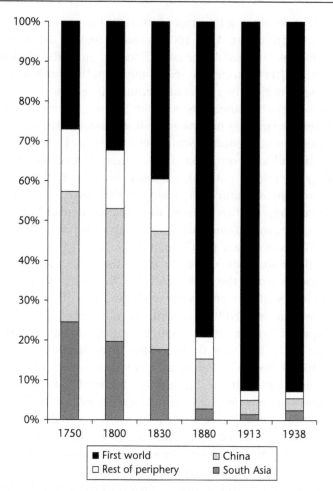

Figure 6.2 Percentage of global manufacturing output by region, 1750–1930

Source: Drawn by author from Williamson (2011) table 5.1, based on estimates by Simmons (1985) and Bairoch (1982).

(Figure 6.2), underwriting what Pomeranz has dubbed the 'great divergence' of rapid rates of growth in Europe and North America and stagnation and decline in Asia (Pomeranz, 2000).

Continental Europe followed, enacting a flurry of no tariff policies catalysed as much by social processes as by economic logic. Britain and France signed the 1860 Cobden–Chevalier reciprocal trade treaty, greatly reducing French tariffs, and free trade spread like an epidemic as Belgium, Prussia, Sweden, Spain, Norway, Holland, the Hanseatic league, Switzerland, Austria, and the German principalities successively entered into a network of bilateral tariff-reduction treaties between 1862 and 1877 (Kindleberger, 1975; O'Rourke and Williamson, 2000). Kindleberger (1975: 39) attributes this fast policy transfer

(Peck, 2002) to Manchesterist ideology: 'Manchester and the English liberals persuaded Britain, which persuaded Europe.'

Yet European competitors soon reversed course, feeling the bite of the English manufacturing prowess. Beginning with France in 1875, European countries increased their tariffs, with the exception of the Netherlands. The revolutions of 1848 accelerated the influence of socialism and thereby of state intervention, a socio-political context under which national sovereignty and freedom came to be associated with protectionism rather than free trade. Germany adopted Friedrich List's infant industry argument in 1879, erecting tariff barriers to protect domestic manufacturing. Protectionism was the general rule in Britain's white settler colonies. The United States initiated protectionism in 1789, and by the end of the nineteenth century, Canada, Australia, and New Zealand had also introduced protectionist measures (Bairoch, 1993). The colonies experienced the sharp end of free trade, reflecting European enlightenment discourses representing these territories as its backward other, requiring discipline before they could join the civilized global North (Said, 1978; Goldberg, 1993; Muthu, 2003). Colonies and independent countries treated as quasi-colonies (the Latin American republics, China, Thailand, the Ottoman Empire) were enjoined under British pressure to adopt the 'unequal treaties'. These restricted import tariffs to a maximum of 5 per cent, opening their markets to European (and, later, American and Japanese) manufactures (Bairoch, 1993).

In terms of socio-spatial positionality and uneven connectivity, Britain's industrial revolution, rationalized in terms of a comparative advantage in manufacturing combined with British ingenuity, was significantly enabled by how its position at the core of the British Empire provided a capacity to manipulate global manufacturing geographies. Shortly after the American revolution provided political independence, the US calculated that trade connections with Britain were not mutually beneficial, raising tariff barriers to protect domestic manufacturing capitalism and initiate a transition from an agricultural to an industrial economy. In Europe, Germany and other continental European powers came to the same conclusion. The altered trade connectivities that this made possible enabled the US and Germany to overtake British industrial production by 1913 (Sheppard et al., 2009b: 425). No such options were made available to (quasi-)colonial economies, where freer trade was accompanied by economic stagnation and ongoing reliance on a politically constructed 'comparative advantage' of primary commodity specialization and trade.[5]

---

[5] By politically constructed, I refer to the colonial policies that converted colonized territories into producers of food and raw materials for the European motherland. Brazil never had a natural comparative advantage in sugar cane or coffee; these products were foisted on Brazil as a result of colonial strategies for supplying cheap calories and energy to an emergent European workforce.

6.3.2 *After Bretton Woods: The False Promise of Free Trade*

At the Bretton Woods conference, a formerly protectionist and newly hegemonic United States saw free trade as the key to opening global markets for its
now powerful industrial corporations. Thus it used its considerable political
and economic muscle to push the other allied powers to break up their
colonial empires.

The nation-state was seen as the predominant scale at which economic
interests should be managed, and trade policy was an important management
tool. The US economy prospered from its ability to take advantage of international trade after 1944, fuelled by burgeoning demand in post-war Western
Europe and Japan catalysed by the Marshall Plan, as well as the newly opened
colonial regimes. Reminiscent of England after Corn Law repeal, free trade
after Bretton Woods was presented as a key to this era of prosperity—even
though the size and diversity of the US means that it is not particularly
dependent on its trade fortunes (Krugman, 1994). Tariff levels fell, but the
US never pursued the zero-tariff policy of nineteenth-century Britain. Lower
tariffs were also offset with more complex non-tariff barriers, selective 'retali-
atory' tariffs, and national financial policies manipulating interest and
exchange rates of the US dollar to periodically alter global comparative advantage in favour of the US. As issuer of the *de facto* currency for international
payments, the US was uniquely positioned to take advantage of such policies
(Brett, 1983; Porter and Sheppard, 1998).

For newly independent colonies, national sovereignty meant that they were
now in a position to make their own decisions about specialization and trade.
Mainstream trade theory provided a strategy, one that was pushed by a free
trading US and the Bretton Woods financial institutions that it could heavily
influence. A comparative advantage in labour intensive primary commodity
production, to be traded for manufactures from the North Atlantic region,
Japan, Australia, and South Africa, was presented as the former colonies' best
chance to get on an equal footing and catch up with wealthy former colonizers and white settler economies. Trading primary commodities for manufactures, so the reasoning went, would create a neo-Ricardian win–win situation,
with greater global output and increased economic growth for all countries.
Ricardian trade theory is agnostic about how the gains from trade would
be distributed among partner countries, but its logic implies that everyone
should be better off than before.

Political economic theorists were sceptical, reasoning that the lion's share of
this larger pie would end up in the hands of the wealthy manufacture-
exporting economies, thereby increasing economic inequality between former colonies and these countries, and there is significant evidence to support
this interpretation (Spraos, 1983; Sarkar, 1986; Sarkar and Singer, 1991). The

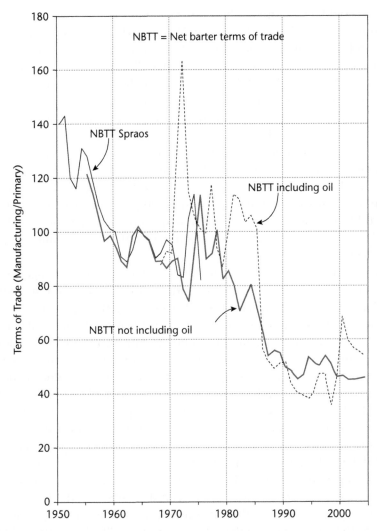

Figure 6.3 Terms of trade for primary commodities relative to manufactures, 1950–2004

Source: Sheppard et al. (2009b), Figure 16.4. Calculated by author, based on global bundles of primary and manufactured commodity exports. Data are from UNCTAD *Handbook of International Trade and Development Statistics* (1965–2003), United Nations *International Trade Statistics Yearbook* (1965–2003), and Spraos (1983).

terms of trade governing the global trade of primary commodities for manu- factures (Figure 6.3) show a steady decline in purchasing power, from the perspective of former colonies—and increased purchasing power from that of countries exporting manufactures. In short, the gains from this trade have been accruing in favour of the richer countries, a pattern that even the OPEC oil cartel could only temporarily counteract (and this, of course, only for oil-exporting former colonies, between 1973 and 1981). It is former colonies that have conformed more closely to the high degree of specialization recommended by mainstream trade theory, to their disadvantage. This asymmetry is reinforced by place-based differences: the multi-year production cycle for many primary commodities, considerable year-on-year primary commodity price uncertainty, low global market size and bargaining power for post-colonial economies, higher wages in manufacturing economies underwriting rapid increases of prosperity there under Fordism, and subsidies for first world agriculture. It is further reinforced by asymmetric connectivities: tariffs and non-tariffs in manufacturing exporting countries creating barriers for former colonies seeking to export manufacturing goods, foreign direct investment by first world corporations in primary commodity production in former colonies, and global logistics networks centered on the North Atlantic realm (Sheppard et al., 2009b).

Encountering these barriers, former colonies have sought to re-engineer their comparative advantage by 'getting the prices wrong' and promoting industrialization. In the 1970s, certain Latin American countries pioneered import-substituting industrialization (ISI) by following the protectionist lead of the US and Germany, enhancing domestic economic growth. Yet such protectionism proved difficult to duplicate in peripherally positioned economies: they still had to import the upstream capital goods necessary to produce consumer durable manufactures, and that production often took place in branch plants owned by North Atlantic-based transnational corporations. By the 1980s, the neoliberal structural adjustment policies of the Washington Consensus precluded ISI by fiat—telling these countries not to pursue the policies that had enabled the US itself to succeed (Chang, 2002). East and southeast nations were more successful in industrializing, pursuing a state-organized combination of ISI and export-oriented manufacturing (Amsden, 1989; Wade, 1990; Webber and Rigby, 1996). Many of these countries (Korea, Taiwan, Singapore, Hong Kong) further benefited from their strategic positionality during the Cold War, bringing long-term American and British support (Glassman and Young-Jin, 2014). And then there's China, whose deliberate strategy to open its economy to the world by the 1990s dramatically reshaped its socio-spatial positionality. Combined with place-based characteristics, the sheer size of China's economy and the determination and effectiveness of its socialist state, this resulted in an explosion of export-oriented low wage industrialization to become the new 'workshop of the world' (a strategy now being modified as the state enables rising wages and an upgraded manufacturing base).[6]

---

[6] An appellation originally applied to nineteenth-century Britain.

For all the attention devoted to rapid industrialization in east Asia, and other BRICS (Brazil, Russia, India, South Africa), much of the third world remains trapped in primary commodity specialization and trade. Repeated international political attempts have been made to rectify this imbalance: the Group of 77, the United Nations Commission on Trade and Development, the OPEC oil cartel, General Agreements on Tariffs and Trade negotiations, and the World Trade Organization. Yet none of these have enabled many former colonies to improve their deteriorating terms of trade. First world proponents of free trade remain more guilty than most of abandoning the doctrine when this serves domestic interests. The World Trade Organization symbolizes the willingness of territories to cede sovereignty over trade, and their acceptance of the free trade doctrine. Yet this has not levelled the playing field, due to vast differences in the power of different nation-states to make their argument effectively, as well as decision-making structures, such as the WTO's 'green room', that prioritize first world interests (Hoekman and Kostecki, 2001). As a result, the current Doha round of trade negotiations, dedicated to development, remain acrimonious and unresolved after fifteen years of recrimination and disruptive civil society protests (most notably at the 1999 Seattle and 2003 Cancun WTO meetings) (Wolfe, 2015). Even some mainstream development economists have become highly critical (Chapter 1; Stiglitz and Charlton, 2005).

6.4 Conclusion

In this chapter, I have argued that the free trade doctrine is more an ideological construct than a scientific principle. It is justified on the basis of a theoretical imaginary—a socio-spatial ontology—that disentangles trade under globalizing capitalism from all the other processes that dialectically co-evolve with it (processes at the centre of economic geographical analysis). Yet the uneven historical geography of who benefited from global trade belies the doctrine's assertions.

The doctrine became a global discourse and practice on the coat-tails of Britain's turn to free trade in 1846. Britain had been able to position itself to benefit from free trade by dint of having forced deindustrialization on South Asia. Britain pursued free trade until 1918, with other European countries following. But Britain's position as the workshop of the world posed barriers to industrialization elsewhere under the free trade regime, incentivizing Germany, but also Japan and the United States to contest the doctrine by protecting domestic industry. The United States, having prospered under protectionism, becoming the world's largest manufacturing economy, replaced Britain as the world's free trade proponent at Bretton Woods.

Since 1946, those countries envisaged to have the most to gain from free trade—newly independent former colonies positioned within the global division of labour as suppliers of raw materials—found themselves on a hiding to nothing. Attending to socio-spatial positionality and temporality leads to the conclusion that the post-colonial global South was not simply a victim of place-based characteristics. Rather, the actions of the firms, governments, and at times organized labour, of wealthy powerful capitalist countries—in the name (if not the practice) of free trade—have channelled this region into disadvantaged specialization: historically in primary commodities and now in low wage export-oriented assembly production. Certain post-colonial countries have found their way out of this trap, through state-led actions to alter the terms of their 'comparative advantage'. One consequence of this has been deindustrialization and lowered working conditions in parts of the global north; a second is a polarization between emergent manufacturing economies, particularly in east, southeast, and south Asia, and the remainder of the global south.

Given these problems with the free trade doctrine, disentangled from the other processes co-evolving with trade, what alternatives are worthy of consideration?

7

Geographies of Unequal Global Exchange

Arghiri Emmanuel coined the term unequal exchange to refer to what he argued is an inequitable trade of the labour value of commodity production, a net flow from former colonies to the 'advanced' capitalist economies of the North Atlantic (Emmanuel, 1972). While his calculations have been criticized, the term is useful nonetheless. If global commodity trade under globalizing capitalism is such that less prosperous (often post-colonial) territories gain less from trade than their more prosperous partners, then that is an inequity that should disturb all but the most trenchant proponents of globalizing capitalism.

Having identified in Chapter 6 that such inequities exist, in this chapter, I explore the basis for an economic geographical theory of global trade. Economic geographers have had remarkably little to say about global trade (for an overview, see Sheppard, 2012), a silence that no doubt partly reflects their averseness to the danger of being swept into the strange attractor created by the theories justifying the free trade doctrine. These theories have been subject to almost two centuries of criticism inside and outside economics, criticism that has been absorbed as cautionary tales, or as exceptions that prove the rule, without undermining the consensus surrounding the doctrine (McGovern, 1994; Irwin, 1996; Sheppard, 2005). The relentlessly mathematical and statistical nature of the literature on international trade is also a source of discomfort for many economic geographers, given a (mistaken) tendency to see quantification as incompatible with critical theory. There is a cost, however, to avoiding engaging with mainstream international trade theory, particularly now that it is integrated into a geographical economics that has gained unprecedented attention for 'economic geography' among global policy-making elites (Krugman, 1991; Fujita, Krugman, and Venables, 1999). No matter how quixotic it may seem to challenge mainstream trade theory, geographers' collective failure to do so only reproduces its hegemony.

One starting point is the dated literature theorizing trade from a Marxian and post-Keynesian political economy perspective, but there are limits to its claims about North–South unequal exchange (Section 7.1). By contrast,

I argue, the more nuanced (and realistic) socio-spatial ontology of geographical political economy (Chapter 2) creates space for teasing out the nature and implications of uneven, asymmetric trade flows (Section 7.2). Drawing from these insights, in Section 7.3 I argue that alternatives to free trade (ranging from state-led protectionism to local-scale barter) are worthy of serious consideration.

7.1 Alternative Trade Theories: Stillborn Heterodoxies

A remarkable feature of international trade theory has been the paucity of alternative theorizations from radical political economists, notwithstanding their extreme scepticism about mainstream theory.[1] These alternatives can be subdivided into Marxian and post-Keynesian approaches (also haunted by Marx).

7.1.1 Marxist Theories of Unequal Exchange

Examining two countries and neglecting transport costs, Emmanuel argued that when two countries exchange products at equivalent prices of production, this does not generally result in the exchange of equivalent labour values (Emmanuel, 1972), but a net movement of labour value from poorer (formerly colonized) to wealthier (formerly colonizing and/or white settler) countries.[2] He argues that two general conditions cause a country to suffer a net loss of labour value through international trade. Unequal exchange in the 'broad' sense occurs if a country's specialization entails a lower organic composition of capital, and in the 'narrow' sense if it pays lower wages. The latter case was of particular interest to Emmanuel. A net loss of labour value means that surplus value is transferred to the other country, favouring capital accumulation there. Thus he concludes that lower wages in the periphery favour capital accumulation in the core, enhancing uneven geographical development.

Anwar Shaikh seeks to explicate what Marx's theory of international trade would have been, by extending his law of value to the international scale

---

[1] Çagatay (1994) provides a concise overview of the differences between mainstream, post-Keynesian, and Marxian trade theories.

[2] Marx's critique of capitalism is based on the divergence of labour value, the socially necessary labour time to produce a commodity using socially necessary technologies, from prices of production, the market prices that equalize average profit rates in all sectors/regions. This divergence creates exploitation, legitimating struggles over the distribution of economic surplus between economic classes.

(Shaikh, 1979, 1980).[3] He finds that absolute advantage is more important than comparative advantage (cf. Milberg, 1994, 2002). Using the two-country case with no transport costs ('developed and underdeveloped regions of the capitalist world economy', Shaikh, 1980: 57), he assumes that the prices of production adjust internationally so that rates of profit equalize across sectors and countries, and that labour values are set globally (as globally socially necessary labour time). He argues that differences between Marx's and Ricardo's theories of money entail different conclusions about trade between an underdeveloped and a developed region.[4] In Ricardo's theory, if one country has absolute advantages in both commodities, then gold must flow from the more expensive to the cheaper region (from England to Portugal, in his example), to pay for the trade deficit with the cheaper country. An increasing quantity of gold in Portugal would drive up prices there relative to Britain, until Britain can export the commodity in which it has a comparative advantage at a lower cost than it could be produced in Portugal.[5] At this point trade would equilibrate.

Given that Marx' theory of money does not tie price levels to the quantity of money in an economy, Shaikh argues that international flows of specie would not enable England (less productive in both sectors, and thus less developed) to compete with Portugal. Instead 'eventually the £ must collapse, and with it the level of trade between England and Portugal. . . . England must eventually succumb to the consequences of its backwardness and restrict imports to the level consistent with its capacity to export. . . . [I]n the case of Ricardo's extreme example England has no capacity to export. . . . [However,] even an underdeveloped capitalist region . . . may nonetheless produce certain commodities in which it has an absolute advantage' (Shaikh, 1980: 38–9). Thus trade between core and periphery systematically disadvantages the latter. When trade occurs between countries with similar technologies and levels of productivity (i.e. within the developed or the underdeveloped region of the world), 'factors such as climate, location, availability of resources, experience, innovations, and above all the competitive struggle between capitalists, became decisive in determining the pattern of absolute advantage' (Shaikh, 1980: 41), and thereby specialization and trade.

The Argentinian Keynesian economist Raúl Prebisch (1959) was the first to attribute poverty and economic stagnation in Latin America to the unequal

---

[3] The abstraction that forms the basis of Marx's theory of value was implicitly conceptualized at the scale of a national economy (methodological nationalism). His notes for a fourth volume of Das Kapital offer few clues about how Marx would have theorized value, trade, and production at the supranational scale, had he lived to complete what he envisioned as a six volume work (Marx, 2000 [1862]: ch. 17).

[4] I replicate Shaikh's problematic (developmentalist) terminology, to be faithful to his account.

[5] In fact, gold flowed from Portugal to England. Portugal's deteriorating terms of trade meant that much of the gold exported from Brazil to Portugal ended up in England (Sideri, 1970).

effects of international trade. His argument was based on: (i) a higher rate of growth of productivity in manufacturing than in primary commodities, (ii) elevated wages in industrialized capitalist countries (reflecting struggles there between organized labour and capitalists) that can be passed on as higher prices to primary commodity exporting former colonies due to unequal global political and economic power, and (iii) stagnating prices for primary commodities (benefiting industrialized countries) in the absence of significant wage struggles in the periphery. As a consequence, the bulk of the gains from trade accrue to industrialized core countries, exacerbating global uneven development.

The Franco-Egyptian Marxist scholar Samir Amin, writing from Senegal, offers a theoretical explanation. Constructing a two world region model—advanced capitalist core and third world periphery—he argues that the third world has a 'natural advantage (abundant supply of ore and tropical products)' (Amin, 1974a: 13). Capital flows to the third world to finance extraction of these, because lower wages in the periphery make production more profitable than in the core: 'The products exported by the periphery are important to the extent that—ceteris paribus, meaning equal productivity—the return to labour will be less than it is at the center' (1974a: 13). Geopolitical processes emanating from colonialism, making the periphery dependent on the core, are a precondition. Wage rates in the periphery will be 'as low as the economic, social and *political* conditions allow' (1974a: 13), resulting in small and distorted peripheral domestic markets. At the same time, the emergence of domestic, comprador peripheral elites creates a limited market for luxuries, to be supplied (when he was writing) by domestic import-substituting industrialization.

Dependency and world-system scholars offer historical accounts complementing such analytics (cf. Amin, 1974b; Frank, 1978b; Wallerstein, 1979; Amin et al., 1982). Unequal exchange between a powerful core and a dependent periphery created a global division of labour between industrial and primary commodities, with organized labour in the core negotiating higher wages, subsidized by low wages in a disempowered periphery. Low wages result in a domestic market that is too small to support domestic peripheral capitalism, perpetuating what Frank dubbed the development of underdevelopment. Peripheral elites support this pattern of global dependency because it is in their interest (e.g. Galtung, 1971).[6]

---

[6] Some more mainstream development economists have also focused on core–periphery issues, as 'North–South' models. Krugman's initial foray into international economics was such a model, producing results 'reminiscent of the Hobson–Lenin theory of imperialism' (Krugman, 1981: 149). These models have had no significant impact, however, on mainstream theory (Darity Jr and Davis, 2005).

A variety of criticisms can be offered of these theories from within the Marxian tradition. Emmanuel's empirical argument is based on wages, but his theoretical basis for unequal exchange in the narrow sense depends on differences in the rate of exploitation, not wages (Sheppard and Barnes, 2015 [1990]: 170). Further, Emmanuel's formulation erroneously assumes that Marx's original solution to the transformation problem between value and exchange value is strictly correct. If prices and labour values are calculated correctly, unequal exchange is possible but no predictions can be made about the direction of inequality (Mainwearing, 1974; Gibson, 1980). Shaikh agrees: wage differentials 'in and of themselves...do not necessarily give rise to a transfer of surplus value' (Shaikh, 1980: 59). Thus a higher rate of exploitation and lower organic composition in a country need not imply unequal exchange in Emmanuel's sense. But Emmanuel's and Shaikh's theories share difficulties rooted in their dependence on Marx's value theory (less clearly for Amin, who draws more loosely on the labour theory of value).[7] In a spatially differentiated capitalist economy producing accessibility as a commodity, labour values are geographically variegated in ways that are elided in Marxian value theory. As a consequence, labour value cannot be regarded as independent of prices of production when rates of profit equalize, as Amin and Shaikh aver (Sheppard, 2004). Dependency theory also neglects the rapid industrialization and economic growth in selected third world countries that has transformed global trade and production during the past two decades: Uneven development within the post-colonial world (an empirical problem that world-system theory seeks to redress).

7.1.2 *Post-Keynesian Theories*

Post-Keynesian theorists are sceptical of Marx's value theory, but nevertheless theorize capitalism in ways that are consistent with the economic interdependencies, uncertainties, and contradictions of capitalism emphasized by Marx (e.g., Holt and Pressman, 2001). *Inter alia*, post-Keynesian theory has demonstrated that neoclassical macroeconomic theory, fundamental to the modern trade theory that mainstream economists still utilize to explain North–South trade, is logically inconsistent. This generated a post-Keynesian theory of international trade.

Piero Sraffa, iconoclastic Italian economist at Cambridge University, confidante of Ludwig Wittgenstein and supporter of Antonio Gramsci (Roncaglia, 2000), pioneered this fundamental critique of neoclassical aggregate production theory (Sraffa, 1960). In the neoclassical world of modern trade theory, a

[7] Shaikh criticizes Amin for the 'crucial error' of assuming that intra-industry profit rates will equalize, instead of reflecting inter-firm differences in efficiency and technology.

country with abundant labour relative to capital should specialize in and export commodities requiring labour-intensive technologies, whereas a country with abundant capital should specialize in and export commodities requiring capital-intensive technologies. Sraffa showed that there is no necessary equivalence between factor abundance and factor intensity, that 'reswitching' is possible (Chapter 2, Section 2.2.3). A national, economy-wide 'capital intensive' production technology can replace a 'labour intensive' technology as wages increase, as in neoclassical theory. However, as wages increase further, it is possible that the labour-intensive technology will become more profitable again—impossible in neoclassical theory.[8] In this case when wages are high (and capital cheap) in one country, with the converse holding in another, then the former may export *labour*-intensive commodities in exchange for more capital-intensive exports from the latter (Steedman and Metcalfe, 1979).

This poses two deep problems for how the modern theory of trade explains comparative advantage (Jones, 1956—57). The possibility of what Wong (1995) calls 'factor intensity reversal' (i.e. capital reswitching) undermines core propositions: The Heckscher–Ohlin theory is not universally valid, the factor price equalization theorem is undermined (although weaker conclusions are possible, that average factor prices converge across countries), and the Rybczynski theorem, providing the micro-economic foundation for comparative advantage, does not hold (Wong suggests it is not even meaningful).

Utilizing the example of a single 'small open' economy, Ian Steedman (1979) explored the implications of Sraffa's critique for the Heckscher–Ohlin–Samuelson theory. He concluded that comparative advantage could be resurrected, by the direct method of simply comparing the prices of production for different commodities. A country should specialize in the commodity whose relative price of production is lowest under prevailing technologies, irrespective of how it is produced or whether this is consistent with micro-foundations. Wong similarly concludes that comparative advantages can still be determined, although it depends also on the trade equilibrium (Wong, 1995: 94). Yoshinori Shiozawa (2007) generalizes this to the case of M countries and N (>M) commodities, neglecting transport costs, to show that an international pattern of specialization exists that minimizes production prices and thus maximizes global production.

Sraffa's analysis highlights a second, deeper critique, undermining any attempt to conceptualize production factors as exogenous inputs. Recognizing the importance of exogeneity, Ohlin had devoted a chapter to trying to

---

[8] The neoclassical parable is only guaranteed under the unrealistic assumption that every sector of each economy uses the identical mix of inputs from other all other sectors. Ironically, Marx' solution to the transformation problem, foundational to his value theory, is also immune to mainstream critiques under these conditions (Harcourt, 1972; Sheppard and Barnes, 2015 [1990]).

conceptualize factors of production in this exogenous sense, in terms of kinds of labour (skilled, unskilled, technical), natural resources, and capital (long and short, safe, and risky) (Ohlin, 1933: ch. V). Sraffa shows, however, that capital goods are produced using other produced commodities, not from some exogenous homogeneous 'putty-clay' stuff called capital. Indeed, all 'production factors'—money capital, labour, land, biophysical resources—are increasingly commodified (Polanyi, 2001 [1944]; Harvey, 2003). Yet post-Keynesian trade theory still treats production factors and technologies as fixed, place-based characteristics.[9]

7.1.3 Assessment

These various attempts to construct political economic alternatives to mainstream trade theory—with the potential to deconstruct the free trade doctrine—have had remarkably little purchase, even within radical political economy. They emerged as a cluster of intellectual innovations in the 1970s, but only world-systems analysis received sustained attention and is now also out of fashion. There is also little consensus—heterodoxy is the rule within these marginalized heterodox alternatives: Marxian value theorists disagree on the nature, degree, and causes of unequal exchange, whereas post-Keynesians are critical of value theory *tout court*. This has left the field open for mainstream theory. Beyond this, these alternatives tend to reiterate aspects of mainstream economics' problematic, disentangled socio-spatial ontology: the economy, only, methodological nationalism, absent or exogenous geography (reduced to fixed, place-based characteristics), and limited temporality. Geographical political economy has the potential to do better.

7.2 Toward a Geographical Theory of Global Trade

Geographical political economy resists the disentanglements characterizing mainstream economics, and to a lesser degree political economic alternatives (Sheppard, 2011a). This implies distinct theorizations of trade, challenging the free trade doctrine. Such theories are at best nascent. Thus, to explore this claim I examine two of the six entanglements of trade identified in Chapter 6: spatio-temporal, and more-than-economic.

---

[9] Feminist trade theory has become an active area of recent research (Elson, Grown, and Çagatay, 2007; Van Staveren et al., 2007), incorporating issues of the gendered division of labour, care, and gendered inequality into existing theories. This is a different line of criticism to that developed here.

7.2.1 Entanglements of Space

I begin within the confines of a capitalist economy. This enables me to interrogate how attending to the co-constitution of economy and spatiality departs from both the disentangled mainstream theories as well as heterodox economic theories of global trade. Consider the case of defined spatial territories (e.g. nation-states), within which a variety of interdependent economic sectors evolve, with technologies that vary by sector, firm, and location. When such interdependencies transcend national borders, they are recorded as international trade. Three spatialities are of particular import: connectivity, methodological nationalism, and spatio-temporality.

Consider, first, connectivity. Once the production of accessibility as a commodity is incorporated (Chapter 2), endogenizing the transportation and communications sectors, transport costs are no longer a fixed cost undermining productivity (cf. the iceberg model), but co-evolve with the capitalist space economy. This has two crucial implications (Sheppard and Barnes, 2015 [1990]). First, capitalists (and workers) face genuine uncertainty about the consequences of their actions. Not only can they not know whether they will realize their intentions, but the economy's endogenous spatiality also reduces the likelihood that they can do so. Second, inter-sectoral interdependencies are fungible. Every shift in prices and location patterns, even when technological interdependencies remain unaltered, can alter spatial interdependencies (i.e. trade flows). Uneven geographical development can evolve, then, in a variety of ways (Bergmann, 2012).

Post-Keynesian theorists demonstrate how the entanglements of a relational economy undermine modern trade theory's factor-abundance principle of comparative advantage. Yet this critique remains incomplete because it presumes that geographies are fixed (and that labour and capital are exogenous to the economy). If no unambiguous basis for comparative advantage can be established except in equilibrium (of which, more below), then the possibility that all trading territories benefit from specialization and trade is further compromised.[10] Such complications would need to be teased out in political economic theories of international trade before making definitive judgements, but they imply:

Proposition 1: Incorporating transportation as an endogenous sector of commodity production can undermine central claims of existing trade theories.

---

[10] The implications of this for 'new' trade theory remain unclear. Note, however, that this theory neglects inter-sectoral interdependencies, assumes that all firms (and sectors) use identical technologies, and presumes a zero-profit (net of fixed costs), balance-of-trade equilibrium. Geographical political economy has the capability of analysing 'intra' and inter-industry trade without making such assumptions.

A second entanglement of space is territoriality. The world is not flat. Nation-states are neither equally empowered, nor are they homogeneous, sovereign territorial units with well-defined interests and goals. Yet the inclination in international economics, like realist international relations, is to resort to methodological nationalism (Agnew, 1994; Brenner, 2004). By treating nation-states as separate units of analysis, methodological nationalism also has the effect of aligning them onto a single teleological development trajectory along which free trade lifts all boats (Sheppard, 2011b).

Nation-states differ vastly, of course, in size and internal coherence, itself a difficult problem for methodological nationalism. Beyond this, they are differentially empowered with respect to one another: unequal socio-spatial positionality (Sheppard, 2006b). Recall that socio-spatial positionality is relational, implying that locational (dis)advantage cannot be reduced to an exogenous geography redolent of environmental determinism (e.g. tropicality or landlockedness). Differences in positionality form the basis for distinct interests, perspectives, identities, and strategies that reflect, reproduce, but also contest existing power relations.[11]

Such positional differences are assumed away in the bulk of mainstream and post-Keynesian trade theory (except for the neglected subfield of North–South models, and recent mainstream work incorporating geography as fixed relative location). By contrast, Marxist trade theorists presuppose a binary positionality: core vs. periphery. This highlights one aspect of unequal socio-spatial positionality: how powerful nations have historically used that power to turn international trade to their advantage, creating asymmetries and dependencies that fly in the face of the free trade doctrine. This provides a fixed datum for their quasi-equilibrium analyses of unequal exchange. Consider, however, the emergence of selected manufacturing powers within the post-colony. South Korea and Taiwan came to occupy favourable positionalities by comparison to other formerly colonized countries, shifting from primary commodity to manufacturing commodity exporters, and China has been transforming itself (and global trade flows) through a similar strategy. As these examples demonstrate, socio-spatial positionality can be reconfigured, not just reproduced (cf. Deleuze, 1994 [1968]): On occasion, the multiple gaps and contingencies underlying all power relationships enable a broader power shift. Given their complex dynamical nature, such possibilities and contingencies remain unpredictable, but their conditions of possibility can be identified:

---

[11] Here, I restrict discussion of socio-spatial positionality to the national scale, mindful of how any territory is riven by heterogeneities that reflect the different socio-spatial positionalities of its inhabitants.

Proposition 2: By attending to the socio-spatial positionality of territorial units, geographical political economy can contribute to theorizations of periodic restructurings of trade relations and uneven geographical development.

The entanglements of connectivity and territoriality entail a third aspect: space/time. Marxian theories of the capitalist space-economy fundamentally question the utility of examining potential equilibrium outcomes—the dominant predilection in mainstream economics. Agents cannot be presumed to know equilibrium outcomes and act on the basis of such knowledge, particularly given the additional complexities and possibilities of unintended consequences in a spatially differentiated economy. Even in geographical economics, seemingly rational actions taken far from equilibrium need not drive the space economy toward equilibrium (Fowler, 2007, 2011), and anyway individuals frequently do not act on the basis of a perfectly rational calculation of their self-interest (cf. Thaler and Sunstein, 2003). Beyond this, the politics of production, compounded at the international scale, have the potential to destabilize any equilibrium outcome that is serendipitously reached. In the real world, trade is not in balance, markets do not clear, labour and capital are often underemployed, and profits are positive (e.g. Subasat, 2003; Unger, 2007; Fletcher, 2009). It is thus strange that even Marxist trade theories have focused on equilibrium outcomes.

Attempts to theorize trade as an evolutionary process, often far from any potential equilibrium, remain rare. Marxisant approaches occasionally narrate accumulation dynamics mathematically, to determine the conditions under which equilibrium is an emergent feature or what kinds of out-of-equilibrium dynamics result (e.g. Duménil and Lévy, 1993; Webber and Rigby, 1999; Foley, 2003; Bergmann et al., 2009). Yet none of these incorporate spatiality, address commodity trade, or attend to destabilizing struggles over the economic surplus.[12]

Proposition 3: Entanglements of economy and space require an out-of-equilibrium theorization of trade and uneven development, incorporating evolutionary and historical perspectives (e.g. Smith and White, 1992; Fry and Wilson, 2012).

7.2.2 Entanglements with the More-than-economic

Consider, first, the political governance of trade. It is necessary to conceptualize the multi-scalar context shaping the national territories whose

---

[12] Bergmann (2012) analyses the first two.

boundaries define what is counted as international trade. Nation-states' actions are embedded within shifting supra-national frameworks (the United Nations, the World Trade Organization, international financial institutions, the Group of 77, transnational corporations, global finance markets, ATTAC, the World Social Forum). This constitutes a geopolitics of trade, which positionally differentiated nations are unequally empowered to influence, and which unevenly shapes actions at the national scale (cf. Grant, 1993, 1994; Gibb and Michalak, 1996; Poon, Thompson, and Kelly, 2000; Hughes, 2006). Nation-states also are territorially and socially differentiated into sub-national, and transcended by trans-local, regions, which also shape, and are shaped by, national scale trade and industrial policy. Geographical political economists have contributed to a powerful theorization of the production and politics of scale (cf. Delaney and Leitner, 1997; Swyngedouw, 1997b; Collinge, 1999; Brenner, 2001; Leitner and Miller, 2007) that has yet to be applied to trade. As for socio-spatial positionality, inter-scalar relations are shaped by unequally empowered agents whose contestations make possible reconstitutions of scales and hierarchies. Power need not emanate from the top (contra. Marston et al., 2005) or the bottom as mainstream economic theory asserts (Chapter 2), and occasionally it is up for grabs.

Consider also how the economic is entangled with culture, emotion, identity, discourse, and materialities. Notwithstanding the centrality of such entanglements to contemporary shcolarship, geographical political economists have had very little to say about how these are co-implicated in the production processes associated with commodity trade. Here, I can only gesture toward how the more-than-economic can be incorporated into a geographical theory of global trade. Commodity trade always has had a vital cultural aspect. From the earliest day, traders have acted as cultural brokers, embodying the mobility of cultural difference between places, and posing problems for societies that seek to take advantage of their space-transcending proclivities while retaining already-existing cultural norms. A persistent strategy was to confine 'foreign' traders to peripheral spaces in receiving societies (cf. Sjoberg, 1960; Curtin, 1984). The process of trade itself is encultured. Forms and norms of exchange resonate with cultural difference (cf. Gudeman, 2001, 2008). Participants in those places through which trade is realized—ships, trucks, airplanes, and markets—find their economic activities bound up with their (often) itinerant identity as traders (Robins, 1995; Casale, 2007; Hughes, 2007).

It is not just the traders, but also the commodities traded, that are entangled with culture. Indeed, many of the cultural debates surrounding globalizing capitalism have revolved around the question of the degree to which global vectors of trade constitute a stalking horse for western cultural hegemony, undermining national cultural heritage, or are productive of cultural hybridity

127

and difference. With respect to gender and sexuality, there has been considerable research into the gendering of places of trade and the transportation/communication systems connecting them. Marketplaces are highly gendered, in ways that vary geographically and are often contested (cf. Mintz, 1971; McDowell, 1997; Seligmann, 2001; Mandel, 2004; Wright, 2004), as are the mobile workplaces producing the accessibility that facilitates trade (Norling, 1996; Bunnell, 2007; Fajardo, 2008).[13]

Entanglements of trade with the more-than-human world fall into two overlapping but somewhat separable themes. First, is the question of how trade is co-implicated with the more-than-human world. A number of geographers have examined this with respect to particular commodities, how the material attributes of, particularly, primary commodities comingle with the trade and commodity chains that bring them to first world consumers (e.g. Whatmore and Thorne, 1997; Whatmore, 2001; Cook et al., 2004, 2006). There are, of course, much larger questions about how global trade vectors, and the processes driving these, are entangled with broader scale biophysical processes. What is the carbon footprint of global trade, how is this distributed geographically, and whose responsibility is it (Bergmann, 2013)? How does free trade compound the ecological unsustainability argued to accompany capitalism's imperative to accumulate (Harvey, 1996; O'Connor, 1998)? Is local trade more sustainable and, if so, how can it be encouraged and what are its implications? There has been considerable theoretical and empirical research into these questions outside geography (Hertwich and Peters, 2009), but their complex spatialities remain under-researched (Bergmann, 2013).

The entanglements of trade with materialities also connect with questions of science and technology (cf. Latour, 1987; Pickering, 1995; Stengers, 1997). Contesting attempts in mainstream trade theory to treat technology as a malleable capital input whose evolution is either treated as exogenous to the economy (a time trend), or endogenously as 'human capital' (e.g. the new growth theory: Romer, 1990), economic geographers have taken up the insight from science and technology studies that technology is neither exogenous to nor reducible to political economic processes. The pressure for new trading, transportation, and communications technologies is central to capitalism (Chapter 2). They accelerate the production and circulation of commodities and extend the geographical reach of trade and production networks (enhancing capitalists' and states' capacities to eke out the economic opportunities associated with geographical inequality and difference).

---

[13] Interestingly, the limited geographical scholarship on gender and transportation has tended to focus on short distance personal commuting and daily travel; to date, the study of identity and long distance freight transportation has been dominated by non-geographers (Goetz, Vowles, and Tierney, 2009).

Technologies co-evolve with, helping constitute, trading practices and possibilities in marketplaces—enhancing and disrupting market functionality (Callon, 1998; Mackenzie et al., 2008; Mackenzie, 2009). This is also the case for the vehicles transporting commodities, whose functionality and capacity depend on geographical knowledge and emergent geographical technologies of navigation, transportation, and communication (particularly, today, electronic trade and commerce) (Latour, 1993; Law, 1996; Dodge and Kitchin, 2004; Zook, 2005).

Proposition 4: Entanglements with the non-economic profoundly complicate theorizations of trade, in ill-understood ways.

7.3 Conclusion

In this chapter, summarized in the preceding four propositions, I have argued that a geographical approach to trade and globalizing capitalism has the potential to deconstruct the free trade doctrine. Careful attention to entanglements of space, particularly connectivity, calls into question mainstream trade theory's hard-core propositions. Theoretically, trade is bound up with the production of accessibility, that quintessentially geographical commodity. Empirically, logistics remains a sector of increasing economic import for globalizing capitalism. One of the most immediate dramatic impacts of the 2008–09 global crisis was on freight transportation: around the world, containers piled up in ports, ships were idled outside harbours, logistics companies faced crises of profit realization, and economies based heavily on logistics (e.g. Singapore) were thrown into a particular kind of crisis. Yet this mobile arena of commodity production and profit realization remains largely a most unfortunate lacuna in economic geography.

There are profound consequences associated with replacing the socio-spatial ontology of mainstream trade theory with the relational and dialectical one of geographical political economy. First, as I have argued throughout, this shift fundamentally calls into question modernist teleological accounts, in the spirit of Walter Rostow (1960; Sachs, 2005), of development as a universal sequence of stages that all countries can and must pass through to attain prosperity—emulating the United States and other 'advanced' capitalist countries (Blaut, 1993; Massey, 1999; Sheppard, 2011b). Rather, the produced geopolitical and socionatural geographies of uneven development that have accompanied really-existing globalizing capitalism require that if precarious bodies and places are to escape impoverishment they must break with the free trade doctrine. A geographical account of globalizing capitalism undermines the claims of the free trade doctrine, implying that the variety of already existing alternatives is worthy of exploration and examination. Some are narrow forms of protectionism: state-led interventions into territorial trade policy that seek to tweak capitalism when it undermines the constituted interests of a territory. Protectionism can be venal, seeking to enhance the interests of territorial elites or powerful states at the expense of others. Consider, for example, US, Japanese, and European Union protectionist subsidies for their farmers, or Chinese policies that advance the interests of capitalists over those of workers. Yet it may also be used to protect disadvantaged bodies and places from the ravages of uneven development (Stiglitz and Charlton, 2005; Fletcher, 2009). In addition to fair trade initiatives, alternative food networks, and LETS (Hughes, 2005), these include the Bolivarian Alternative for the Americas (ALBA, Harris and Azzi, 2006). Such alternatives resonate with more-than-capitalist exchange and production (Gibson-Graham, 2006): Barter, Ithaca hours, exchange values incorporating living wages and environmental protection, and the politics of trading Cuban doctors for Venezuelan oil.

There are no panaceas, of course: 'The best-laid schemes . . . Gang aft agley' (Burns, 1786). Others have documented how alternative logics can become absorbed into capitalism (e.g. Walmart marketing fair trade coffee; Nestlé selling organic baby food), or be compromised by the always conflicting interests and unequal power relations of participants in trade (Fridell, 2006; Raynolds and Long, 2007). The answer to the deep problems of the free trade doctrine cannot be a ban on trade. But a geographical approach to globalizing capitalism can contribute to creating an intellectual space that acknowledges and critically assesses alternative trading movements and initiatives, rethinking and decentring hegemonic doctrines.

8

Capitalism's Raggedy Edges

People, Earth, Finance

Thus far I have focused my geographical analysis of globalizing capitalism largely on how our understanding is altered once we account adequately for its socio-spatial relations. I have shown that spatialities matter to the conditions of possibility and evolutionary trajectories of capitalism, arguing that too little attention has been paid to a particular aspect: socio-spatial positionality. Put otherwise, the possibilities faced by bodies and places depend *inter alia* on the always uneven, asymmetric connectivities of globalizing capitalism. Yet thinking geographically about capitalism, indeed about anything, also means thinking beyond the economic—acknowledging how those aspects of society conventionally classified as economic co-evolve with other societal and more-than-human processes (Chapter 1; Sheppard, 2015). The conceit of capitalism is that it is potentially all-embracing; everything can be commodified and brought to (capitalist) market: bodies, carbon, ecosystems, air, etc. Indeed, Marxian analysis suggests that capitalism requires the ongoing commodification of everything: this is both a precondition for capitalism coming into existence (primitive accumulation), and essential to its survival (accumulation by dispossession). In this view, to avoid an existential crisis the processes driving capitalism have to continually identify new phenomena to commodify—body parts, the ether, the oceans, or recirculate former commodities out of and back into capitalism—waste, recycling (e.g. Luxemburg, 1951 [1913]; Marx, 1967 [1867]; Harvey, 1982b, 2003, 2014; O'Connor, 1991; Gidwani and Reddy, 2011; Gidwani, 2012).

In this chapter, I turn to those edges of capitalism dubbed 'fictitious commodities' by Karl Polanyi, each of which has been the subject of considerable geographical scholarship in recent years—while largely neglected in geographical economics: people, the more-than-human world, and finance. As Polanyi (2001 [1944]: 75) puts it: 'labor, land, and money are obviously *not* commodities; the postulate that anything that is bought and sold must have been produced for sale is emphatically untrue with regard to them'. I dub these raggedy edges because any line separating them from capitalist economic processes is continually up for grabs, but also because in my view it remains impossible to legislate a priori whether, in the final analysis, these edges are functional to the sustainability of capitalism or undermine it.

Polanyi's discussion of fictitious commodities was central to his analysis of the Great Depression, which he argued was a consequence of the 'great transformation' of the North Atlantic economy under British free trade suzerainty between 1846 and 1914. As he saw it, the great transformation triggered the dissolution of social bonds with the commodification of labour, ecological crisis accompanying the commodification of nature, and financial crises consequent on the commodification of money. The Keynesian/Fordist response of the 1930s marked what he called the double movement: the metastasization of capitalist markets and commodification, counteracted by attempts to limit this by social institutions and political movements. (He thought that the latter had prevailed, but neoliberalization suggests otherwise.) Polanyi's threefold analysis of crisis, of the consequences of market-rule in the domains of fictitious capital, exemplifies thinking beyond the economic (extending the analyses of Chapter 5), and invokes parallels between what he observed at the culmination of British hegemony and what we experienced after 2007—a crisis that is simultaneously economic, ecological, and reproductive (Fraser, 2014). In the sections that follow, rather than attempting to summarize the voluminous literatures in each area, I examine how these raggedy edges co-evolve with uneven connectivities and socio-spatial positionality.

8.1 People

Economic theory, both mainstream and political economic, is inclined to reduce societal complexity to individual economic agents. They may also act collectively on the basis of shared interests, but their actions are of interest only to the extent that they contribute to capitalist production and consumption—to the Gross National Product. As innumerable scholars have established, there is far more to sustaining capitalism than this. It is important to extend any analysis of capitalism beyond such accounting conventions if we are to recognize the occluded societal conditions of possibility for capitalist agency that such conventions make invisible (Waring, 1988; Stiglitz et al., 2010).

8.1.1 *More-than-capitalist Society: Nurturing or Challenging Capitalism?*

Underlying the abstract bodies of the worker (and capitalist)—the automatons of economic theory—is a raft of societal processes enabling economic agents' participation in labour markets, commodity production, and capital accumulation. I call these more-than-capitalist because they are neither fully external to nor subsumable within capitalism—they are dialectically inter-related. Yet they are invisible in, and excluded from, conventional mainstream and political economic theory.[1]

One obvious component of more-than-capitalist society is social reproduction, which is what Polanyi had in mind:

> Social reproduction is the fleshy, messy and indeterminate stuff of everyday life.... At its most basic, it hinges upon the biological reproduction of the labor force, both generationally and on a daily basis, through the acquisition and distribution of the means of existence, including food, shelter, clothing and health care.... Apart from the need to secure the means of existence, [this] calls forth a range of cultural forms and practices that are also geographically and historically specific, including those associated with knowledge and learning, social justice and its apparatus, and the media. (Katz, 2001: 711)

Yet there are other ways that more-than-capitalist processes can underwrite capitalism.[2] Those who find themselves engaged in the informal economy not only produce for one another, but also subsidize capitalist commodity production by providing cheaper goods and services (Portes, Castells, and Benton, 1989). Such activities, also excluded from GNP calculations because they are not reported to state agencies, are ubiquitous; but they are particularly prevalent in the post-colony. Estimates suggest that informal sector employment constitutes 60 per cent of the global labour force, and as much as 93 per cent of all employment in India including 84.2 per cent of all non-agricultural employment (Sen and Kolli, 2009; Williams, 2013; Roberts, 2014). Informal employment also includes highly exploited labour: forms of slavery, indentured, trafficked, and forced labour that to date co-evolve with capitalist labour relations rather than being replaced by them (Brysk and Choi-Fitzpatrick, 2012).

Finally, there are the activities associated with what has come to be known as diverse economies. Diverse economies references the great diversity of economic activities that are not primarily driven by the logic of commodity production: 'the huge variety of economic transactions, labor practices and economic organizations that contribute to social well-being worldwide, in both positive and unsavory ways' (Gibson-Graham, 2008: 615). One marker of the persistence of such diversity, notwithstanding European enlightenment attempts to push this under the mat, is the local and global re-emergence of

[1] Exchange value may not be realized when potential commodities remain unsold or become devalued, but there is at least the intent to accumulate.

[2] In Fordist and state-oriented space-times, the state has also been cajoled into underwriting key aspects of social reproduction, albeit in geographically variegated ways: education, health, utilities, and welfare, in particular. Many such practices remained within the spaces of civil society and the household, however.

economic practices driven by religious principles, such as Sharia and Hindu economics (Sandikci and Rice, 2011; Vinod, 2012). These are post-secular times, and not just in the post-colony (Chakrabarty, 2000; Habermas, 2008). To label this diversity as non-capitalist is too simplistic; like (indeed, overlapping with) the informal sector, they are not some dualist other of globalizing capitalism but articulate with it. Yet they are more-than-capitalist in the sense described above.

As befits their conceptual marginalization in economic thought, and notwithstanding their capacity to nurture capitalism, such more-than-capitalist activities are archetypically associated with bodies and places represented as peripheral to the capitalist space-economy. Those participating in such activities are disproportionately female and non-white, working in domestic, impoverished and informally occupied spaces deemed as having limited value for commodity production. Consider, for example, their flourishing in the currently devalued spaces of inner city Detroit—triggering attempts to remake it into a 'proper' city—as well as in Mumbai's slums or Jakarta's kampungs (Nijman, 2010; Peck, 2012a; Simone, 2014).

Pro-capitalist discourses often represent the bodies and places of more-than-capitalist practices as ill-developed domains of economic prosperity, spaces of arrested development whose incorporation into capitalism would enable both personal emancipation and economic growth (de Soto, 2000). In this view, capitalism makes it possible for anyone who is hard working and responsible to achieve prosperity and social influence, irrespective of their positionality; cultural diversity should not be a basis for discrimination as it can be a valued economic resource (e.g. multiculturalism). Indeed, the neoliberalization of globalizing capitalism entails major efforts to commodify and marketize all kinds of more-than-capitalist societal practices: Maids, professional cleaners, personal trainers, farmers' markets, charter schools, the corporatization of Basque's Mondragon cooperative movement, the marijuana industry, the social economy, etc. (e.g. Amin, Cameron, and Hudson, 2003). It follows that failure to develop or prosper reflects the deficient nature of these bodies and places—place-based explanations of poverty and inequality that amount to little more than sexism, racism, and placism. Yet, as I have argued throughout, such accounts overlook a profound vector through which inequality is perpetuated (within capitalism, but also relative to its alternatives): unequal and asymmetric connectivities reflecting differences in socio-spatial positionality.

For its critics, however, globalizing capitalism's persistent failure to deliver on its promise, that is, its tendency to reproduce socio-spatial inequality, necessitates the pursuit of more-than-capitalist economic activities; indeed, capitalism requires such 'constitutive outsides'. Such activities also can prioritize forms of social practices and imaginaries that receive little recognition in economic thought: ethics and justice rather than self-interest, care and nurturing rather than efficiency and productivity, collaboration rather than competition, collective action rather than possessive individualism (Sayer, 2007). Not all more-than-capitalist activities are desirable or ethical, of course; some are emancipatory and exemplary but others will be deeply exploitative (Samers, 2005). Further, none can constitute ubiquitous best practice. Yet they can act as barriers to the expansion of globalizing capitalism and represent a resource for those seeking alternative economic experiments and imaginaries (Gibson-Graham, 1996, 2006; Gibson-Graham et al., 2013). Their capacity to constitute alternatives to globalizing capitalism is subject to passionate debate, however, between those arguing that nothing less than a global revolution is necessary, and those advocating for the positive potential of grassroots alternatives (compare Gibson-Graham, 2006; Leitner et al., 2007a; Harvey, 2014).

In brief, the trading zones between capitalist commodity production and more-than-capitalist practices stalk Earth, replete with already existing unequal socio-spatial positionalities. Beyond the complex differentiations of socio-spatial positionality within spaces of capitalist commodity production and exchange (inter and intra-class, compounded by gender, race, sexuality, and location, etc.), are those that connect but differentiate these from more-than-capitalist practices and spaces. Indeed there is a deep dialectic here: more-than-capitalist economic activities marginalize those participating in them even as they represent a diverse ecosystem of alternatives to capitalism. In what follows, I will briefly review ways in which such differentiated positionalities are incorporated into globalizing capitalism, as well as ways in which they disrupt it.

8.1.2 Commodifying More-than-capitalist Practices

An important trend in globalizing capitalism—in geographically very uneven ways—has been the emancipation of marginalized bodies and spaces by extending the scope of the capitalist labour market. The expansion of capitalist employment opportunities, combined with shifting valuations of social difference, has enabled some women and non-whites to enter such markets, improving their economic and social status and influence. Yet, as is well known, sexual and racial inequality and the stereotypes deployed to legitimize it have not dissipated. Within capitalism, these demographic groups too often find themselves tethered to lower wage and lower status jobs, butt up against glass ceilings, and find themselves among the first to be fired in the space-times of economic crisis and restructuring. These opportunities may well be an improvement for those able to take advantage, but the promises of capitalism remain unfulfilled (unfulfillable, I have argued). On the one hand, such extensions of capitalism always remain incomplete, reproducing burdens for those newly able to commodify their labour. On the other, the accrued benefits for some tendentially exacerbate the challenges faced by others: relational impoverishment. I offer some vignettes to illustrate how this works.

Consider, first, the household scale. The entry of women into the labour market increases their income and that of the household, but at the cost of the double burden of commonly being expected to provide the bulk of the domestic work of social reproduction. Domestic work, unvalued but unavoidable, extends the effective working day and acts as a costless subsidy to reproduction of the labour force. Its responsibilities put homemakers in motion (between work, home, garden, schools, doctors, etc.), constraining where and under what conditions they can enter the labour market (e.g. Hanson and Pratt, 1995), and reinforcing constructions of women as insufficiently dedicated to their capitalist employers. This spills over into stereotypes about female capitalist entrepreneurs themselves, who are judged, inappropriately, by the standards of male colleagues unburdened by social reproduction (Blake and Hanson, 2005).[3]

Wealthier households can compensate for such burdens by commodifying the work of social reproduction—hiring child minders, cleaners, gardeners, drivers, etc.—options available only to those who have accumulated the means to employ others. This creates a secondary circuit of employment, bringing often female and non-white workers into the household but away from their own responsibilities for social reproduction in the generally more impoverished places where they reside. Of course, the opportunities for income and advancement disproportionately favour those employing domestic labour, relative to those employed as such. Because of the often informal nature of this kind of employment, the lack of state regulation and enforcement, and the disadvantaged socio-spatial positionality of those hired to perform the work of social reproduction (including undocumented migrants), abuses are legion. Some such workers find themselves trapped in the homes where they work, others are exploited, sexually harassed, underpaid, or unpaid (Fussell, 2011; Minkler et al., 2014). The conditions of possibility for households to realize adequate social reproduction also exceed the household scale: wealthier neighbourhoods tend to have better quality education and healthcare, a more healthful physical environment, etc., correlating geography with capitalist economic opportunity (Chatty et al., 2014).

Consider, next, the intra-urban scale. Informal work concentrates in low income and marginal neighbourhoods, where those employed in the social reproduction of others also typically reside. In cities like Los Angeles, there is

---

[3] Of course, this describes how such relations play out in a conventional, heterosexual, western-style nuclear family. In other contexts, the gender divisions will differ and extended families also become involved.

regular daily traffic between wealthy and poor neighbourhoods as cleaners, maids, nurses, and dog-walkers commute from the latter to the former neighbourhoods (often with very limited public transit accessibility). Day labourers commute to work centres and DIY superstore parking lots, hoping to be picked up. While economic benefits accrue to both sides, they favour the better off households and neighbourhoods. In cities like Jakarta, the kampungs— spaces of informal housing and employment—also provide such social reproduction labour for wealthier communities. In addition, informal (often quasi-capitalist) economies operate out of the kampungs, producing and marketing cheap food, clothing and other relatively low-end commodities (relatively direct substitutes for domestic social reproduction) to middle income households and office workers. But informal settlements also are centres of calculation for wide-ranging—even global—networks of informal trade and bootlegged commodities. In short, social reproduction and informal economies connect poor with wealthy neighbourhoods in ways that can be mutually beneficial but nevertheless widen the economic gulf between them.

The geography of diverse economies is more complex. Cities certainly are places of experimentation with more-than-capitalist economic relations: Community gardens, community supported agriculture, labour sharing, local exchange and trading systems, etc. We do not know a great deal about the kinds of connectivities between differently positioned bodies and neighbourhoods that these reflect and stimulate, but one relatively well-researched aspect is alternative food networks (AFNs). These connect urban households with rural farmers as well as urban gardeners. In some contexts, notably the European Union, AFNs have been documented to enhance the welfare of marginalized farmers by catalysing markets for organic and local food; in the post-socialist Baltic states, however, where diverse economies have a very different evolution (Smith and Stenning, 2006), small farmers struggle to benefit systematically from AFNs (Blumberg, 2014).

At the global scale, a core aspect of the narrative of globalizing capitalism is that it has largely replaced earlier, more exploitative forms of employment (associated with feudalism and slavery) with a 'free' labour market and pluralist representative democracies. Even Marx, no friend of capitalism, underlined this as a positive development. Yet, contra stageist readings of historical materialism (e.g. Warren, 1980), recent research into the history of capitalism suggests a far more dialectical relationship. Historians and geographers have identified a broad range of processes by means of which European colonialism enabled the conditions of possibility for globalizing capitalism, ranging from the provision of cheap resources and food, to gold and silver, agricultural and industrial technologies, slavery and the factory system (Blaut, 1993; Frank, 1998; Hobson, 2004; Baucom, 2005; Johnson, 2013; Beckert, 2014).

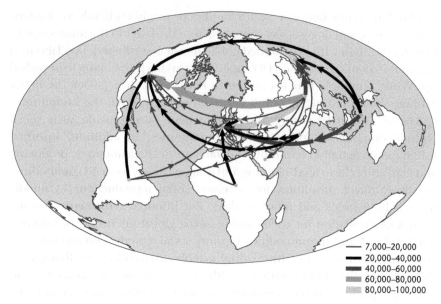

——	7,000–20,000
■■	20,000–40,000
■■■	40,000–60,000
▨▨▨	60,000–80,000
▨▨▨	80,000–100,000

Figure 8.1 Embedded labour flows in the global economy, 2004

Arrows flow from the country where labour is employed for commodity production to where these commodities are consumed. Arrow width measures the total embedded labour flow—the labour directly and indirectly utilized in commodity production.

Source: Computed by Luke Bergmann from a social accounting matrix, based on the Global Trade Analysis Program 7 database. Used by permission.

In the contemporary era, embedded labour is transferred from the post-colony to the North Atlantic region and to Japan even within the formal economy—asymmetric connectivities much like Emmanuel's (1972) notion of unequal exchange in labour value terms subsidizing economic growth in the most prosperous economies (Figure 8.1). This is only reinforced by international migration flows, a further vector of documented and undocumented migration from the post-colony to the prosperous capitalist economies of the North Atlantic, amounting to a net flow of approximately 13.7 million people between 2005 and 2010 (Abel and Sander, 2014). A further approximately 6.4 million migrated to the booming economies of the Arabian gulf. The International Labour Organization estimates that there are some 232 million migrant workers worldwide (Figure 8.2). These include foreign labour migration under contract but working in largely unregulated labour markets, such as agricultural labour in North America and construction labour in the Middle East (Mohammad and Sidaway, 2012). It includes Filipina and other south-east and south Asian women hired as maids by wealthy North American, European, and Asian households (Asis, Huang, and Yeoh, 2004; Kelly and Lusis 2006; Pratt, 2012). It includes undocumented migration from Latin

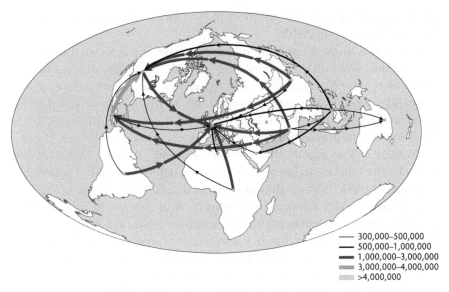

300,000–500,000
500,000–1,000,000
1,000,000–3,000,000
3,000,000–4,000,000
>4,000,000

Figure 8.2 Net migration flows between world regions, 2005–2010
The width of the flow represents the volume of migration.
Source: Abel and Sander (2014), by permission.

America and the Caribbean into the US, from Africa and Asia into Europe, and from Bangladesh and Burma to Australia, Indonesia, and Malaysia, seeking informal work and residency. It includes nurses and doctors, trained in Africa and Asia but seeking employment in the North Atlantic economies (Kingma, 2006). It includes Asian wives sought out by lonely men in Japan (Faier, 2009). It includes trafficked women, and men, indentured into sexual slavery (Altink, 2013).

Even as this raggedy edge of more-than-capitalist practices is brought within the ambit of globalizing capitalism, the latter too often fails to deliver on its promise. At the scale of bodies, those already marginalized agents participating in more-than-capitalist activities find themselves in irregular and poorly regulated markets for labour, with limited possibilities to enhance their wealth, opportunities, or influence. This can be the case within households, and along lines of gender, race, or sexuality, as well as between employees and employers. For example, undocumented international migrant workers place themselves at personal risk as they migrate, and at their destination if they arrive. Women migrating for care work or as healthcare workers face a spatially extended double burden, leaving behind their own children and relying on others to provide the work of social reproduction at home, even as they enhance social reproduction for those in the place of destination (Herod and Aguiar, 2006; Lawson, 2010).

Further, the uneven connectivities between places associated with such practices may well enhance pre-existing spatial inequalities. Mainstream geographical economists are inclined to argue that migration reduces spatial inequalities by mitigating spatial imbalances in the supply of and demand for labour, moving toward inter-regional equilibrium (e.g. World Bank, 2009). Migration scholarship comes to very different conclusions, however. Places of origin tend to lose exactly those residents (young, skilled, pro-active) who would be the most desirable to retain, and spatial inequalities in wealth and economic growth do not diminish. Indeed, places of origin often have invested in the skills acquired by migrants—skills that are lost as a result of migration (also often lost to skilled migrants themselves, as a doctor from, say, Tanzania becomes a taxi driver in London). This is compounded by immigration filters developed by North Atlantic economies, offering citizenship to wealthy Asians, Africans, and Latin Americans while keeping the barriers high for poor immigrants (Ong, 2006).[4] Proponents of globalizing capitalism argue that such losses can be compensated for by the remittances sent home by migrants working abroad, or by persuading successful former migrants to reinvest in their place of origin. Indeed, remittance flows have exploded alongside documented and undocumented migration, as migrants willingly forgo personal income and wealth to support families back home. Yet such remittances are often used to enhance the status of the migrant's extended family there, rather than promoting economic well-being for all.

In all these ways, even the enrolment of more-than-capitalist practices and places into globalizing capitalism contributes to relational impoverishment (e.g. Elwood, Lawson, and Nowak, 2014)—to the processes through which wealth accumulation by prosperous bodies and places is at the expense of the impoverishment of precarious bodies and places.

8.1.3 *The Triple Movement: More-than-capitalist Contestations*

Such mechanisms of enrolment are always incomplete. In part, this is because of globalizing capitalism's failure to make good on its promise of opportunity for all, necessitating a search for alternatives. But in good part it is also because of the persistence of and desire for other ways of living, organized around mutual aid (Kropotkin, 1922) rather than possessive individualism. This adds

---

[4] Colonialism created a channel by means of which European countries could readily expel the surplus populations that so concerned Malthus to white settler and other colonies; today, those wealthy countries' immigration controls largely foreclose this option for countries of the post-colony.

a third, civil society, dimension to Polanyi's state and market: a triple movement, as it were (Fraser, 2013).

First, the rationales and desires underlying more-than-capitalist imaginaries and practices are irreducible to individuals' rational choices among scarce alternatives (contra Becker, 1973). They involve an ethics of care—not only for humans we know, but also for broader more-than-human moral communities (geoethics) (Lynn, 1998; Smith, 1998; Lawson, 2007). They involve an orientation toward collaborative and collective action: working together to meet challenges and improve livelihoods, and acting together to resist inimical developments and advocate for radical change. Such actions are always fraught with difficulties in identifying, and acting appropriately with respect to: one's moral community; the politics of collaboration, particularly when different participants are unequally positioned and empowered; and the complex alliance and transversal politics that always accompany collective action (Yuval-Davis, 1999). Yet, once we accept that humans are social animals rather than self-interested individuals, collaboration can no longer be reduced to overcoming the free rider problem (Barnes and Sheppard, 1992). Rather, the question is reversed: why do humans eschew their collectivity in favour of self-interest? One answer is that they have been subject to four centuries of discourses, emanating from the North Atlantic sphere, alleging that humans are possessive individualists by nature, and the better for it (Macpherson, 1962).

Broadly speaking, more-than capitalist imaginaries and practices can be parsed into contestation and resistance (Leitner et al., 2007b). Contestation references those actions, from household care to alternative economic systems and livelihood practices, that are tangential to the commodity logic of capitalism. These include imaginaries and practices that long preceded globalizing capitalism and continue to operate outside or tangential to it; they also include alternatives turned to by people who find their encounters with capitalism and its developmental imaginary disabling. Such practices are particularly salient in post-colonial spaces, where the promise of capitalist development has repeatedly failed (Escobar, 1995, 2001; Guha, 1997; Chatterjee, 2001), yet they are also practised within the heartlands of capitalism (Williams, 2005). They are commonly associated with subaltern positionalities (with people of colour, women, formerly colonized peoples), yet are also practised by middle class and elite families seeking to advance their collective interest (Simone, 2004; Benjamin, 2008; Bayat, 2009; Roy, 2009). Of course, socio-spatial positional inequalities enable those with greater political and cultural capital to more effectively marshal more-than-capitalist practices in ways that enhance their livelihood chances.

Resistance references those actions and imaginaries mobilized in response to the perceived predations of globalizing capitalism—actions seeking to push back its advances in the name of an alternative economic and political order. These would include social movements and contentious politics of many kinds—anti-capitalist, feminist, environmentalist, etc. Some initiatives seek to replace capitalist with other forms of economic activity locally; others seek global resonance. Some articulate with political parties and movements, others resolutely ignore representative democratic politics and are quite anarchic. For both contestations and resistance, there is also abundant evidence that the spatial organization and strategies of such initiatives can be crucial to their prospects for success (Leitner et al., 2008; Miller, Beaumont, and Nicholls, 2013).

The unanswerable question, a priori, is whether and how such contestations and forms of resistance destabilize globalizing capitalism. On the one hand, as can be seen with such recent examples of direct action as the Arab Spring movements, the Occupy initiatives, anti-WTO and anti-G8 protests, ATTAC, and the World Social Forum, immensely creative initiatives often run into sand. They can be taken over by undesirable more-than-capitalist imaginaries (military autocracy, patriarchy, religious fundamentalism), suppressed by police and military action, or disabled by internal disagreement. On the other hand they do not disappear, and attempts to commodify them are always incomplete.

Conceptually, extending Polanyi's framework to a triple movement (with the third leg including, but not confined to, movements seeking emancipation, *pace* Fraser) enables us to see that there is more to the future of capitalism than the question of the shifting role of the state and the market. Polanyi's imaginary confines us to thinking along a two-dimensional continuum, extending from the (mythical, as Polanyi was the first to point out) free market/nightwatchman state at one end, to state-led capitalism (or, *in extremis*, socialism) at the other. This is a rather North Atlantic perspective on political possibilities, notwithstanding their global resonance. The triple movement makes space for a variety of experiments, actions within civil society and subaltern populations that are not bound to the state–market continuum but possessed of their own agency.

The persistence, indeed necessity, of this third dimension means that the coherence and sustainability of capitalism is always under question—and rightly so given its internal contradictions and failure to deliver. But it also points to a complex spatio-temporal dynamic linking the uneven geographies of globalizing capitalism with those of more-than-capitalist practices. Just as capitalism cannot be best practice for all, the same must inevitably be the case for more-than-capitalist practices. There is no single best practice alternative waiting in the wings to replace capitalism, but all kinds of experiments emerging from and stretching across different socio-spatial positionalities, which will be differentially effective and unequally desirable in different geohistorical contexts. The first step is to acknowledge their potential significance; the second is to put them in mutual critical engagement with one another.

8.2 Earth

In mainstream economic theory, nature is conceptualized as a bundle of resources—attributes of the lithosphere, biosphere, hydrosphere, and atmosphere that are of economic value for commodity production, circulation, and consumption. Yet the more-than-human world is far more dynamic and complex than this, of course, as is its relation to human society. Transforming the more-than-human world into such resources is a complex cultural, political as well as economic process: It entails cultural valuations of and relations to nature, political processes determining access to a resource and the capacity to exploit it (e.g. the Treaty on the Non-proliferation of Nuclear Weapons), and technological-economic processes shaping the geography of resource exploration and exploitation. Put otherwise, the more-than-human world is not a bundle of separable resources but a complex dynamical and dialectical system within which human society is embedded (Levins and Lewontin, 1985; Smolin, 1997).[5] Potentially commodifiable aspects co-evolve with one another, reflecting intersecting processes of insolation, plate tectonics, erosion, chemical weathering and sedimentation, carbon and hydrologic cycles, species evolution, ecosystem change, etc. Since such processes are irreducible to economic logics, the challenge becomes how to enrol the more-than-human world into that of capitalism. As with more-than-capitalist practices, discussed above, as for any economic system capitalism's material foundation makes it dependent on such processes—on transforming the more-than-human world into commodities. Yet, Earth can never be completely enrolled into the economy; indeed, its processes recurrently exceed all such attempts with such unintended consequences as anthropocentric global warming. Even as the more-than-human world is enrolled into globalizing capitalism, more than human agency challenges its sustainability.

8.2.1 Enrolling the More-than-human World into Capitalism

Given that the more-than-human world is an indispensible condition of possibility for globalizing capitalism, operating with its own multiple co-evolving logics, how can it be made available to capitalist commodity

---

[5] Of course, human bodies also contain within them aspects of the more-than-human world—underlining the impossibility of separating humans from Earth.

production? It must be converted into commodities. One aspect of this has received particular attention in the political economy literature: land. It is from land (and sea) that most natural resources must be extracted; land is also where most economic activities must be located. Given its fixed material nature, land is relatively malleable to commodification: to fencing it in, exerting private ownership, and bringing to market. All that is required is a legal system recognizing private property and a surveyor. The geography of land markets has been extensively studied (going back to Ricardo), from which come theories of land rent, and of the profit-maximizing geography of land use and land use change (the rent gap) (Harvey, 1982a; Sheppard and Barnes, 1984; Katz, 1986; Smith, 1987; Slater, 2015).

The commodification of land is an ongoing process, an example of Harvey's notion of accumulation by dispossession. Major contemporary issues surrounding its commodification include land 'grabs' and urban tenure 'reform'. Rural land grabs entail the enclosure of agricultural commons in order to organize cash cropping for export: 'to a large extent the result of the liberalisation of land markets, which . . . has contributed to the commoditisation of land' (Zoomers, 2010: 431; McMichael, 2012). Dubbed by Zoomers 'the foreignisation of space', these enclosures archetypically connect countries where land is made available, by national governments seeking foreign rural investment, with countries seeking crops and whose firms organize the cash crop production. These uneven connectivities often dispossess local peasants, undermining their livelihoods and occasionally re-employing them as agricultural workers. Land grabs also include dispossessions in the name of special economic zones (dedicated to producing low wage manufactures for export) and urban development (Levien, 2012).

Urban land tenure reform refers to World Bank-led attempts to 'regularize' the complex land tenure arrangements in many cities of the post-colony, particularly in informal settlements, by surveys designed to convert these into European-style privatized leasehold or freehold, as envisioned by John Locke. The rationale is that this will enable the urban poor to leverage their entrepreneurial acumen (de Soto, 2000). Once such land rights have been assigned, those lucky enough to accrue them are in a position to sell their land—creating temporary land markets in informal settlements that enable large developers, backed by international finance, to assemble land for residential developments for the middle class and industrial estates. This is not simple dispossession (although those unable to access land rights experience it as such) but displacement, again bound up with enclosure in the name of creating a land market (Jeffrey, McFarlane, and Vasudevan, 2012; Ince, 2014; Sevilla-Buitrago, 2015).

Mineral and fossil fuel reserves also are fixed in place and relatively easy to commodify. The trick here is finding economically viable locations and concentrations, and then exploiting them. The conditions of possibility for turning a reserve into an exploitable resource are geographically differentiated, dependent on geological processes of mineral deposition as well as the socio-cultural processes discussed above. The biophysical properties of the raw materials extracted (and the exploitative technologies) also matter, potentially shaping the societies that have come to rely on them (Bakker and Bridge, 2006; Mitchell, 2011). Such conditions co-evolve with the complex and uneven economic geography of exploration and exploitation (Rees, 1990; Hayter, Barnes and Bradshaw, 2003; Sheppard et al., 2009b: ch. 18). The commodification of resources connects resource peripheries with industrializing cores, an exchange of raw materials for manufactured products that often disadvantages already poorer resource peripheries (Chapter 6).

Commodification of the more-than-human world becomes more complex for biological, hydrological, and climatic processes. Agricultural commodity production (including forests and fisheries) involves manipulating the biological world in order to optimize its profitability for supporting human life. Under globalizing capitalism, such anthropomorphic intervention requires the commodification of ecosystems, as the basis for the profit-rate maximizing production of food and other biological inputs. This often involves isolating one element of the more-than-human world (corn, tuna) socio-culturally constructed as worthy of commodification, separating it from the broader ecosystem (and, often, socio-cultural system) in which it is entangled, exerting private property rights over it, and manipulating (domesticating, farming, selectively breeding, genetically engineering) its productivity to maximize the rate of profit on capital advanced.

This last step involves assembling labouring bodies, technologies, and other inputs, managing spatially extensive systems of production and consumption. But it also means modulating the uncertainties of a highly dynamic, spatio-temporally variegated, heterogeneous, and unpredictable biophysical world: Soil fertility, other species seeking food and shelter or in ecological competition, climatic fluctuation, rainfall, etc. Globalizing capitalism has qualitatively altered the nature of agriculture (from agroecological practices to agro-industry—and selectively back to the former with the revival of organic farming), as well as its socio-spatial scale (from variegated local practices embedded in socio-ecological systems, to global food regimes dominated by transnational agricultural and chemical corporations, McMichael, 2009). Other aspects of the biological world also are progressively being commodified: Nature reserves, generating tourist income; non-agricultural ecosystems, generating income under REDD+ and other ecosystem services schemes; local knowledge about the properties of plants, extracted—often without compensation—on the basis of an intellectual property regime legalizing bioprospecting (Shiva, 1991; Robertson, 2004; Adams and Hutton, 2007).

Consider, however, the mobile flows of the more-than-human world—water and air circulation, insolation, hydrological and carbon cycles, the migration of species, etc. The unruly and shape-shifting materiality of these phenomena makes their commodification extraordinarily challenging. Unless they can be pinned down, and private property rights exerted over them, they cannot be brought to market. Even in mainstream welfare economics, such phenomena may be tagged as public goods, implying that the state rather than capitalist markets should organize their provision even if property rights could be exerted.

Water has become a cause célèbre for such challenges. Of all such flows, water is the easiest to channel and bound: into reservoirs, pipelines, and bottles. State control over water came under increasing question with neoliberalization. Global water corporations moved to commodify both water itself and delivery systems, particularly in the post-colony (Harris, Goldin, and Sneddon, 2015). Yet these initiatives, introduced with much fanfare as an example of the power of neoliberalizing capitalism to manage nature, proved highly problematic in practice (Bakker, 2009). They have reinforced what Bakker has termed archipelagos of water provision: plentiful and cheap water for those with the ability to pay, alongside poor quality, more expensive, and insufficient water for those who cannot. This is not only the case in cities of the post-colony, like Mumbai, Jakarta, Cape Town, or Guayaquil, but also in the heart of the global economy. Southern California's wealthy communities continue to water their lawns and golf courses, even as Hispanic towns in the Central Valley struggle to access water (Bakker, 2003; Swyngedouw, 2004; Peters and Oldfield, 2005; Gandy, 2008; Marcum, 2014).

For even more unruly flows resistant to commodification, such as air and carbon, quasi-capitalist market structures have been designed in collaboration between states and capitalists to 'internalize the externalities' of the more-than-human world.[6] Cap-and-trade markets have been institutionalized in an attempt to control carbon and other emissions; other examples of such market solutions include environmental services and carbon offsets. These remain controversial 'capital-accumulation strategies that devolve governance over the atmosphere to supra-national and nonstate actors and to the market' (Bumpus and Liverman, 2008: 127). Cap and trade reinforces uneven geographies of emissions, as well as proving difficult to implement because of the politics of setting initial prices and credits (Betsill and Hoffmann, 2011). Meanwhile, the carbon flows embedded in the trade vectors of globalizing capitalism demonstrate how the carbon emitted in countries of the post-colony (particularly China) subsidizes the wealthy North Atlantic economies

---

[6] In mainstream economic lingo, externalities are the unpriced and thus unaddressed side-effects of markets—a cost or benefit involuntarily incurred by an individual.

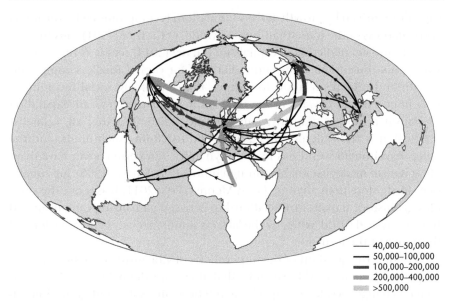

Figure 8.3 Embedded carbon flows in the global economy, 2004

Source: Bergmann (2013) Figure 1.

Arrows flow from regions where carbon is emitted during production and consumption to where the eventual investment in economic futures is supported by those emissions. Arrow widths are proportional to the carbon emissions 'embodied' within a given interregional interaction.

Source: Computed by Luke Bergmann from a social accounting matrix, based on the Global Trade Analysis Program 7 database. Used by permission.

(Figure 8.3, see Bergmann, 2013)—unequal global connectivities much like those for labour (Figure 8.1).

8.2.2 *How Earth Exceeds Globalizing Capitalism*

Notwithstanding the enormous strides made in extending the reach of globalizing capitalism across the more-than-human world, biophysical processes continue to exceed and confound the logics of commodity production and exchange. Examples can be found at every geographical scale, from bacterial resistance to drugs, to species evolving resistance to insecticides and herbicides, to anthropogenic climate change. Almost by definition, these challenges are unpredictable in terms of their spatio-temporal imprint and socio-ecological impact—the outcome of complex nonlinear socio-ecological dynamics. If economic actors struggle to devise strategies that realize their intended consequences within the logic of a capitalist space economy, this is all the more so in this socio-ecological context.

The vulnerabilities triggered by how Earth exceeds capitalism can be parsed, briefly, on several levels. First, is the question of whether the logic of capitalism, driven by growth and accumulation, is compromised by the limits and otherness of the more-than-human world. O'Connor (1991) calls this the second fundamental crisis of capitalism; Harvey (2014) sees is as the basis for two of his three 'dangerous contradictions' for capital (endless compound growth and capital's relation to nature—the third being social revolution). It is important to beware of overly Malthusian narratives—an expanding capitalism running up against natural ecological limits. After all, capitalist innovation is endlessly pushing against and redefining such limits, and the more-than-human world has its own dynamics. But cornucopian narratives, of capitalism made sustainable through innovation (Simon, 1998), are equally one-sided. More than anyone, Jason Moore (2003, 2011) teases out the complex geohistorical dialectical relationship between globalizing capitalism and the biophysical world, whereby the latter is simultaneously generative for and disruptive of the former.

Second, is the question of the implications of globalizing capitalism for the more-than-human world. To note that these are dramatic is self-evident: climate change, accelerated species extinction, air, water and ground pollution, etc. Yet the implications of this for the more-than-human world are complex to assess as it depends on what constitutes the assessor's moral community. Ours is inevitably an anthropomorphically positioned assessment, but that will vary with socio-spatial positionality. Humans feel close to and connected to certain species (primates, large mammals), regretting their loss much more than, say, the Anopheles mosquito (Mitchell, 2002). Yet some humans find themselves in a positionality from which the poaching and killing of such valued animals enables them to make a buck. For some farmers, the changing temperature and rainfall regimes associated with global warming undermine vegetative productivity and livelihood possibilities, for others, in different (cooler) locations, they enhance livelihood possibilities.

Third, and more straightforward to assess, are the implications for human actors of the relationship between globalizing capitalism and the more-than-human world: questions of political ecology, of environmental and climate equity, and of justice. Globalizing capitalism can be characterized as contributing to unequal socio-geographical relations between humans and the non-human-world. On the one hand, are inequities in terms of drawing on the biophysical world, as measured for example by an ecological footprint (Wackernagel and Rees, 1998): the bulk of what are constituted as resources are consumed by wealthy bodies in prosperous places, with poorly remunerated bodies in peripheral spaces dependent on their extraction and export (cf. Figure 8.3). On the other, are inequities in proximity to environmental goods and bads. Wealthy bodies in prosperous places are more likely to be shielded from technological hazards (and natural hazards, unless they choose to take the risk); poorer bodies—often non-white—find themselves in locations with higher exposure to natural and technological hazards (Pulido, 1996; Bullard, 2000). Third, are inequalities in terms of vulnerability to environmental events: wealthy bodies in prosperous communities can rely on insurance, personal and community resources, and state emergency services when things go wrong; poor bodies in precarious places are more likely to have to fend for themselves (Turner et al., 2003; Hewitt, 2014).

Such inequities exist in all manner of economic systems, but political ecologists provide abundant evidence that they are compounded by the political struggles among actors occupying unequal socio-spatial positionalities that accompany globalizing capitalism (Watts, 1983; Blaikie, 1984; Peet and Watts, 1996; Rocheleau, Thomas-Slayter, and Wangari, 1996; Robbins, 2004; Heynen et al., 2007; Harcourt and Nelson, 2015). Such inequities have triggered substantial collective action around issues of environmental and climate justice, and justice to the more-than-human world (Low and Gleeson, 1998), seeking both distributive and procedural redress. Such action by people identifying with environmental issues, while at times unproductively finding themselves in tension along lines of differentiated socio-spatial positionality—green vs. brown or North vs. South—show how the challenges that the more-than-human world poses to globalizing capitalism are entangled with Fraser's triple movement (Section 8.1.3).

8.3 Finance

While it is self-evident that the more-than-human world (including people) exceeds capitalism—in terms of the processes creating it and its materialities—this is far from obvious for finance. When Polanyi was writing, the gold standard linked money to a material object, giving it a tangible material foundation. Since gold had to be mined, the production of money could be assigned a production price relative to other commodities (Marx' universal equivalent) and its availability depended on more-than-human processes (cf. Schoenberger, 2015). Yet the gold standard did not survive Richard Nixon and the 1971 US monetary crisis, and Polanyi's case for the fictitiousness of the money commodity was different: 'money...is merely a token of purchasing power which, as a rule, is not produced at all, but comes into being through the mechanism of banking or state finance' (Polanyi, 2001 [1944]: 75–6). If anything, with contemporary financialization, money is becoming the ultimate commodity: increasingly immaterial, highly fluid, shape-shifting, and universally in demand—a universal equivalent indeed. In these neoliberal times, Polanyi's definition also seems outdated: central and supra-national banks are as active as ever, but the availability of finance is increasingly shaped by non-state processes: Currency speculation, hedge funds, high-frequency trading, offshore banking, etc. Marx's (1972 [1885]) version of fictitious capital seems more apposite:

> The potentiality for 'fictitious capital'...is...associated with the emergence of credit money....The lender...holds a piece of paper, the value of which is backed by an unsold commodity....If the pieces of paper...begin to circulate as credit money, then it is fictitious value that is circulating. A gap is thereby opened up between credit moneys (which always have a fictitious, imaginary component) and 'real' moneys tied directly to a money commodity. (Harvey, 1982b: 267)

Yet one aspect of Polanyi's thinking carries forward. Money and finance are simultaneously necessary for, and disruptive of, globalizing capitalism. Further, irrespective of its contemporary immateriality and fluidity, finance is bound up globalizing capitalism's uneven connectivities and socio-spatial inequalities: In the world of finance, geography *matters* (contra O'Brien, 1992).

8.3.1 *The Necessity of Finance*

Marx (1972 [1867–96]) was obsessed with the complexities of ensuring that money was available to complete the market transactions necessary for commodities to circulate. This has been, from the beginning, a spatio-temporal challenge—that of extending markets across space and time. In terms of extending markets across space, any money commodity needed certain material characteristics; it had to be easy to transport and physically durable (not decaying on the back of a camel crossing the Asian steppe). It also had to carry the cultural value of being intrinsically trustworthy. Eventually the many materialities of money—cowrie shells, cattle, leather—resolved into silver and gold, the sourcing of which drove much colonial exploitation. In terms of extending economic transactions through time, gold and silver are ideal ways of burying treasure but cannot function as credit. Credit instruments were devised to enable capital to be advanced now and paid for later, necessary for the large up-front expenditures increasingly faced by globalizing capitalism. Credit became increasingly necessary to pay for the means of transportation, for infrastructure, and for capital-intensive commodity production.

The spatialities of financial markets have co-evolved with those of globalizing capitalism. Transnational European banking networks expanded contemporaneously with the spread of colonialism, creating enormous wealth for those able to advance credit and make good on the interest charged (Fuggers, Medici, etc.). By the early seventeenth century, a continuous stock exchange had emerged in Amsterdam, the headquarters of the Dutch East India Company (the first joint stock corporation). This was where derivatives trading first emerged. Once nation-states became the default way of governing globalizing capitalism after the 1648 Treaty of Westphalia, stock exchanges became national institutions, and were complemented by the emergence of central banks (underwriting fictitiousness à la Polanyi). The Bank of England (1694) was copied by other European central banks during the nineteenth century, and the Bank of Japan was founded in 1882 (mimicking that of Belgium). Beginning with the US Federal Reserve (1913), during the twentieth century central banks were founded across post-colonial Latin American states and other white settler colonies.

Arrighi (2010) documents certain spatio-temporal moments when financialization came to dominate economic transactions and social life in the geographical centre of globalizing capitalism, culminating in a financial crisis and geopolitical shift: in Genoa (1557), Amsterdam (1760s), and London (1929). Each crisis, he argues, marked the end of hegemony there, after which its geographical centre shifted to another, larger political entity (the US, since Bretton Woods).

Even today, when the discourses and practices of finance seem so deeply embedded in everyday life across the planet as to feel ubiquitous and inescapable, and when financial policies are increasingly harmonized across nation-states, profound geographical inequities persist (Martin, 1999; Clark and Wójcik, 2007; French, Leyshon, and Wainwright, 2011; Christophers, 2013; Dixon, 2014). Trading places still matter: even as the clusters of human bodies are disappearing from stock exchanges (London, New York, Tokyo, Frankfurt, Hong Kong, Shanghai), proximity to these exchanges remains vital. Place, including face-to-face contact, still matters for financial firms, with employment and transactions highly geographically concentrated in these global nodes (Leyshon and Thrift, 1997). Trading and proximity are now features of cyberspace, with the latter measured in nanoseconds, but colocation of trading computers remains vital (Lewis, 2014).

The contemporary global financial landscape is one of complex socio-spatial financial cores and peripheries, linked by uneven connectivities that tend to reproduce inequities in access to finance and wealth accumulation (global financial networks, cf. Coe, Lai, and Wójcik, 2014). Wealthy bodies and prosperous places have little difficulty accessing finance as they conform to norms of what constitutes minimal risk or a risk worth taking; money and credit flows to these people and places, and wealth accumulates there. Others, by contrast, are excluded, at scales ranging from nation-states to neighbourhoods (Brett, 1985; Christopherson, 1996; Pollard, 1996; Dymski and Li, 2003). Lending is extended to riskier clients during spatio-temporal moments when there are financial gluts (often with little attention by the lender to due diligence) only to be withdrawn when the next crisis hits, leaving those clients and spaces worse off than before. By contrast the bulk of lenders who find themselves in trouble at such moments are bailed out by state institutions who fear a global crisis and see them as too big to fail, thereby allowing them to escape relatively unscathed. There have been notable attempts to help poorer bodies access finance in precarious places (particularly women), through microloans. While these have made a difference, they have become a source of financialization and wealth creation by lenders—microfinance— and entail new forms of indebtedness for the borrowers (Rankin, 2002; Roy, 2010).

Up to and including the period of North Atlantic Fordism, the functionality of finance for globalizing capitalism was placed in the hands of nation-states. This included central bank policy-making—imagined to be independent from political intervention, finance ministries, and the supra-national Bretton Woods financial institutions—created in lieu of Keynes' Bretton Woods vision of a global central bank to manage deficiencies in global financial flows. Armed with Keynesian macroeconomics, it was expected that financial markets would function at least as well as other commodity markets. Yet this has been far from the case, and a key reason has been the ability of finance to slip the bonds of national and global regulation—to find wild, deregulated 'offshore' spaces. With neoliberalization, such wild spaces are reimagined as the kinds of spaces where financial markets can function free of political interference. Yet the 2007 crisis emanated from deregulated contexts.

8.3.2 *How Finance Exceeds Globalizing Capitalism*

The financialization of the 1990s and 2000s was rationalized by the claim that digitized finance, flowing costlessly through such wild spaces, enables the efficient markets hypothesis to be performed (Fama, 1970; Clarke, Jandik, and Mandelkar, 2001). Computer trading algorithms can be imagined to have the rational decision-making capacity of a Turing machine that humans lack, and are themselves programmed in such a way as to perform quasiperfect markets (Mackenzie and Millo, 2003). The persistent recurrence of financial crises belies this representational narrative, however, raising serious questions not only about taming finance, but also about globalizing capitalism's capacity to deliver on its promise of opportunities for all. For reasons of space, I focus here on how these issues have played out at the global scale since Bretton Woods.

Socio-spatial positionality is important to understanding the trajectory of the international financial crises since 1944. In particular, the United States' powerful positionality, as the country whose currency is the default for all international payments and that also financially and politically dominates the Bretton Woods institutions, has shaped this trajectory (Brett, 1985; Sheppard et al., 2009b: chs. 22, 23). Thus President Nixon could unilaterally abrogate the

Bretton Woods agreement that fixed currencies to gold, seeking to resolve a domestic crisis of stagnating economic productivity, rising wages, high Vietnam war-related expenditures, and a run on the dollar by other countries. This created the global currency market that now trades $5 trillion daily, enough to dominate national scale monetary policy of central banks, pushing nation-states to conform to the perceptions of the market. In response to US attempts to exert control over the global dollar market, and to the surplus funds accumulated by OPEC countries seeking investment opportunities during the 1970s oil boom, offshore Eurodollar and petrodollar markets emerged. Flush with this cash, North Atlantic financial institutions leant heavily to select third world nations, underwriting industrialization and development.

A further US domestic crisis in the late 1970s, at the end of the period of Atlantic Fordism, devalued and raised interest rates on the US dollar, triggering the early 1980s third world debt crisis as Mexico and other countries found themselves unable to pay dollar-denominated debt payments that had escalated relative to domestic currencies. The Bretton Woods institutions' answer to this was Structural Adjustment, a Washington Consensus foisting neo-liberal economic and monetary policy on every third world country seeking external funding (Williamson, 2003). By the early 1990s, a new glut of global money resulted in new lines of private credit being extended into 'emerging' third world nations, particularly in southeast Asia. The boom this triggered, compounded by loose lending practices, culminated in the rapid departure again of foreign credit, and the 1997 Asian financial crisis. During both crises socio-spatial positionality also played out at the national scale: national elites in affected countries were able to sequester money abroad, whereas the majority of citizens lost their shirts.

'Smart' money then flowed back into the North Atlantic realm, to find itself embroiled in the 1990s dot.com crisis (targeting the San Francisco Bay Area) and then the 2007 global financial crisis emanating out of the London and New York financial centres. In the meantime, the countries worst affected in 1997 (also in South America) abandoned their faith in the Bretton Woods institutions. Those institutions responded by fostering a post-Washington 'consensus' of 'good' governance and poverty reduction (Jayasuriya, 2001; Bergeron, 2003; Jomo and Fine, 2006; Montiel, 2007; Sheppard and Leitner, 2010). Nevertheless, there has been an explosion of state-organized sovereign wealth funds giving better-heeled former borrowing nations a cushion of domestic funding to fall back on in times of crisis, rather than having to go hat in hand to Washington DC (Clark, Dixon, and Monk, 2013). Other parallel funding streams have also been crafted, including Islamic finance (seeking to align Sharia law with the advancement of credit, cf. Pollard and Samers, 2007), and experiments with alternative multilateral lending organizations (the Banco del Sur in Latin America, China's newly created Asian

Infrastructure Investment Bank, and current discussions among the BRICS about creating a New Development Bank).

8.3.3 *Fictitious Finance and Globalizing Capitalism*

The fictitiousness flowing through uneven, asymmetric global financial networks is quite different from that associated with people and Earth. If anything, rather than rubbing up against the logics of commodity production underlying globalizing capitalism (Tsing, 2005) fictitious capital compounds them. We find ourselves in a world in which monetary exchange value can disappear with the click of a button (Easley, de Prado, and O'Hara, 2011), in which global indebtedness exceeds credit and continues to grow, and in which the global value of finance is growing faster than that of the production of other commodities. Arrighi (2010) diagnoses this last trend as foreshadowing globalizing capitalism's next phase shift in geopolitical and geoeconomic hegemony, from the US to China. Whether or not that turns out to be the case, it is clear that financialization has agency that exceeds its putative role of smoothing out spatio-temporal lesions in the credit system. Global financial networks are not self-regulating, and beyond this it is far from clear what the value of finance is. With money reduced to bytes, a commodity that can be produced at zero marginal cost, its value becomes a psychological or cultural question.

Access to finance remains regulated, however, by economic well-being. At scales ranging from the globe to the household, the uneven connectivities of financial networks tend to reinforce, not modulate, already existing differences in socio-spatial positionality. Bodies, institutions and places regarded as good risks have privileged access to finance and the capacity to borrow more. Global wealth accumulates in and is hoarded by such privileged positionalities—such as the US, Goldman Sachs, and HNWIs (high net worth individuals). Those regarded as poor risks have little access. Their cash flow problems cannot be addressed by borrowing money, an ongoing impoverishment largely unaffected by financial crises—a precarious positionality occupied by many sub-Saharan African countries and much of the global precariat. Those in between are constituted as good risks when money is in surplus and seeking new opportunities, but are the first to have those funds withdrawn during financial crises—a hazardous positionality (occupied by countries like Greece and Thailand, middle class families and individuals offered micro-loans) that can be mitigated only by accumulating rainy-day funds during good times. While it is possible, of course, that the positionality of bodies and places with respect to finance can shift—particularly for those occupying hazardous positionalities—it is far from clear that finance makes it any easier for precariously positioned bodies and spaces to prosper. Indeed, there is much evidence to the contrary.

8.4 Conclusion

Thinking geographically means attending to how economic processes co-evolve with their constitutive outsides—geography's radical intra-disciplinarity (Sheppard, 2015). Focusing on Polanyi's three fictitious commodities—people, earth, and finance—I have argued that these constitute globalizing capitalism's raggedy edges. They are realms of socionature that are dialectically related to the production and consumption of commodities, and to the socio-spatial distribution of the economic costs and benefits thereof. On the one hand, people, earth, and finance are continually enrolled into globalizing capitalism, particularly in recent years as it runs up against internal economic limits. Yet, on the other hand, globalizing capitalism cannot do without them, putting them in a position to disrupt it. Put otherwise, globalizing capitalism's limitations are not simply internal but also external, even as this boundary is constantly under renegotiation.

Fictitiousness functions somewhat differently across these three edges, however. For people and earth, as intuited by Polanyi, it means that even as they are commodified they never function as pure commodities. The logics of social reproduction, of more-than-capitalist economic activities and of biophysical processes are never fully reducible to commodity production. Notwithstanding abstract theoretical claims that this is possible in principle—for example through the internalization of externalities or full cost pricing—globalizing capitalism's failure to make good on its imaginary of untrammelled development opportunities for all suggests otherwise. Given that capitalism depends on bodies and the material world, and that these are not fully commodifiable, disruption remains the order of the day. It takes various forms. Civil society rubs up against globalizing capitalism through resistance and contestation—Fraser's triple movement (or the multitude, cf. Hardt and Negri, 2004). The more-than-human world does so through globalizing capitalism's dependencies on and unintended consequences for biophysical processes. These two domains of fictitious commodities are also mutually interdependent—human life on the more-than-human world and environmental depredation as a motivating force for civil society contestation. The fictitiousness of finance, however, hangs on the uncertainty associated with its increasingly virtual—digital—nature. This uncertainty includes questions of what constitutes finance, of how to measure it (independently of financial value), and about what money is worth. In terms of its relationship with capitalism, while global financial networks seem to constitute the realization of capitalism pure—the efficient markets hypothesis—in practice they exacerbate globalizing capitalism's internal contradictions.

These raggedy edges have their own complex associations with globalizing capitalism's uneven socio-spatial positionalities. Culture and identity are typically invoked around its outer edges—as an explanation for impoverishment. Culture and identity are constructed as the other of rational choice and entrepreneurialism, attributes that get in the way of wealth creation unless they are commodified. Similarly, 'nature' is what happens around the edges of capitalism, where primary commodity producing peripheries and those labouring within suffer from the resource curse. Here, again, the impoverishment associated with globalizing capitalism is blamed on its outsides—on aspects of the world that are not (yet) commodified, disguising how poverty is not simply an inherent attribute of such bodies and places but a result of the uneven, asymmetric ways they are connected with commodity production. After all, culture and identity, and materiality, are always already within the heart of capitalism: entrepreneurialism is cultural (valued positively) just as whiteness is racial (superiority), and the more-than-human world constitutes every commodity (except, perhaps, finance). Finance, notwithstanding its seeming liberation from the material bounds of earth as bytes circulating in cyberspace, tends to reproduce the unequal socio-spatial positionalities of globalizing capitalism. This reinforces the uneven geographical development that globalizing capitalism's proponents (attributing failure to its outsides) claim it can overcome. Yet there is a silver lining: the disruptive potential associated with these raggedy edges (even finance?), opening space for the purchase of more-than-capitalist imaginaries and practices.

9

Conclusion

The argument I have sought to prosecute here is that when we look at capitalism through geographical lenses it turns out to be far from the rose-tinted vision of enabling prosperity for all offered by mainstream/geographical economists. I have called my object of analysis globalizing capitalism to emphasize how its core features have been shaped through its particular historical geography. The bulk of the variegated local forms of capitalism that coexisted across the trading nodes of the old world by the fourteenth century withered on the vine, once Western Europe embarked on its colonial adventures as the fifteenth century came to a close. Fuelled by colonialism and slavery, the phenomenon that we have come to know as capitalism emerged in northwestern Europe by the end of the eighteenth century, globalizing from there in differentiated forms ever since (Sheppard 2015). Further, capitalism is globalizing, never global: other more-than-capitalist political economic systems coexist and co-evolve with its variegations.

Thinking geographically about capitalism means much more than acknowledging this. I have focused on two aspects in the preceding chapters. On the one hand is the socio-spatial dialectic: how capitalist economic processes produce, but also are shaped by, spatiality in its various manifestations. This is economic geography as socio-spatial theory. On the other hand is the acknowledgement that economic processes cannot be studied in isolation: their coevolution with political, social, cultural, and biophysical processes must be part of our analysis. This is geography as the discipline that embraces the cross-cutting study of nature–society relations.

Putting the socio-spatial ontology of mainstream/geographical economics in conversation with that of critical economic geography reveals how each of these leads to very different narratives about, and assessments of the possibilities associated with, globalizing capitalism. From the mainstream perspective, globalizing capitalism is the single best form of organizing economic activities yet conceived by humans. It is one that carries with it the possibility of prosperity for all (albeit with considerable disagreement about what kinds of state interventions are necessary to realize this). In this view, the bodies and spaces that fail to prosper, the precarious people and places, are marked by their failure to adapt to the logic of capitalism: precarious places fail to display good governance or suffer from bad latitude; precarious bodies are inadequately entrepreneurial, rational, and self-interested. A corollary of this argument is that economic development is equated with a universal, teleological trajectory of capitalist development to be followed by all, with prosperous (North Atlantic) economies offering a vision that other 'less developed' places should follow. Achieving development, then, means emulating the North Atlantic political economies (or at least following whatever advice their experts now offer, whether or not it is consistent with their own past practices: Chang, 2002). More-than-capitalist economic practices should be eschewed because they are diversionary to achieving this goal.

A geographical perspective fundamentally calls this narrative into question. Taking the socio-spatial dialectic seriously (particularly the production of accessibility as a commodity) leads to the conclusion that through uneven geographical development globalizing capitalism reproduces socio-spatial precarity and impoverishment, rather than overcoming it. A key, somewhat neglected aspect of this process of uneven geographical development is the role of the uneven, asymmetric connectivities of globalizing capitalism: commodity trade, financial flows, foreign direct investment, migration, transportation and communications networks, the diffusion and patenting of innovations, etc. Once we attend to such connectivities, it is no longer possible to explain the precarity of certain bodies and places in terms of their own inadequate attributes—place-based explanations. Rather, we examine how and why precarious bodies and places often find themselves occupying deleterious socio-spatial positionalities within these uneven connectivities and flows. Once we acknowledge this, it follows that precarity and poverty also reflect the broader uneven spatial dynamics of globalizing capitalism—connectivity-based explanations.

This geographical narrative of globalizing capitalism also generates a very different assessment of its possibilities. Notwithstanding many progressive attributes of capitalism relative to its predecessors (acknowledged, *inter alia*, by Marx), there are inherent limits to capitalist globalization. It is constitutionally unable to deliver on its promise of prosperity for all who act appropriately because prosperity for certain bodies and places is achieved at the expense of precarity and poverty elsewhere. Put otherwise, impoverishment is relational. A corollary of this is that globalizing capitalism is not the answer for those who find themselves positionally disadvantaged in its landscape of connectivities and flows. Thus a geographical perspective undermines the teleological imaginary of capitalist development, creating intellectual space in which experimentation with more-than- (and anti-)capitalist alternatives becomes both desirable and necessary. Such experimentation is fraught with good and bad possibilities. Thinking geographically, there can be no single best practice for all bodies and places (whether capitalist or non-capitalist). Rather, there are multiple alternatives (some already existing, others not yet conceived) to be explored, and to be assessed against one another on ethical grounds as well as in terms of their performance.

For those who find this argument persuasive and wish to advance it, there are some significant gaps in the current empirical research agenda of critical economic geography that must be redressed, if we are adequately to account for the role of uneven asymmetric connectivities in shaping globalizing capitalism and its uneven geographical development. First, is constructing a nuanced spatial history of capitalism. The history of capitalism has emerged as a vibrant field of economic history in recent years, breaking down conceptual barriers between what Marx also conceived as successive phases: feudalism, slavery, capitalism. Yet there is a geography to this evolution, which needs to be teased out if we are to avoid what Chakrabarty would call a history 1 of capitalism.

Second, critical economic geographers have failed to study adequately the production of accessibility—the geographical political economy of transportation and communications. Strangely, transportation geography was a high priority theme during economic geography's spatial science era, but has not been so since (perhaps because it was too heavily identified with spatial science's models of spatial interaction). We need to better understand the logics through which particular transportation modes and routes are developed, logistics (e.g. Cowen, 2014), and the implications for the evolution of asymmetric and uneven connectivities. We also need to attend to the mobile workplaces and workforces through which these accessibilities are reproduced and reshaped on a daily basis (e.g. Bunnell, 2016). A second such gap is the geographical political economy of telecommunications and cyberspace (Zook, 2005). This includes developing a better understanding of how virtual and material space co-evolve, of the corporations and state institutions shaping this industry, and of the global workforces underlying it. But it also entails the study of the geographies behind, and mobilized through, the collection, commodification and deployment of digital information and 'big data'. Within this domain there are huge changes afoot in globalizing capitalism that we ignore at our peril.

Third, geographers must redouble their efforts to decentre, without marginalizing, the role of economic analysis in understanding globalizing capitalism. Cultural political economy, feminist and post-colonial economic geography, discourse analysis, political as well as industrial ecology should all be integral to economic geography's broad and colorful palette. Within this,

159

specialization is vital to making advances on various fronts, of course, but economic geography comes into its own when such specialized analyses are put into constructive mutual critical engagement with one another.

Finally, economic geographers must pay more attention to the potential and limits of the more-than-capitalist experiments that are all around us, working with and learning from their practitioners. It is all very well to critique globalizing capitalism on theoretical grounds, as I have assayed here, but critique only gains traction through rigorous analysis of the relative merits of such alternatives in the wild. If I have helped kick open the conceptual door blocking any desire to take such alternatives seriously, beating down the door entails engaging in spatio-temporally differentiated more-than-capitalist praxis.

References

Abel, G.J. and Sander, N. (2014) Quantifying global international migration flows. *Science* 343: 1520–2.

Abu-Lughod, J. (1991) *Before European Hegemony: The world system A.D. 1250–1350*, New York: Oxford University Press.

Acemoglu, D. and Robinson, J. (2012) *Why Nations Fail: The origins of power, prosperity, and poverty*, New York: Crown Publishing.

Acemoglu, D., Johnson, S., and Robinson, J.A. (2002) Reversal of fortune: Geography and institutions in the making of the modern world income distribution. *Quarterly Journal of Economics* 117: 1231–94.

Acemoglu, D., Johnson, S., and Robinson, J.A. (2003) Disease and development in historical perspective. *Journal of the European Economic Association* 1: 397–405.

Adams, W.M. and Hutton, J. (2007) People, parks and poverty: Political ecology and biodiversity conservation. *Conservation and Society* 5: 147–83.

Aglietta, M. (1979) *A Theory of Capitalist Regulation*, London: New Left Books.

Agnew, J. (1987) *Place and Politics: The geographical mediation of state and society*, London: Unwin Hyman.

Agnew, J.A. (1994) The territorial trap: The geographical assumptions of international relations theory. *Review of International Political Economy* 1: 53–80.

Agnew, J. (2009) *Globalization and Sovereignty*, Lanham, MD: Rowman & Littlefield.

Alonso, W. (1964) *Location and Land Use*, Cambridge, MA: Harvard University Press.

Altink, S. (2013) *Stolen Lives: Trading women into sex and slavery*, London: Routledge.

Amin, A. (1989) Flexible specialization and small firms in Italy: Myths and realities. *Antipode* 21: 13–34.

Amin, A. and Thrift, N. (1992) Neo-Marshallian nodes in global networks. *International Journal of Urban and Regional Research* 16: 571–87.

Amin, A. and Thrift, N. (1994) Holding down the global. In: Amin, A. and Thrift, N. (eds) *Globalization, Institutions and Regional Development in Europe*. Oxford: Oxford University Press, 257–60.

Amin, A. and Thrift, N. (2000) What kind of economic theory for what kind of economic geography? *Antipode* 32: 4–9.

Amin, A., Cameron, A., and Hudson, R. (2003) *Placing the Social Economy*, London: Routledge.

Amin, S. (1974a) Accumulation and development: A theoretical model. *Review of African Political Economy* 1: 9–26.

Amin, S. (1974b) *Accumulation on a World Scale*, New York: Monthly Review Press.

Amin, S., Arrighi, G., Frank, A.G., et al. (1982) *Dynamics of the Global Crisis*, New York: Monthly Review Press.

Amsden, A.H. (1989) *Asia's Next Giant: South Korea and late industrialization*, Oxford: Oxford University Press.

Anderson, B. and McFarlane, C. (2011) Assemblage and geography. *Area* 43: 124–7.

Anderson, J.E. (1979) A theoretical foundation for the gravity hypothesis. *American Economic Review* 69: 106–16.

Anderson, J.E. and van Wincoop, E. (2004) Trade costs. *Journal of Economic Literature* 42: 691–751.

Anderson, P., Arrow, K.J., and Pines, D. (eds) (1988) *The Economy as an Evolving Complex System*, New York: Addison-Wesley, Pages.

Aoyama, Y. and Sheppard, E. (2003) The dialectics of geographic and virtual space. *Environment and Planning A* 35: 1151–6.

Arrighi, G. (2010) *The Long Twentieth Century: Money, power and the origins of our times*, London: Verso.

Arrow, K.J. (1994) Methodological individualism and economic knowledge. *American Economic Review* 84: 1–9.

Arthur, W.B., Durlauf, S.N., and Lane, D.A. (eds) (1997) *The Economy as an Evolving Complex System II*, New York: Addison-Wesley.

Asis, M.M.B., Huang, S., and Yeoh, B.S.A. (2004) When the light of the home is abroad: Unskilled female migration and the Filipino family. *Singapore Journal of Tropical Geography* 25: 198–215.

Aune, J.A. (2001) *Selling the Free Market: The rhetoric of economic correctness*, New York: Guilford.

Bairoch, P. (1982) International industrialization levels from 1750 to 1980. *Journal of European Economic History* 11: 269–333.

Bairoch, P. (1993) *Economics and World History*, Chicago: University of Chicago Press.

Bakker, K. (2003) Archipelagos and networks: urbanization and water privatization in the South. *The Geographical Journal* 169: 328–41.

Bakker, K. (2009) *Privatizing Water: Governance failure and the world's water crisis*, Ithaca, NY: Cornell University Press.

Bakker, K. and Bridge, G. (2006) Material worlds? Resource geographies and the matter of 'nature'. *Progress in Human Geography* 30: 5–27.

Baldwin, R. (2006) Globalisation: The great unbundling(s), Helsinki: Prime Minister's Office, Economic Council of Finland.

Baran, P. and Sweezy, P. (1966) *Monopoly Capital: An essay on the American economic and social order*, New York: Monthly Review Press.

Barca, F. (2009) An agenda for a reformed cohesion policy: A place-based approach to meeting European Union challenges and expectations. *Independent Report Prepared at the Request of Danuta Hübner, Commissioner for Regional Policy*. Brussels: European Commission.

Barca, F., McCann, P., and Rodriguez-Pose, A. (2012) The case for regional development intervention: Place-based versus place-neutral approaches. *Journal of Regional Science* 52: 134–52.

Barnes, T.J. (1996) *Logics of Dislocation: Models, metaphors, and meanings of economic space,* New York: Guilford Press.

Barnes, T.J. (2000) Inventing Anglo-American economic geography, 1889–1960. In: Sheppard, E. and Barnes, T.J. (eds) *Companion to Economic Geography.* Oxford: Blackwell, 11–26.

Barnes, T.J. (2004) Placing ideas, genus loci, heterotopia and geography's quantitative revolution. *Progress in Human Geography* 28: 1–31.

Barnes, T.J. and Sheppard, E. (1992) Is there a place for the rational actor? A geographical critique of the rational choice paradigm. *Economic Geography* 68: 1–21.

Barnes, T.J. and Sheppard, E. (2010) 'Nothing includes everything'. Towards engaged pluralism in Anglophone economic geography. *Progress in Human Geography* 34: 193–214.

Barnes, T.J., Peck, J., and Sheppard, E. (eds) (2012) *The Wiley-Blackwell Companion to Economic Geography,* New York: Wiley-Blackwell.

Barnett, C. (2005) The consolations of 'neoliberalism'. *Geoforum* 36: 7–12.

Barnett, C., Clarke, N., Cloke, P., et al. (2008) The elusive subjects of neoliberalism. *Cultural Studies* 22: 624–53.

Bartels, C.P.A., Booleman, M., and Peters, W.H. (1978) A statistical analysis of regional-unemployment series. *Environment & Planning A* 10: 937–54.

Basile, R., Capello, R., and Caragliu, A. (2012) Technological interdependence and regional growth in Europe: Proximity and synergy in knowledge spillovers. *Papers in Regional Science* 91: 697–722.

Bassett, K. and Haggett, P. (1971) Towards short-term forecasting for cyclic behaviour in a regional system of cities. In: Chisholm, M. (ed.) *Regional Forecasting.* London: Butterworth, 389–413.

Bathelt, H. and Glückler, J. (2003) Toward a relational economic geography. *Journal of Economic Geography* 3: 117–44.

Bathelt, H. and Taylor, M. (2002) Clusters, power and place: Inequality and local growth in time-space. *Geografiska Annaler* 84: 93–109.

Bathelt, H., Malmberg, A., and Maskell, P. (2004) Clusters and knowledge: Local buzz, global pipelines and the process of knowledge creation. *Progress in Human Geography* 28: 31–56.

Baucom, I. (2005) *Specters of the Atlantic: Finance capital, slavery, and the philosophy of history,* Durham, NC: Duke University Press.

Baumol, W.J. (1990) Entrepreneurship: Productive, unproductive, and destructive. *Journal of Political Economy* 98: 893–921.

Baumol, W.J. and Litan, R. (2007) *Good Capitalism, Bad Capitalism, and the Economics of Growth and Prosperity,* New Haven, CT: Yale University Press.

Bayat, A. (2009) *Life as Politics: How ordinary people change the Middle East,* Stanford, CA: Stanford University Press.

Becker, G. (1973) A Theory of Marriage: Part I. *Journal of Political Economy* 81: 813–46.

Becker, G. (1974) A Theory of Marriage: Part II. *Journal of Political Economy* 82: 11–27.

Beckert, S. (2014) *Empire of Cotton: A new history of global capitalism,* London: Penguin.

Beckmann, M. and Puu, T. (1985) *Spatial Economics: Density, potential and flow,* Amsterdam: North Holland.

References

Behrens, K., Gaigné, C., Ottaviano, G., et al. (2003) Interregional and international trade: Seventy years after Ohlin. CEPR Discussion Paper.

Benjamin, S. (2008) Occupancy urbanism: Radicalizing politics and economy beyond policy and programs. *International Journal of Urban and Regional Research* 32: 719–29.

Bergeron, S. (2003) The post-Washington consensus and the economic representations of women in development at the World Bank. *International Feminist Journal of Politics* 5: 397–419.

Bergmann, L. (2012) A coevolutionary approach to the capitalist space economy. *Environment & Planning A* 44: 518–37.

Bergmann, L. (2013) Bound by chains of carbon: Ecological–economic geographies of globalization. *Annals of the Association of American Geographers* 103: 1348–70.

Bergmann, L., Sheppard, E., and Plummer, P. (2009) Capitalism beyond harmonious equilibrium: Mathematics as if human agency mattered. *Environment & Planning A* 41: 265–83.

Bernard, A.B., Redding, S.J., and Schott, P.K. (2007) Comparative advantage and heterogeneous firms. *Review of Economic Studies* 71: 31–66.

Berndt, C. and Boeckler, M. (2009) Geographies of circulation and exchange: Constructions of markets. *Progress in Human Geography* 33: 535–51.

Bernstein, E. (1902) *Die Voraussetzungen des Sozialismus und die Aufgaben der Sozialdemokratie*, Stuttgart: J.H.W. Dietz.

Bernstein, H. (1971) Modernization theory and the sociological study of development. *The Journal of Development Studies* 7: 141–60.

Berry, B.J.L. (1991) *Long-wave Rhythms in Economic Development and Political Behavior*, Baltimore: MD: Johns Hopkins University Press.

Betsill, M. and Hoffmann, M.J. (2011) The contours of 'cap and trade': The evolution of emissions trading systems for greenhouse gases. *Review of Policy Research* 28: 83–106.

Bettelheim, C. (1972) Appendix I: Theoretical Comments. In: Emmanuel, A.G. (ed.) *Unequal Exchange: A study of the imperialism of trade.* New York City: Monthly Review Press.

Birkin, M.H., Clarke, G. and Clarke, M. (2002) *Retail Geography and Intelligent Network Planning*, West Sussex, England: John Wiley & Sons Ltd.

Blaikie, P. (1984) *The Political Economy of Soil Erosion*, London: Longman.

Blake, M.K. and Hanson, S. (2005) Rethinking innovation: Context and gender. *Environment & Planning A* 37: 681–701.

Blaut, J. (1987) Diffusionism: A uniformitarian critique. *Annals of the Association of American Geographers* 77: 30–47.

Blaut, J. (1993) *The Colonizer's Model of the World*, New York: Guilford.

Blaut, J. (1999) Environmentalism and Eurocentrism. *Geographical Review* 89: 391–408.

Blaut, J. (2000) *Eight Eurocentric historians*, New York: Guilford.

Blumberg, R. (2014) The spatial politics and political economy of alternative food networks in post-Soviet Latvia and Lithuania. PhD University of Minnesota: Geography.

Borjas, G.J. (2001) The economics of migration. In: Smelser, N. and Baltes, P.B. (eds) *International Encyclopedia of the Social and Behavioral Sciences.* New York: Pergamon, 9803–9.

Borts, G.H. and Stein, J.L. (1964) *Economic Growth in a Free Market*, New York: Columbia University Press.

Boschma, R.A. and Frenken, K. (2006) Why is economic geography not an evolutionary science? Towards an evolutionary economic geography. *Journal of Economic Geography* 6: 273–302.

Boschma, R.A. and Frenken, K. (2009) Some notes on institutions in evolutionary economic geography. *Economic Geography* 85: 151–8.

Boschma, R.A. and Frenken. K. (2011) The emerging empirics of evolutionary economic geography. *Journal of Economic Geography* 11: 295–307.

Boschma, R.A. and Lambooy, J.G. (1999) Evolutionary economics and economic geography. *Journal of Evolutionary Economics* 9: 411–29.

Boschma, R.A. and Martin, R. (eds) (2010) *The Handbook of Evolutionary Economic Geography*, London: Edward Elgar.

Boschma, R.A. and Wenting, R. (2007) The spatial evolution of the British automobile industry. Does location matter? *Industrial and Corporate Change* 16: 213–38.

Bosker, M. and Garretsen, H. (2007) *Trade Costs, Market Access and Economic Geography: Why the empirical specification of trade costs matters*. Munich: Ifo Institute for Economic Research.

Bowman, C. and Ambrosini, V. (2009) How value is created, captured and destroyed. *European Business Review* 22: 479–95.

Bowman, C. and Toms, S. (2010) Accounting for competitive advantage: The resource-based view of the firm and the labour theory of value. *Critical Perspectives on Accounting* 21: 183–94.

Brakman, S., Garretsen, H., and von Marrewijk, C. (2009) *A New Introduction to Geographical Economics*, Cambridge: Cambridge University Press.

Brenner, N. (1997) State territorial restructuring and the production of spatial scale: Urban and regional planning in the FRG 1960–1990. *Political Geography* 16: 273–306.

Brenner, N. (1998) Global cities, glocal states: Global city formation and state territorial restructuring in contemporary Europe. *Review of International Political Economy* 5: 1–37.

Brenner, N. (1999) Beyond state-centrism? Space, territoriality, and geographical scale in globalization studies. *Theory and Society* 28: 39–78.

Brenner, N. (2001) The limits to scale? Methodological reflections on scalar structuration. *Progress in Human Geography* 25: 591–614.

Brenner, N. (2004) *New State Spaces: Urban governance and the rescaling of statehood*, Oxford: Oxford University Press.

Brenner, N. and Theodore, N. (eds) (2002) *Spaces of Neoliberalism: Urban restructuring in North America and Western Europe*. Oxford: Blackwell Publishing.

Brenner, N., Jessop, B., Jones, M., et al. (eds) (2003) *State/Space: A reader*, New York: Wiley.

Brenner, N., Peck, J., and Theodore, N. (2010) Variegated neoliberalization: Geographies, modalities, pathways. *Global Networks* 10: 182–222.

Brenner, R. (2006) *The Economics of Global Turbulence: The advanced capitalist economies from long boom to long downturn, 1945–2005*, London: Verso.

References

Brenner, R. (2009) *What is Good for Goldman Sachs is Good for America: The origins of the current crisis*, Los Angeles: Center for Social Theory and Comparative History.

Brett, E.A. (1983) *International Money and Capitalist Crisis*, London: Heineman.

Brett, E.A. (1985) *The World Economy since the War: The politics of uneven development*, London: Macmillan.

Brysk, A. and Choi-Fitzpatrick, A. (eds) (2012) *From Human Trafficking to Human Rights: Reframing contemporary slavery*. Philadelphia, PA: University of Pennsylvania Press.

Buck-Morss, S. (1995) Envisioning capital: Political economy on display. *Critical Inquiry* 21: 434–67.

Bullard, R.D. (2000) *Dumping in Dixie: Race, class, and environmental quality*, Boulder, CO: Westview Press.

Bumpus, A.G. and Liverman, D. (2008) Accumulation by decarbonization and the governance of carbon offsets. *Economic Geography* 84: 127–55.

Bunge, W. (1966) *Theoretical Geography*, Lund: C.W.K. Gleerup.

Bunnell, T. (2007) Post-maritime transnationalization: Malay seafarers in Liverpool. *Global Networks* 7: 412–29.

Bunnell, T. (2016) *From World City to the World in One City: Liverpool through Malay lives*, London: Wiley-Blackwell.

Burmeister, E. (1980) *Capital Theory and Dynamics*, Cambridge: Cambridge University Press.

Burns, R. (1786) To a Mouse. In: Burns, R. (ed.) *Poems, Chiefly in the Scottish Dialect*. Kilmarnock.

Butos, W.N. and Kopl, R.G. (1997) The varieties of subjectivism: Keynes and Hayek on expectations. *History of Political Economy* 29: 327–59.

Çaliskan, K. and Callon, M. (2010) Economization, part 2: A research programme for the study of markets. *Economy & Society* 39: 1–32.

Callon, M. (1986) Some elements of a sociology of translation: Domestication of the scallops and the fishermen of St Brieu Bay. In: Law, J. (ed.) *Power, Action and Belief: A new sociology of knowledge*. London: Routledge, 196–223.

Callon, M. (ed.) (1998) *The Laws of the Markets*. Oxford: Blackwell.

Camerer, C., Loewenstein, G., and Rabin, M. (eds) (2003) *Advances in Behavioral Economics*. Princeton, NJ: Princeton University Press.

Casale, G. (2007) The ethnic composition of Ottoman ship crews and the 'Rumi Challenge' to Portuguese identity. *Medieval Encounters* 13: 122–44.

Castells, M. (1996) *The Information Age: Economy, Society and Culture volume 1: The rise of the network society*, Oxford: Blackwell.

Castree, N. and Braun, B. (1998) The construction of nature and the nature of construction: Analytical and political tools for building surivable futures. In: Braun, B. and Castree, N. (eds) *Remaking Reality: Nature at the millennium*. London: Routledge, 3–42.

Çagatay, N. (1994) Themes in Marxian and post-Keynesian theories of international trade: A consideration with respect to new trade theory. In: Glick, M. (ed.) *Competition, Technology and Money: Classical and post-Keynesian perspectives*. Aldershot: Edward Elgar, 237–50.

Chakrabarty, D. (2000) *Provincializing Europe*, Princeton, NJ: Princeton University Press.

Chaney, T. (2008) Distorted gravity: The intensive and extensive margins of international trade. *American Economic Review* 98: 1701–21.

Chang, H.-J. (2002) *Kicking away the Ladder: Development strategy in historical perspective*, London: Anthem Press.

Chatterjee, P. (2001) On civil and political society in post-colonial democracies. In: Kaviraj, S. and Khilnani, S. (eds) *Civil Society: History and Possibilities*. Cambridge: Cambridge University Press, 165–78.

Chatty, R., Hendren, N., Kline, P., et al. (2014) Where is the land of opportunity? The geography of intergenerational mobility in the united states. Cambridge, MA: National Bureau of Economic Research.

Chaturvedi, S. (2003) Towards a critical geography of partition(s): Some reflections on and from South Asia. *Environment & Planning D: Society & Space* 21: 148–54.

Chibber, V. (2013) *Postcolonial Theory and the Specter of Capital*, London: Verso.

Chorley, R. and Haggett, P. (1974) *Network Analysis in Human Geography*, London: E. Arnold.

Christophers, B. (2013) *Banking across Boundaries: Placing finance in capitalism*, New York: John Wiley.

Christopherson, S. (1996) 'Fast money': Financial exclusion in the Mexican economic adjustment model. *Environment and Planning A* 28: 1157–78.

Christopherson, S. and Storper, M. (1989) The effects of flexible specialization on industrial politics and the labor market: The motion picture industry. *Industrial and Labor Relations Review* 42: 331–47.

Clark, G.L. and Wójcik, D. (2007) *The Geography of Finance*, Oxford: Oxford University Press.

Clark, G.L., Dixon, A.D., and Monk, A.H.B. (2013) *Sovereign Wealth Funds: Legitimacy, governance, and global power*, Princeton, NJ: Princeton University Press.

Clarke, J., Jandik, T., and Mandelkar, G. (2001) The efficient markets hypothesis. In: Arffa, R.C. (ed.) *Expert Financial Planning: Investment strategies from market leaders*. New York: Wiley, 126–41.

Clarke, N., Barnett, C., Cloke, P., et al. (2007) Globalising the consumer: Doing politics in an ethical register. *Political Geography* 26: 231–49.

Clarke, S. (1994) *Marx's Theory of Crisis*, London: Macmillan.

Coase, R. (1937) The nature of the firm. *Economica* 4: 386–405.

Cobden, R. (1846) *Free Trade with All Nations. A speech delivered in Manchester, England, January 15, 1846*. Available at: http://www.cooperative-individualism.org/cobden-richard_free-trade-with-all-nations-1846.htm accessed March 11, 2016.

Cockshott, W.P. (2005) Robust correlations between prices and labour values: A comment. *Cambridge Journal of Economics* 29: 309–16.

Cockshott, W.P., Cottrell, A.P., Michaelson, G.P., et al. (2009) *Classical Econophysics*, London: Routledge.

Coe, N. and Yeung, H.W.-c. (2015) *Global Production Networks: Theorizing economic development in an interconnected world*, Oxford: Oxford University Press.

Coe, N. and Wrigley, N. (eds) (2009) *The Globalization of Retailing*, Cheltenham: Edward Elgar.

Coe, N., Hess, M., Yeung, H.W.-c, et al. (2004) 'Globalizing' regional development: A global production networks perspective. *Transactions of the Insititute of British Geographers* NS29: 468–84.

Coe, N., Lai, K.P.Y., and Wójcik, D. (2014) Integrating finance into global production networks. *Regional Studies* 48: 761–77.

Collier, P. (2006) Africa: Geography and growth. *Proceedings: Federal Reserve Bank of Kansas City*: 235–52.

Collier, P. (2007) *The Bottom Billion: Why the poorest countries are failing and what can be done about it*, Oxford: Oxford University Press.

Collinge, C. (1999) Self-organisation of society by scale: A spatial reworking of regulation theory. *Environment and Planning D: Society and Space* 17: 557–74.

Comaroff, J. and Comaroff, J.L. (2011) *Theory from the South: Or, how Euro-America is evolving toward Africa*, Boulder, CO: Paradigm Publishers.

Commons, J.R. (1934) *Institutional Economics: Its place in political economy*, New York: Macmillan.

Connell, R. (2007) *Southern Theory: The global dynamics of knowledge in social science*, London: Polity.

Cook, I., et al. (2004) Follow the thing: Papaya. *Antipode* 36: 642–64.

Cook, I., et al. (2006) Geographies of food: following. *Progress in Human Geography* 30: 655–66.

Cook, I. and Woodyear, T. (2012) Lives of things. In: Barnes, T.J., Peck, J., and Sheppard, E. (eds) *The Wiley-Blackwell Companion to Economic Geography*. Oxford: Wiley-Blackwell, 226–41.

Cooke, P. and Morgan, K. (1998) *The Associational Economy: Firms, regions, and innovation*, Oxford: Oxford University Press.

Coriat, B. and Dosi, G. (1998) Learning how to govern and learning how to solve problems: On the co-evolution of competencies, conflicts and organizational routines. In: Chandler Jr, A.D., Hagström, P. and Sölvell, Ö. (eds) *The Dynamic Firm*. Oxford: Oxford University Press, 103–33.

Costanza, R. (1980) Embodied energy and economic valuation. *Science* 210: 1219–24.

Courant, P.N. and Deardorff, A.V. (1992) International trade with lumpy countries. *Journal of Political Economy* 100: 192–210.

Cowen, D. (2014) *The Deadly Life of Logistics: Mapping violence in global trade*, Minneapolis, MN: University of Minnesota Press.

Cowen, M.P. and Shenton, R.W. (1996) *Doctrines of Development*, London: Routledge.

Cox, K.R. (2013) Territory, scale, and why capitalism matters. *Territory, Politics, Governance* 1: 46–61.

Crafts, N. and Venables, A.J. (2001) *Globalization in History: A geographical perspective. Globalization in Historical Perspective*. NBER. Working Papers. Cambridge, MA: National Bureau of Economic Research.

Cravey, A. (1998) *Women and Work in Mexico's Maquiladoras*, Lanham, MD: Rowman & Littlefield.

Crozet, M. and Koenig-Soubeyran, P. (2004) Trade liberalization and the internal geography of countries. In: Mayer, T. and Muccielli, J.L. (eds) *Multinational Firms, Location and Economic Geography*. Cheltenham: Edward Elgar, 91–109.

Cukrowski, J. and Fischer, M.M. (2000) Theory of comparative advantage: Do transportation costs matter? *Journal of Regional Science* 40: 311–22.

Curry, L. (1970) Geographical specialization and trade. In: Wilson, A.G. (ed.) *Urban and Regional Planning.* London: Pion, 85–95.

Curry, L. (1972) A bivariate spatial regression operator. *The Canadian Geographer* 16: 1–14.

Curry, L. (1989) Spatial trade and factor markets. *Economic Geography* 65: 271–9.

Curry, L. and Sheppard, E. (1982) Spatial price equilibria. *Geographical Analysis* 14: 279–304.

Curtin, P.D. (1984) *Cross-cultural Trade in World History,* Cambridge: Cambridge University Press.

Darity Jr, W. and Davis, L.S. (2005) Growth, trade and uneven development. *Cambridge Journal of Economics* 29: 141–70.

Davis, D.R. and Weinstein, D.E. (2003) Market access, economic geography and comparative advantage: An empirical test. *Journal of International Economics* 59: 1–23.

de Soto, H. (2000) *The Mystery of Capital: Why capitalism triumphs in the west and fails everywhere else,* New York: Basic Books.

Deardorff, A.V. (1998) Determinants of bilateral trade: Does gravity work in a neoclassical world? In: Frankel, J.A. (ed.) *The Regionalization of the World Economy.* Chicago: Chicago University Press, 7–22.

Debreu G. (1959) *Theory of Value: An axiomatic analysis of economic equilibrium,* New Haven, CT: Yale University Press.

DeLanda, M. (2006) *A New Philosophy of Society: Assamblage theory and social complexity,* London: Continuum.

Delaney, D. and Leitner, H. (1997) The political construction of scale. *Political Geography* 16: 93–7.

Deleuze, G. (1994 [1968]) *Difference and Repetition,* New York City: Columbia University Press.

Démurger, S., Sachs, J., Woo, W.T., et al. (2002) Geography, economic policy, and regional development in China. *Asian Economic Papers* 1: 146–97.

Denike, K. and Parr, J. (1970) Production in space, competition and restricted entry. *Journal of Regional Science* 10: 49–63.

Diamond, J. (1997) *Guns, Germs and Steel,* New York: Norton.

Diamond, J. (2005) *Collapse: How societies choose to fail or succeed,* New York: Penguin.

Dicken, P. (1992) *Global Shift: The internationalization of economic activity,* New York: Guilford.

Dicken, P. (2003) 'Placing' firms: Grounding the debate on the 'global' corporation. In: Peck, J. and Yeung, H.W.-c (eds) *Remaking the Global Economy: Economic–geographical perspectives.* London: Sage, 27–44.

Dicken, P., Kelly, P.F., Olds, K., et al. (2001) Chains and networks, territories and scales: Towards a relational framework for analysing the global economy. *Global Networks* 1: 89–112.

Disdier, A.-C. and Head, K. (2008) The puzzling persistence of the distance effect on bilateral trade. *The Review of Economics and Statistics* 90: 37–48.

References

Dixit, A.K. and Stiglitz, J.E. (1977) Monopolistic competition and optimum product diversity. *American Economic Review* 67: 297–308.

Dixon, A.D. (2014) *The New Geography of Capitalism: Firms, finance and society*, Oxford: Oxford University Press.

Dodge, M. and Kitchen, R. (2001) *Mapping Cyberspace*, London: Routledge.

Dodge, M. and Kitchin, R. (2004) Flying through code/space: The real virtuality of air travel. *Environment & Planning A* 36: 195–211.

Domar, E.D. (1946) Capital expansion, rate of growth and employment. *Econometrica* 14: 137–47.

Domencich, T. and McFadden, D. (1975) *Urban Travel Demand: A behavioral analysis*, Amsterdam: North-Holland.

Doran, J. and Fingleton, B. (2013) Economic shocks and growth: Spatio-temporal perspectives on Europe's economies in a time of crisis. *Papers in Regional Science* 93 (S1): S137–65.

Dow, G.K. (1993) Why capital hires labor: A bargaining perspective. *American Economic Review* 83: 118–34.

Duménil, G. and Lévy, D. (1987) The dynamics of competition: A restoration of the classical hypothesis. *Cambridge Journal of Economics* 11: 133–64.

Duménil, G. and Lévy, D. (1991) Micro adjustment toward long-term equilibrium. *Journal of Economic Theory* 53: 369–95.

Duménil, G. and Lévy, D. (1993) *The Economics of the Profit Rate: Competition, crises and historical tendencies in capitalism*, Aldershot: Edward Elgar.

Dunford, M. (1990) Theories of regulation. *Environment and Planning D: Society and Space* 8: 297–322.

Dymski, G.A. and Li, W. (2003) The macrostructure of financial exclusion: Mainstream, ethnic, and fringe banks and money/space. *Espaces, Populations, Societes* 1: 183–201.

Earle, C. (1982) The geography of strikes in the United States, 1881–1894. *Journal of Interdisciplinary History* 31: 63–84.

Easley, D., de Prado, M.L. and O'Hara, M. (2011) The microstructure of the 'Flash Crash': Flow toxicity, liquidity crashes and the probability of informed trading. *The Journal of Portfolio Management* 37: 118–28.

Easterly, W. (2006) *The White Man's Burden: Why the west's efforts to aid the rest have done more harm than good*, New York City: Penguin Press.

Easterly, W. and Levine, R. (2003) Tropics, germs, and crops: How endowments influence economic development. *Journal of Monetary Economics* 50: 3–39.

Eaton, J. and Kortum, S. (2002) Technology, geography, and trade. *Econometrica* 70: 1741–79.

Elson, D., Grown, K., and Çagatay, N. (2007) Mainstream, heterodox, and feminist trade theory. In: Van Staveren, I., Elson, D., Grown, K., et al. (eds) *The Feminist Economics of Trade*. London: Routledge, 33–52.

Elwood, S., Lawson, V. and Nowak, S. (2014) Middle-class poverty politics: Making place, making people. *Annals of the Association of American Geographers* 105: 123–43.

Emmanuel, A.G. (1972) *Unequal Exchange: A study of the imperialism of trade*, New York: Monthly Review Press.

Engels, F. (1962 [1878]) *Anti-Dühring*, Moscow: Foreign Languages Publishing House.

England, K. and Ward, K. (eds) (2007) *Neoliberalization: States, networks, peoples*, Oxford: Blackwell.

Escobar, A. (1995) *Encountering Development*, Princeton, NJ: Princeton University Press.

Escobar, A. (2001) Culture sits in places: Reflections on globalism and subaltern strategies of localization. *Political Geography* 20: 139–74.

Escobar, A. (2008) *Territories of Difference: Place, movements, life, redes*, Durham, NC: Duke University Press.

Essletzbichler, J. (2009) Should economic geographers count? *Geography Compass* 3: 237–55.

Essletzbichler, J. and Rigby, D. (2007) Exploring evolutionary economic geographies. *Papers in Evolutionary Economic Geography*, Utrecht: Utrecht University.

Essletzbichler, J. and Rigby, D. (2010) Generalized Darwinism and evolutionary economic geography. In: Boschma, R.A. and Martin, R. (eds) *The Handbook of Evolutionary Economic Geography*. Cheltenham: Edward Elgar, 43–61.

Faier, L. (2009) *Intimate Encounters: Filipina women and the remaking of rural Japan*, Berkeley, CA: University of California Press.

Fajardo, K.B. (2008) Translating Filipino and Filipino American tomboy masculinities through global migration and seafaring. *GLQ: A Journal of Lesbian and Gay Studies* 14: 403–24.

Fama, E. (1970) Efficient capital markets: A review of theory and empirical work. *Journal of Finance* 25: 383–417.

Fama E. (1991) Efficient capital markets: II. *The Journal of Finance* XLVI: 1575–615.

Faye, M.L., McArthur, J.W., Sachs, J., et al. (2004) The challenges facing landlocked developing countries. *Journal of Human Development* 5: 31–68.

Featherstone, D. (2003) Spatialities of transnational resistance to globalization: The maps of grievance of the Inter-Continental Caravan. *Transactions of the Institute of British Geographers* NS28: 404–21.

Featherstone, D. (2008) *Resistance, Space and Political Identities: The making of counter-global networks*, New York: Wiley.

Featherstone, D. (2012) *Solidarity: Hidden histories and geographies of internationalism*, London: Zed Press.

Fine, B. and Milonakis, D. (2009) *From Economics Imperialism to Freakonomics: The shifting boundaries between economics and other social sciences*, London: Routledge.

Fingleton, B. (2000) Spatial econometrics, economic geography, dynamics and equilibrium: A 'third way'? *Environment and Planning A* 32: 1481–98.

Fingleton, B. and McCann, P. (2007) Sinking the iceberg? On the treatment of transportation costs in the new economic geography. In: Fingleton, B. (ed.) *New Directions in Economic Geography*. Cheltenham: Edward Elgar, 168–203.

Fletcher, I. (2009) *Free Trade Doesn't Work: Why America needs a tariff*, Washington DC: U.S. Business and Industry Council.

Florida, R. (2002) *The Rise of the Creative Class*, New York City: Basic Books.

Foley, D.K. (2000) Recent developments in the labor theory of value. *Review of Radical Political Economics* 32: 1–39.

Foley, D.K. (2003) Endogenous technical change with externalities in a classical growth model. *Journal of Economic Behavior and Organization* 52: 167–89.

References

Foster, J. (2011) Evolutionary macroeconomics: A research agenda. *Journal of Evolutionary Economics* 21: 5–28.

Foster, J.B. and Magdoff, F. (2009) *The Great Financial Crisis: Causes and consequences*, New York: Monthly Review Press.

Fowler, C.S. (2007) Taking geographical economics out of equilibrium: Implications for theory and policy. *Journal of Economic Geography* 7: 265–84.

Fowler, C.S. (2011) Finding equilibrium: How important is general equilibrium to the results of geographical economics? *Journal of Economic Geography* 11: 457–80.

Francois, P. and Lloyd-Ellis, H. (2003) Animal spirits through creative destruction. *American Economic Review* 93: 530–50.

Frank, A.G. (1978a) *Dependent Accumulation and Underdevelopment*, London: Macmillan.

Frank, A.G. (1978b) *World Accumulation 1492–1789*, New York: Monthly Review Press.

Frank, A.G. (1998) *ReORIENT: Global economy in the Asian age*, Berkeley, CA: Unuversity of California Press.

Fraser, N. (2013) A triple movement? Parsing the politics of crisis after Polanyi. *New Left Review* NS 81: 119–32.

Fraser, N. (2014) Can society be commodities all the way down? Post-Polanyian reflections on capitalist crisis. *Economy and Society* 43: 541–58.

Freeman, C., Clark, J.A., and Soete, L. (1982) *Unemployment and Technical Innovation: A study of long waves and economic development*, London: Francis Pinter.

French, S., Leyshon, A., and Wainwright, T. (2011) Financializing space, spacing financialization. *Progress in Human Geography* 35: 798–819.

Fridell, G. (2006) Fair trade and neoliberalism: Assessing emerging perspectives. *Latin American Perspectives* 33: 8–28.

Friedman, M. (1953) The methodology of positive economics. In: Friedman, M. (ed.) *Essays in Positive Economics*. Chicago: University of Chicago Press, 3–43.

Friedman, T. (2005) *The World is Flat*, New York: Farrar, Strauss and Giroux.

Fröbel, F., Heinrichs, J. and Kreye, O. (1980) *The New International Division of Labour*, Cambridge: Cambridge University Press.

Fry, H. and Wilson, A.G. (2012) A dynamic global trade model with four sectors: Food, natural resources, manufactured goods and labour. *UCL Working Papers*. London: UCL.

Fujita, M., Krugman, P., and Venables, A.J. (1999) *The Spatial Economy: Cities, regions and international trade*, Cambridge, MA: MIT Press.

Fulbrook, E. (ed.) (2004) *A Guide to What's Wrong with Economics*. London: Anthem Press.

Fussell, E. (2011) The deportation threat dynamic and victimization of Latino migrants: Wage theft and robbery. *The Sociological Quarterly* 52: 593–615.

Gallup, J.L., Sachs, J.D., and Mellinger, A.D. (1999) Geography and economic development. *International Regional Science Review* 22: 179–232.

Galtung, J. (1971) A structural theory of imperialism. *Journal of Peace Research* 2: 81–116.

Gandy, M. (2008) Landscapes of disaster: Water, modernity, and urban fragmentation in Mumbai. *Environment and Planning A* 40: 108–30.

Garcia-Perpet, M.-F. (2007) The social construction of a perfect market: The strawberry auction at Fontaines-en-Sologne. In: Mackenzie, D., Muniesa, F., and Siu, L. (eds) *Do Economists make Markets?* Princeton, NJ: Princeton University Press, 20–53.

Garegnani, P. (1966) Switching of techniques. *Quarterly Journal of Economics* 80: 554–67.

Garegnani, P. (2012) On the present state of the capital controversy. *Cambridge Journal of Economics* 36: 1417–32.

Garretsen, H. and Martin, R. (2010) Rethinking (new) economic geography models: taking geography and history more seriously. *Spatial Economic Analysis* 5: 127–60.

Georgescu-Roegen, N. (1971) *The Entropy Law and the Economic Process*, Cambridge, MA: Harvard University Press.

Gereffi, G. (1996) Global commodity chains: New forms of coordination and control among nations and firms in international industries. *Competition & Change. The Journal of Global Business and Political Economy* 1: 427–39.

Gibb, R. and Michalak, W. (1996) Regionalism in the world economy. *Area* 28: 446–58.

Gibson, B. (1980) Unequal exchange: Theoretical issues and empirical findings. *Review of Radical Political Economics* 12: 15–35.

Gibson-Graham, J.K. (1996) *The End of Capitalism (as we knew it)*, Oxford: Blackwell.

Gibson-Graham, J.K. (2006) *A Postcapitalist Politics*, Minneapolis: University of Minnesota Press.

Gibson-Graham, J.K. (2008) Diverse economies: performative practices for 'other worlds'. *Progress in Human Geography* 32: 613–32.

Gibson-Graham, J.K., Resnick, S.A., and Wolff, R.D. (2000) *Class and its Others*, Minneapolis, MN: University of Minnesota Press.

Gibson-Graham, J.K., Cameron, J., and Healy, S. (2013) *Take Back the Economy, any Time, any Place*, Minneapolis, MN: University of Minnesota Press.

Giddens, A. (1984) *The Constitution of Society: Outline of the theory of structuration*, Berkeley, CA: University of California Press.

Gidwani, V. (2012) Waste/value. In: Barnes, T.J., Peck, J., and Sheppard, E. (eds) *The Wiley-Blackwell Companion to Economic Geography*. Oxford: Wiley-Blackwell, 275–88.

Gidwani, V. and Reddy, R.N. (2011) The afterlives of 'waste': Notes from India for a minor history of capitalist surplus. *Antipode* 43.

Gidwani, V. and Wainwright, J. (2014) On capital, not-capital, and development after Kalyan Sanyal. *Economic and Political Weekly* XLIX: 40–7.

Glaeser, E. (2011) *The Triumph of the City: How our greatest invention makes us richer, smarter, greener, healthier, and happier*, New York: Penguin.

Glassman, J. and Samatar, A. (1997) Development geography and the third-world state. *Progress in Human Geography* 21: 164–98.

Glassman, J. and Young-Jin, C. (2014) The chaebol and the US military–industrial complex: Cold War geopolitical economy and South Korean industrialization. *Environment and Planning A* 46: 1160–80.

Glyn, A. and Sutcliffe, B. (1972) *British Capitalism, Workers and the Profit Squeeze*, Harmonsworth: Penguin.

Goetz, A.R., Vowles, T.M., and Tierney, S. (2009) Bridging the qualitative–quantitative divide in transport geography. *The Professional Geographer* 61: 323–35.

Goldberg, D.T. (1993) *Racist Culture: Philosophy and the politics of meaning*, Oxford: Blackwell.

Goodwin, R.M. (1967) A growth cycle. In: Feinstein, C.H. (ed.) *Socialism, Capitalism and Economic Growth*. Cambridge: Cambridge University Press, 54–8.

References

Goss, J. (1995) We know who you are and we know where you live: The instrumental rationality of geo-marketing information systems. *Economic Geography* 71: 171–98.

Gould, S.J. (1996) *Full House: The spread of excellence from Plato to Darwin*, New York: Three Rivers Press.

Grabher, G. (2006) Trading routes, bypasses, and risky intersections: Mapping the travels of 'networks' between economic geography and economic sociology. *Progress in Human Geography* 30: 163–89.

Grabher, G. (2009) Yet another turn? The evolutionary project in economic geography. *Economic Geography* 85: 119–27.

Graham, S. and Marvin, S. (2001) *Splintering Urbanism: Networked infrastructures, technological mobilities and the urban condition*, London: Routledge.

Granovetter, M. (1973) The strength of weak ties. *American Journal of Sociology* 78: 1360–80.

Granovetter, M. (1985) Economic action and social structure: The problem of embeddedness. *American Journal of Sociology* 91: 481–510.

Grant, R. (1993) Trading blocs or trading blows—the macroeconomic geography of United-States and Japanese trade policies. *Environment and Planning A* 25: 273–91.

Grant, R. (1994) The geography of international trade. *Progress in Human Geography* 18: 298–312.

Griffith, D.A. (2007) Spatial structure and spatial interaction: 25 years later. *The Review of Regional Studies* 37: 28–38.

Grossman, G.M. and Helpman, E. (1991) *Innovation and Growth in the Global Economy*, Cambridge, MA: MIT Press.

Gudeman, S. (2001) *The Anthropology of Economy*, Oxford: Blackwell.

Gudeman, S. (2008) *Economy's Tension: The dialectics of community and market*, New York: Berghahn Books.

Gudeman, S. and Penn, M. (1982) Models, meanings and reflexivity. In: Parkin, D. (ed.) *Semantic Anthropology*. London: Academic Press, 89–106.

Guha, R. (ed.) (1997) *A Subaltern Studies Reader, 1986–1995*, Minneapolis, MN: University of Minnesota Press.

Habermas, J. (2008) Notes on post-secular society. *New Perspectives Quarterly* 25: 17–29.

Hale, A. and Wills, J. (eds) (2005) *Threads of Labour: Garment industry supply chains from the workers' perspective*. Oxford: Basil Blackwell.

Hall, T. and Hubbard, P. (eds) (1998) *The Entrepreneurial City*. London: John Wiley & Sons.

Hanink, D.M. and Cromley, R.G. (2005) Geographic change with trade based on comparative advantage. *Annals of the Association of American Geographers* 95: 511–24.

Hanson, S. and Pratt, G. (1995) *Gender, Work, and Space*, New York: Routledge.

Haraway, D. (1988) Situated knowledges: The science question and the privilege of partial perspective. *Feminist Studies* 14: 575–99.

Haraway, D. (1997) *Modest_Witness@Second_Millenium.FemaleMan©_Meets_Onco-Mouse™*, London: Routledge.

Harcourt, G.C. (1972) *Some Cambridge Controversies in the Theory of Capital*, Cambridge: Cambridge University Press.

Harcourt, W. and Nelson, I.L. (eds) (2015) *Practicing Feminist Political Ecology*, London: Zed Books.

Hardt, M. and Negri, A. (2004) *Multitude: War and democracy in the age of empire*, London: Penguin.

Hargittai, E. and Centeno, M.A. (2001) Introduction: Defining a global geography. *American Behavioral Scientist* 44: 1545–60.

Harman, C. (2009) *Zombie Capitalism: Global crisis and the relevance of Marx*, Chicago, IL: Haymarket Books.

Harris, D. and Azzi, D. (2006) *ALBA. Venezuela's Answer to 'free trade': The Bolivarian Alternative for the Americas*. Bankok: Focus on the Global South.

Harris, L.M., Goldin, J.A., and Sneddon, C. (eds) (2015) *Contemporary Water Governance in the Global South: Scarcity, marketization and participation*, London: Routledge.

Harris, R.J., Sleight, P. and Webber, R. (2005) *Geodemographics, GIS and Neighbourhood Targeting*, Chichester: Wiley.

Harrod, R. (1948) *Towards a Dynamic Economics*, London: Macmillan.

Hart, G. (2002) *Disabling Globalization: Places of power in post-apartheid South Africa*, Berkeley, CA: University of California Press.

Hart, G. (2008) The provocations of neoliberalism: Contesting the nation and liberation after Apartheid. *Antipode* 40: 678–705.

Harvey, D. (1969) *Explanation in Geography*, London: Edward Arnold.

Harvey, D. (1973) *Social Justice and the City*, London: E. Arnold.

Harvey, D. (1982a) Land rent and the transition to the capitalist mode of production. *Antipode* 14: 17–25.

Harvey, D. (1982b) *The Limits to Capital*, Oxford: Basil Blackwell.

Harvey, D. (1985) Money, space, time and the city. In: Harvey, D. *Consciousness and the Urban Experience*. Oxford: Basil Blackwell, 1–35.

Harvey, D. (1989a) *The Condition of Postmodernity*, Oxford: Basil Blackwell.

Harvey, D. (1989b) From managerialism to entrepreneurialism: The transformation of urban governance in late capitalism. *Geografisker Annaler* 71, Series B: 3–17.

Harvey, D. (1994) Flexible accumulation through urbanization: Reflections on 'postmodernism' in the American city. In: Amin, A. (ed.) *Post-Fordism: A reader*. Oxford: Basil Blackwell, 361–85.

Harvey, D. (1996) *Justice, Nature and the Geography of Difference*, Oxford: Basil Blackwell.

Harvey, D. (2000) *Spaces of Hope*, Berkeley: University of California Press.

Harvey, D. (2003) *The New Imperialism*, Oxford: Oxford University Press.

Harvey, D. (2006) *A Brief History of Neoliberalism*, Oxford: Oxford University Press.

Harvey, D. (2007) Neoliberalism as creative destruction. *The Annals of the American Academy of Social and Political Science* 610: 22–44.

Harvey, D. (2014) *Seventeen Contradictions and the End of Capitalism*, Oxford: Oxford University Press.

Harvey, D. and Wachsmuth, D. (2012) What is to be done? And who the hell is going to do it? In: Brenner, N., Marcuse, P., and Mayer, M. (eds) *Cities for People: Critical urban theory and the right to the city*. London: Routledge, 264–74.

Hassink, R., Klaerding, C., and Marques, P. (2014) Advancing evolutionary economic geography by engaged pluralism. *Regional Studies*: 1–13.

Hausmann, R. (2001) Prisoners of Geography. *Foreign Policy* January/February: 45–53.

Hayek, F.A. (1937) Economics and knowledge. *Economica* N.S.4: 33–54.

Hayter, R., Barnes, T.J., and Bradshaw, M.J. (2003) Relocating resource peripheries to the core of economic geography's theorizing: Rationale and agenda. *Area* 35: 15–23.

Heckscher, E.F. (1919) The effect of foreign trade on the distribution of income. *Ekonomisk Tidskrift* 21: 1–32.

Helpman, E. (1990) Monopolistic competition in trade theory. Department of Economics, Princeton University, Princeton NJ.

Helpman. E. (1999) The structure of foreign trade. *Journal of Economic Perspectives* 13: 121–44.

Helwig, C. (2008) Monetary business cycles (imperfect information). In: Durlauf, S. and Blume, L.E. (eds) *The New Palgrave Dictionary of Economics Online*. London: Palgrave Macmillan http://www.dictionaryofeconomics.com/article?id=pde2008_M000375 accessed March 11, 2016.

Henderson, G. (2013) *Value in Marx: The persistence of value in a more-than-capitalist world,* Minneapolis, MN: University of Minnesota Press.

Hendry, DF. (2001) *Econometrics: Alchemy or science?*, Oxford: Oxford University Press.

Herod, A. (1997) Labor as an agent of globalization and as a global agent. In: Cox, K.R. (ed.) *Spaces of Globalization: Reasserting the power of the local*. New York: Guilford Press, 167–201.

Herod, A. (1998a) Of blocs, flows and networks: The end of the Cold War, cyberspace, and the geo-economics of organized labor at the *fin de milleniare*. In: Herod, A., Ó Tuathail, G. and Roberts, S. (eds) *An Unruly World? Globalization, Governance and Geography*. London: Routledge, 162–95.

Herod, A. (ed.) (1998b) *Organizing the Landscape*. Minneapolis, MN: University of Minnesota Press.

Herod, A. (2001) *Labor Geographies: Workers and the landscapes of capitalism*, New York: Guilford.

Herod, A. and Aguiar, L.L.M. (eds) (2006) *The Dirty Work of Neoliberalism: Cleaners in the global economy*. New York: John Wiley.

Hertwich, E.G. and Peters, G.P. (2009) Carbon footprint of nations: A global, trade-linked analysis. *Environmental Science and Technology* 43: 6414–20.

Hess, M. and Yeung, H.W.-c. (2006) Whither global production networks in economic geography? Past, present, and future. *Environment & Planning A* 38: 1193–204.

Hesse M. (1963) *Models and Analogies in Science,* London: Sheed and Ward.

Hewitt, K. (2014) *Regions of Risk: A geographical introduction to disasters*, London: Routledge.

Heynen, N.C., McCarthy, J., Prudham, S., et al. (eds) (2007) *Neoliberal Environments: False promises and unnatural consequences*, London: Routledge.

Hilferding, R. (1981 [1910]) *Finance Capital*, London: Routledge & Kegan Paul.

Hinde, W. (1987) *Richard Cobden: A Victorian outsider*, New Haven, CT: Yale University Press.

Hobson, J.A. (1922) *The Economics of Unemployment*, London: G. Allen & Unwin.

Hobson, J.M. (2004) *The Eastern Origins of Western Civilisation*, Cambridge: Cambridge University Press.

Hodgson, G.M. (2007) Meanings of methodological individualism. *Journal of Economic Methodology* 14: 211–26.

Hoekman, B.M. and Kostecki, M.M. (2001) *The Political Economy of the World Trading System: The WTO and beyond*, Oxford: Oxford University Press.

Holt, R.P.F. and Pressman, S. (eds) (2001) *A New Guide to Post-Keynesian Economics*, London: Routledge.

Hoover, K. (1988) *The New Classical Macroeconomics: A sceptical inquiry*, Oxford: Blackwell.

Hopkins, T.K. and Wallerstein, I. (1994) Commodity chains: Construct and research. In: Gereffi, G. and Korzeniewicz, M. (eds) *Commodity Chains and Global Capitalism*. Westport, CT: Greenwood Press, 17–20.

Hudson, R. (1999) The learning economy, the learning firm and the learning region: A sympathetic critique of the limits to learning. *European Urban and Regional Studies* 6: 59–72.

Hudson, R. and Sadler, D. (1986) Contesting works closures in Western Europe's old industrial regions: Defending place or betraying class? In: Scott, A.J. and Storper, M. (eds) *Production, Work Territory—The geographical anatomy of industrial capitalism*. London: Allen & Unwin, 172–93.

Hughes, A. (2005) Geographies of exchange and circulation: Alternative trading spaces. *Progress in Human Geography* 29: 496–504.

Hughes, A. (2006) Geographies of exchange and circulation: Transnational trade and governance. *Progress in Human Geography* 30: 635–43.

Hughes, A. (2007) Geographies of exchange and circulation: Flows and networks of knowledgeable capitalism. *Progress in Human Geography* 31: 527–35.

Huntington, E. (1922) *Civilization and Climate*, New Haven, CT: Yale University Press.

Hymer, S. (1972) The multinational corporation and the law of uneven development. In: Bhagwati, J. (ed.) *Economics and World Order: From the 1970's to the 1990's*. Free Press: New York, 113–40.

Iammarino, S. (2005) An evolutionary integrated view of regional systems of innovation. Concepts, measures and historical perspectives. *European Planning Studies* 13: 497–519.

Ince, O.U. (2014) Primitive accumulation, new enclosures, and global land grabs: A theoretical intervention. *Rural Sociology* 79: 104–31.

Irwin, D.A. (1996) *Against the Tide: An intellectual history of free trade*, Princeton, NJ: Princeton University Press.

Irwin, D.A. (2006) Commentary: Shifts in economic geography and their causes. Federal Reserve Bank of Kansas City, fourth quarter: 41–8.

Isard, W. (1951) Interregional and regional input-output analysis: A model of a space-economy. *The Review of Economics and Statistics* 33: 318–28.

Isard, W. (1999) Regional science: Parallels from physics and chemistry. *Papers in Regional Science* 78: 5–20.

Jacks, D.S., Meissner, C.M. and Novy, D. (2009) Trade booms, trade busts, and trade costs. CESIFO Working Paper 2767.

Jackson, P. and Holbrook, B. (1995) Multiple meanings: Shopping and the cultural politics of identity. *Environment and Planning A* 27: 1913–30.

Jayasuriya, K. (2001) Governance, post Washington consensus and the new anti politics. Hong Kong: Southeast Asia Research Centre.

Jeffrey, A., McFarlane, C., and Vasudevan, A. (2012) Rethinking enclosure: Space, subjectivity and the commons. *Antipode* 44: 1247–67.

Jessop, B. (1990) Regulation theories in retrospect and prospect. *Economy and Society* 19: 153–216.

Jessop, B. (1994) Post-Fordism and the state. In: Amin, A. (ed.) *Post-Fordism: A reader.* Oxford: Basil Blackwell, 251–79.

Jessop, B. (1999) Reflections on globalization and its (il)logics. In: Dicken, P., Kelly, P., Olds, K., et al. (eds) *Globalization and the Asia Pacific: Contested territories.* London: Routledge, 19–38.

Jessop, B. (2001) *On the spatio-temporal logics of capital's globalization and their manifold implications for state power.* Available at: http://www.lancaster.ac.uk/fass/resources/sociology-online-papers/papers/jessop-spatio-temporal-logics.pdf accessed March 11, 2016.

Jessop, B. and Sum, N.-l. (2006) *Beyond the Regulation Approach: Putting capitalist economies in their place,* London: Edward Elgar.

Jessop, B., Brenner, N., and Jones, M. (2008) Theorizing sociospatial relations. *Environment & Planning D: Society & Space* 26: 389–401.

Johnson, W. (2013) *River of Dark Dreams: Slavery and empire in the cotton kingdom,* Cambridge, MA: Belknap Press.

Johnston, R.J. (1976) *The World Trade System: Some enquiries into its spatial structure,* London: G. Bell & Sons Ltd.

Jomo, K. and Fine, B. (eds) (2006) *The New Development Economics: After the Washington consensus.* London: Zed Books.

Jones, R.W. (1956–57) Factor proportions and the Hecksher–Ohlin theorem. *Review of Economic Studies* 24: 1–10.

Kaldor, N. (1957) A model of economic growth. *Economic Journal* 67: 591–624.

Kalecki, M. (1968) Trend and the business cycle. *The Economic Journal* 78: 263–76.

Kansky, K.J. (1963) *Structure of Transportation Networks: Relationships between network geometry and regional characteristics,* Chicago: Uniuversity of Chicago Press.

Kaplinsky, R. (2000) Globalization and unequalization: What can be learned from value chain analysis. *The Journal of Development Studies* 37: 117–46.

Katz, C. (2001) Vagabond capitalism and the necessity of social reproduction. *Antipode* 33: 709–28.

Katz, S. (1986) Towards a sociological definition of rent: Notes on David Harvey's *The Limits to Capital. Antipode* 18: 64–78.

Kautsky, K. (1901–2) Krisentheorien. *Die Neue Zeit* 20.

Kautsky, K. (1910 [1892]) *The Class Struggle,* Chicago: Charles H. Kerr.

Keen, S. (2011) *Debunking Economics: The naked emperor dethroned?* London: Zed Books.

Kelly, P. and Lusis, T. (2006) Migration and the transnational habitus: Evidence from Canada and the Philippines. *Environment and Planning A* 38: 831–47.

Keynes, G.M. (1936) *The General Theory of Employment, Interest, and Money,* London: Macmillan.

Kidd, A. (2002) *Manchester,* Edinburgh: Edinburgh University Press.

Kindleberger, C.P. (1975) The rise of free trade in Western Europe. *The Journal of Economic History* 35: 20–55.

Kingma, M. (2006) *Nurses on the Move: Migration and the global health care economy*, Ithaca, NY: Cornell University Press.

Kirsch, S. (1995) The incredible shrinking world? Technology and the production of space. *Environment and Planning D: Society and Space* 13: 529–55.

Kliman, A.J. (2006) *Reclaiming Marx's 'Capital': A refutation of the myth of inconsistency*, Lanham, MD: Lexington Books.

Kliman, A.J. (2009) 'The destruction of capital' and the current economic crisis. *Socialism and Democracy* 23: 47–54.

Knight, F.H. (1921) *Risk, Uncertainty and Profit*, Boston, MA: Houghton Mifflin.

Kropotkin, P.A. (1922) *Mutual Aid: A factor of evolution*, New York: Alfred A. Knopf.

Krugman, P. (1981) Trade, accumulation and uneven development. *Journal of Development Economics* 8: 149–61.

Krugman, P. (1990) *Rethinking International Trade*, Cambridge, MA: MIT Press.

Krugman, P. (1991) *Geography and Trade*, Cambridge, MA: MIT Press.

Krugman, P.R. (1993) First nature, second nature, and metropolitan location. *Journal of Regional Science* 33: 129–44.

Krugman, P. (1994) Competitiveness: A dangerous obsession. *Council on Foreign Relations* 73: 28–44.

Krugman, P.R. (1996) *The Self-organizing Economy*, Oxford: Blackwell.

Krugman, P.R. and Livas Elizondo, R. (1996) Trade policy and the third world metropolis. *Journal of Development Economics* 49: 137–50.

Krugman, P.R. and Venables, A.J. (1995) Globalization and the inequality of nations. *Quarterly Journal of Economics* 110: 857–80.

Kuznets, S. (1955) Economic growth and income inequality. *American Economic Review* XLV: 1–28.

Lakatos, I. (1970) Falsification and the methodology of scientific research programmes. In: Lakatos, I. and Musgrave, A. (eds) *Criticism and the Growth of Knowledge*. Cambridge: Cambridge University Press, 91–195.

Larner, W. (2000) Neoliberalism: Policy, ideology, governmentality. *Studies in Political Economy* 63: 5–25.

Latour, B. (1987) *Science in Action*, Cambridge, MA: Harvard University Press.

Latour, B. (1993) *We Have Never Been Modern*, Cambridge, MA: Harvard University Press.

Latour, B. (1999) On recalling ANT. In: Law, J. and Hassard, J. (eds) *Actor Network Theory and After*. Oxford: Blackwell, 15–25.

Latour, B. (2004) Why has critique run out of steam? From matters of fact to matters of concern. *Critical Inquiry* 30: 25–8.

Latour, B. (2005) *Reassembling the Social: An introduction to actor-network-theory*, Oxford: Oxford University Press.

Law, J. (1996) On the methods of long-distance control: Vessels, navigation and the Portuguese route to India. In: Law, J. (ed.) *Power, Action and Belief: A new sociology of knowledge?* London: Routledge and Kegan Paul, 234–63.

Law, J. (1999) After ANT: Complexity, naming and topology. In: Law, J. and Hassard, J. (eds) *Actor Network Theory and After*. Oxford: Blackwell, 1–14.

References

Lawson, T. (2003) *Reorienting Economics*, London: Routledge.

Lawson, V. (2007) Geographies of care and responsibility. *Annals of the Association of American Geographers* 97: 1–11.

Lawson, V. (2010) Reshaping economic geography? Producing spaces of inclusive development. *Economic Geography* 86: 351–60.

Lebowitz, M.A. (2005) *Following Marx: Method, critique, and crisis*, Chicago: Haymarket Books.

Lee, F.S. (1998) *Post Keynesian Price Theory*, Cambridge: Cambridge University Press.

Lefebvre, H. (1991 [1974]) *The Production of Space*, Oxford: Blackwell.

Leitner, H. (1990) Cities in pursuit of economic growth. *Political Geography Quarterly* 9: 146–70.

Leitner, H. (1994) Capital markets, the development industry, and urban office market dynamics: rethinking building cycles. *Environment & Planning A* 26: 779–802.

Leitner, H. (1997) Reconfiguring the spatiality of power: the construction of a supra-national migration framework for the European Union. *Political Geography* 15: 123–43.

Leitner, H. (2004) The politics of scale and networks of spatial connectivity: Trans-national interurban networks and the rescaling of political governance in Europe. In: Sheppard, E. and McMaster, R. (eds) *Scale & Geographic Inquiry: Nature, society and method.* Oxford: Blackwell, 236–55.

Leitner, H. and Miller, B. (2007) Scale and the limitations of ontological debate: A commentary on Marston, Jones and Woodward. *Transactions of the Institute of British Geographers* 32: 116–25.

Leitner, H., Peck, J., and Sheppard, E. (eds) (2007a) *Contesting Neoliberalism: Urban frontiers*, New York City: Guilford.

Leitner, H., Sheppard, E., Sziarto, K.M., and Maringanti A. (2007b) Contesting urban futures: Decentering neoliberalism. In: Leitner, H., Peck, J. and Sheppard, E. (eds) *Contesting Neoliberalism: Urban frontiers.* New York: Guilford, 1–25.

Leitner, H., Sheppard, E., and Sziarto, K.M. (2008) The spatialities of contentious politics. *Transactions of the Institute of British Geographers* NS 33: 157–72.

Leontief, W. (1928) Die Wirtschaft als Kreislauf. Ph.D. University of Berlin: Economics.

Leontief, W. (1956) Factor proportions and the structure of American trade: Further theoretical and empirical analysis. *Review of Economics and Statistics* 38: 386–407.

Levien, M. (2012) The land question: Special economic zones and the political economy of dispossession in India. *Journal of Peasant Studies* 39: 933–69.

Levine, A., Sober, E. and Wright, E.O. (1987) Marxism and methodological individualism. *New Left Review* 162: 67–84.

Levins, R. and Lewontin, R. (1985) *The Dialectal Biologist*, Cambridge, MA: Harvard University Press.

Levy, D.L. (2008) Political contestation in global production networks. *Academy of Management Review* 33: 943–63.

Lewis, M. (2014) *Flash Boys: a Wall Street revolt*, New York City: WW Norton & Company.

Leyshon. A. and Thrift, N. (1997) *Money/Space: Geographies of monetary transformation*, London: Routledge.

Lipietz, A. (1986) New tendencies in the international division of labor: Regimes of accumulation and modes of regulation. In: Scott, A.J. and Storper, M. (eds) *Production, Work, Territory*. London: Allen & Unwin, 16–40.

Lipietz, A. (1987) *Mirages and Miracles*, London: Verso.

Logan, J. and Molotch, H.L. (1987) *Urban Fortunes*, Los Angeles: University of California Press.

Longino, H. (2002) *The Fate of Knowledge*, Princeton, NJ: Princeton University Press.

Lösch, A. (1954 [1940]) *The Economics of Location*, New Haven, CT: Yale University Press.

Low, N. and Gleeson, B. (1998) *Justice, Society and Nature*, London: Routledge.

Lucas, R.E. and Prescott, E.C. (1974) Equilibrium search and unemployment. *Journal of Economic Theory* 7: 188–209.

Luce, S. (2004) *Fighting for a Living Wage*, Ithaca, NY: Cornell University Press.

Luke ,T.W. and Ó Tuathail, G. (1998) Global flowmations, local fundamentalisms, and fast geopolitics: 'America' in an accelerating world order. In: Herod, A., Ó Tuathail, G., and Roberts, S.M. (eds) *An Unruly World? Globalization, governance and geography*. London: Routledge, 1367–80.

Luxemburg, R. (1951 [1913]) *The Accumulation of Capital—An anti-critique*, London: Routledge & Kegan Paul.

Lynn, W.S. (1998) Animals, ethics and geography. In: Wolch, J. and Emel, J. (eds) *Animal Geographies: Place, politics and identity in the nature-culture borderlands*. London: Verso, 280–98.

McCulloch, J.R. (1824) *A Discourse on the Rise, Progress, Peculiar Objects, and Importance, of Political Economy*, Edinburgh: A. Constable and Co.

McDowell, L. (1991) Life without father and Ford: The new gender order of post-Fordism. *Transactions of the Insititute of British Geographers* NS 16: 400–19.

McDowell, L. (1997) *Capital Culture: Money, sex and power at work*, Oxford: Blackwell.

McDowell, L. (2003) *Redundant Masculinities? Employment change and working class youth*, Oxford: Blackwell.

McFadden, D. (2013) The new science of pleasure. *NBER Working Papers*. Cambridge, MA: National Bureau of Economic Research.

McGovern, S. (1994) A Lakatosian approach to changes in international trade theory. *History of Political Economy* 26: 351–68.

Mackenzie, D. (2009) *Material Markets: How economic agents are constructed*, Oxford: Oxford University Press.

Mackenzie, D. and Millo, Y. (2003) Constructing a market, performing theory: The historical sociology of a financial derivatives exchange. *American Journal of Sociology* 109: 107–45.

Mackenzie, D., Muniesa, F., and Siu, L. (eds) (2008) *Do Economists Make Markets? On the performativity of economics*. Princeton, NJ: Princeton University Press.

MacKinnon, D. (2012) Beyond strategic coupling: Reassessing the firm–region nexus in global production network. *Journal of Economic Geography* 12: 227–45.

MacKinnon, D., Cumbers, A., Pike, A., et al. (2009) Evolution in economic geography: Institutions, political economy and adaptation. *Economic Geography* 85: 129–50.

McMichael, P. (2009) A food regime genealogy. *Journal of Peasant Studies* 36: 139–69.

References

McMichael, P. (2012) The land grab and corporate food regime restructuring. *Journal of Peasant Studies* 39: 681–701.

Macpherson, C.B. (1962) *The Political Theory of Possessive Individualism*, Oxford: Clarendon Press.

Mainwearing, L. (1974) A neo-Ricardian analysis of international trade. *Kyklos* 27: 537–53.

Mair, A. (1997) Strategic localization: The myth of the postnational enterprise. In: Cox, K. (ed.) *Spaces of Globalization: Reasserting the lower of the local*. New York: Guilford, 64–88.

Malmberg. A. and Maskell. P. (2002) The elusive concept of localization economies: Towards a knowledge-based theory of spatial clustering. *Environment and Planning A* 34: 429–49.

Malmberg, A., Sölvell, Ö., and Zander, I. (1996) Spatial clustering, local accumulation of knowledge and firm competitiveness. *Geografiska Annaler* 78B: 85–97.

Malthus, T.R. (1820) *Principles of Political Economy: Considered with a view to their practical application*, London: J. Murray.

Mandel, E. (1995) *Long Waves of Capitalist Development*, London: Verso.

Mandel, J. (2004) Mobility matters: Women's livelihood strategies in Porto Novo, Benin. *Gender, Place and Culture* 11: 257–87.

Mandeville, B. (1795) *The Fable of the Bees*, London. C. Bathurst.

Mann, G. (2007) *Our Daily Bread: Wages, workers, and the political economy of the American west*, Chapel Hill, NC: University of North Carolina Press.

Mansuri, K. (2003) The geographic effects of trade liberalization with increasing returns in tranportation. *Journal of Regional Science* 43: 249–68.

Mansvelt, J. (2012) Making consumers and consumption. In: Barnes, T.J., Peck, J., and Sheppard, E. (eds) *The Wiley-Blackwell Companion to Economic Geography*. Oxford: Wiley-Blackwell, 444–57.

Marcum, D. (2014) 'Hi, do you have water?' In a central California town, answer is often no. *The Los Angeles Times*: http://www.latimes.com/local/great-reads/la-me-c1-east-porterville-20140918-story.html accessed March 11, 2016.

Markose, S.M. (2005) Computability and evolutionary complexity: Markets as complex adaptive systems. *The Economic Journal* 115: F159–92.

Markusen, A. (1985) *Profit Cycles, Oligopoly and Regional Development*, Cambridge MA: MIT Press.

Markusen, A. (1996) Sticky places in slippery space: A typology of industrial districts. *Economic Geography* 72: 293–313.

Markusen, J.R. (2002) *Multinational Firms and the Theory of International Trade*, Cambridge, MA: MIT Press.

Marshall, A. (1890) *Principles of Economics*, London: Macmillan and co.

Marston, S. (2000) The social construction of scale. *Progress in Human Geography* 24: 219–42.

Marston, S.A., Jones, III J.P., and Woodward, K. (2005) Human geography without scale. *Transactions of the Institute of British Geographers* NS30: 416–32.

Marston, S.A, Woodward, K., and Jones, III J.P. (2007) Flattening ontologies of globalization: The Nollywood case. *Globalizations* 4: 45–63.

Martin, R. (1998) The new 'geographical turn' in economics: Some critical reflections. *Cambridge Journal of Economics* 23: 65–91.

Martin, R (ed.) (1999) *Money and the Space Economy*, Chichester: John Wiley.

Martin, R. and Sunley, P. (2006) Path dependence and regional economic evolution. *Journal of Economic Geography* 6: 395–435.

Martin, R., and Sunley, P. (2007) Complexity thinking and evolutionary economic geography. *Journal of Economic Geography* 7: 573–601.

Martin, R., and Sunley, P. (2014) Towards a developmental turn in evolutionary economic geography? *Regional Studies* 49: 712–32.

Martin, R., Sunley, P., and Wills, J. (1994) Unions and the politics of deindustrialization: Some comments on how geography complicates class analysis. *Antipode* 26: 59–76.

Marx, K. (1848) On the question of free trade. Speech to the democratic Association of Brussels, January 9. Brussels.

Marx, K. (1967 [1867]) *Capital: A Critique of Political Economy, Vol. 1*, New York: International Publishers.

Marx, K. (1971) *Theories of Surplus Value*, Moscow: Progress Publishers.

Marx, K. (1972 [1867–96]) *Capital, Volume 2*, Harmondsworth: Penguin.

Marx, K. (1972 [1885]) *Capital, Volume 3*, Harmondsworth: Penguin.

Marx, K. (2000 [1862]) *Theories of Surplus Value*, Amherst, NY: Prometheus.

Massey, D. (1973) Towards a critique of location theory. *Antipode* 5: 33–49.

Massey, D. (1984) *Spatial Divisions of Labour: Social Structure and the Geography of Production*, London: Methuen.

Massey, D. (1991) A global sense of place. *Marxism Today* June: 24–9.

Massey, D. (1994) *Space, Place and Gender*, Minneapolis, MN: University of Minnesota Press.

Massey, D. (1999) Imagining globalization: Power-geometries of time-space. In: Brah, A., Hickman, M. and Mac an Ghaill, M. (eds) *Global Futures: Migration, environment and globalization*. New York: St. Martin's Press, 27–44.

Massey, D. (2005) *For Space*, London: Sage.

Massey, D. and Meeghan, R. (1982) *The Anatomy of Job Loss: The how, why and where of employment decline*, London: Methuen.

Massey, D., Quintas, P., and Wield, D. (1992) *High Tech Fantasies: Science parks in society, science and space*, London: Routledge.

Mattick, P. (1969) *Marx and Keynes*, London: Merlin.

Mauldin, A. (2015) Global Internet Capacity Trends. https://www.ptc.org/assets/uploads/papers/ptc15/1030_Slides_Mauldin_Alan.pdf accessed March 11, 2016.

Medio, A. (2008) Trade cycle. In: Durlauf, S. and Blume, L.E. (eds) *The New Palgrave Dictionary of Economics Online*. London: Palgrave Macmillan http://www.dictionaryofeconomics.com/article?id=pde2008_T000090 accessed March 11, 2016.

Melitz, M.J. and Ottaviano, G.I.P. (2008) Market size, trade, and productivity. *Review of Economic Studies* 75: 295–316.

Metcalfe, J.S. (1988) The diffusion of innovation: An interpretative survey. In: Dosi, G., Freeman, C., Nelson, R., et al. (eds) *Technical Change and Economic Theory*. New York: Columbia University Press, 560–89.

Milanovic, B. (2005) *Worlds Apart: Measuring international and global inequality*. Princeton, NJ: Princeton University Press.

Milberg, W. (1994) Is absolute advantage passé? Towards a post-Keynesian/Marxian theory of international trade. In: Glick, M.A. (ed.) *Competition, Technology and Money: Classical and post-Keynesian perspectives*. Aldershot: Edward Elgar, 219–36.

Milberg, W. (2002) Say's Law in the open economy: Keynes's rejection of the theory of comparative advantage. In: Dow, S.C. and Hillard, J. (eds) *Keynes, Uncertainty and the Global Economy*. Aldershot: Edward Elgar, 239–53.

Miller, B., Beaumont, J., and Nicholls, W. (eds) (2013) *Spaces of Contention: Spatialities and social movements*. Farnham: Ashgate.

Minkler, M., Salvatore, A.L., Chang, C., et al. (2014) Wage theft as a neglected public health problem: An overview and case study from San Francisco's Chinatown district. *American Journal of Public Health* 104: 1010–20.

Minsky, H.P. (1993) The financial instability hypothesis. In: Arestis, P. and Sawyer, M. (eds) *Handbook of Radical Political Economy*. Aldershot: Edward Elgar.

Mintz, S. (1971) Men, women, and trade. *Comparative Studies in Society and History* 13: 247–69.

Mirowski, P. (1984) Physics and the marginalist revolution. *Cambridge Journal of Economics* 8: 361–79.

Mirowski, P. (2013) *Never Let a Serious Crisis go to Waste: Now neoliberalism survived the financial meltdown*, London: Verso.

Mirowski, P., and Plehwe, D. (eds) (2009) *The Road from Mont Pelerin: The making of the neoliberal thought collective*, Cambridge, MA: Harvard University Press.

Mitchell, D. (1996) *The Lie of the Land: Migrant workers and the California landscape*, Minneaplois, MN: University of Minnesota Press.

Mitchell, T. (2002) Can the mosquito speak? In: Mitchell, T. *Rule of experts: Egypt, technopolitics, modernity*. Berkeley, CA: University of California Press, 19–53.

Mitchell, T. (2005) The work of economics: How a discipline makes its world. *European Journal of Sociology* 46: 297–320.

Mitchell, T. (2011) *Carbon Democracy*, London: Verso.

Mohammad, R. and Sidaway, J.D. (2012) Spectacular urbanization amidst variegated geographies of globalization: Learning from Abu Dhabi's trajectory through the lives of South Asian men. *International Journal of Urban and Regional Research* 36: 606–27.

Mohanty, C.T. (2003) 'Under western eyes' revisited: Solidarity through anti-capitalist struggles. In: Mohanty, C.T. *Feminism without Borders: Decolonizing theory, practicing solidarity*. Durham, NC: Duke University Press, 221–51.

Montiel, H.C. (2007) Incompleteness of the post-Washington consensus: A critique of macro-economic and institutional reforms. *International Studies* 44: 103–22.

Moore, D.S. (1998) Subaltern struggles and the politics of place: Remapping resistance in Zimbabwe's Eastern Highlands. *Cultural Anthropology* 13: 344–81.

Moore, J.W. (2003) 'The Modern World-System' as environmental history? Ecology and the rise of capitalism. *Theory and Society* 32: 307–77.

Moore, J.W. (2011) Ecology, capital, and the nature of our times: Accumulation and crisis in the capitalist world-ecology. *Journal of World-Systems Research* 17: 108–47.

Morishima, M. (1973) *Marx's Economics: A dual theory of value and growth*, Cambridge: Cambridge University Press.

Mulligan, G.F. (1995) Myopic spatial competition: Boundary effects and network solutions. *Papers in Regional Science* 75: 155–76.

Mulligan, G.F. and Fik, T.K. (1989) Price variation in spatial oligopolies. *Geographical Analysis* 21: 32–46.

Murdoch, J. (1997) The spaces of actor-network theory. *Geoforum* 29: 357–74.

Murdoch, J. (2005) *Post-structural Geography: A guide to relational space*, Thousand Oaks, CA: Sage Publications.

Murgatroyd, L., Savage, M., Shapiro, D., et al. (1985) *Localities, Class and Gender*, London: Pion.

Muth, R. (1961) Rational expectations and the theory of price movements. *Econometrica* 29: 315–25.

Muthu, S. (2003) *Enlightenment against Empire*, Princteon, NJ: Princeton University Press.

Nagar, R. and Geiger, S. (2007) Reflexivity, positionality and identity in feminist fieldwork: Beyond the impasse. In: Tickell, A., Barnes, T., Peck, J., et al. (eds) *Politics and Practice in Economic Geography*. Thousand Oaks, CA: Sage, 267–78.

Nagar, R., Lawson, V., McDowell, L., et al. (2002) Locating Globalization: Feminist (re)readings of the subjects and spaces of globalization. *Economic Geography* 78: 257–84.

Nagurney, A. (1987) Competitive equilibrium problems, variational inequalities and regional science. *Journal of Regional Science* 27: 503–18.

Neary, J.P. (2009) Two and a half theories of trade. *The World Economy* 33: 1–19.

Nelson, R.R. and Winter, S. (1982) *An Evolutionary Theory of Economic Change*, Cambridge, MA: Harvard University Press.

Nijman, J. (2010) A study of space in Mumbai's slums. *Tijdschrift voor economische en sociale geografie* 101: 4–17.

Nordhaus, W.D. (2006) Geography and macroeconomics: New data and new findings. *Proceedings of the National Academy of Sciences* 103: 3510–7.

Norgaard, R. (1994) *Development Betrayed: The end of progress and a coevolutionary revisioning of the future*, London: Routledge.

Norling, L. (1996) *Iron Men, Wooden Women: Gender and seafaring in the Atlantic world*, Baltimore, MD: Johns Hopkins University Press.

Norman, G. (ed.) (1986) *Spatial Pricing and Differentiated Markets*, London: Pion.

North, D.C. (2005) *Understanding the Process of Economic Change*, Princeton, NJ: Princeton University Press.

O'Brien, R. (1992) *Global Financial Integration: The end of geography*, London: The Royal Institute of International Affairs.

O'Connor, J. (1991) On the two contradictions of capitalism. *Capitalism Nature Socialism* 2: 107–9.

O'Connor, J. (1998) *Natural Causes: Essays in ecological Marxism*, New York: Guilford.

O'Neill, P. and McGuirk, P. (2005) Towards an Antipodean theory of space. *ARCRNISS Workshop*. University of Newcastle, Australia.

O'Rourke, K.H. and Williamson, J.G. (2000) *Globalization and History: The evolution of the Atlantic economy*, Cambridge, MA: The MIT Press.

Obstfeld, M. and Rogoff, K.S. (2000) The six major puzzles in international macroeconomics: Is there a common cause? In: Bernanke, B.S. and Rogoff, K.S. (eds) *NBER Macroeconomics Annual 2000*. Cambridge, MA: MIT Press, 339–90.

Ocampo, J.A. and Parra, M.A. (2006) The commodity terms of trade and their strategic implications for development. In: Jomo, K. (ed.) *Globalization under Hegemony: The changing world economy*. New Delhi: Oxford University Press, 164–94.

Offe, C. (1984) *Contradictions of the Welfare State*, Cambridge, MA: MIT Press.

Ohlin, B. (1933) *Interregional and International Trade*, Cambridge, MA: Harvard University Press.

Ohmae, K. (1995) *The End of the Nation State: The rise of regional economies*, New York: Free Press.

Oinas, P. (2002) Competition and collaboration in interconnected places: Towards a research agenda. *Geografiska Annaler* 84: 65–76.

Okishio, N. (1961) Technical changes and the rate of profit. *Kobe University Economic Review* 7: 85–99.

Olsson, O. and Hibbs, Jr D.A. (2005) Biogeography and long-run economic development. *European Economic Review* 49: 909–38.

Ong, A. (2006) *Neoliberalism as Exception: Mutations in sovereignty and citizenship*, Durham, NC: Duke University Press.

Ong, A. (2007) Neoliberalism as a mobile technology. *Transactions of the Insititute of British Geographers* NS 32: 3–8.

Ormerod, P. (1994) *The Death of Economics*, London: Faber & Faber.

Ottaviano, G. (2010) 'New' new economic geography: Firm heterogeneity and agglomeration economies. *Journal of Economic Geography* 11: 231–40.

Ottaviano, G. and Thisse, J.-F. (2004) Agglomeration and economic geography. In: Henderson, J.V. and Thisse, J.-F. (eds) *Handbook of Urban and Regional Economics, Vol. 4*. Amsterdam: Elsevier, 2564–608.

Painter, J. (1997) Regulation, regime, and practice in urban politics. In: Lauria, M. (ed.) *Reconstructing Urban Regime Theory: Regulating urban politics in a global economy*. Thousand Oaks, CA: Sage Publications, 122–44.

Paluzie, E. (2001) Trade policy and regional inequalities. *Papers in Regional Science* 80: 67–85.

Parry, B. (2012) Economies of bodily commodification. In: Barnes, T.J., Peck, J., and Sheppard, E. (eds) *The Wiley-Blackwell Companion to Economic Geography*. Oxford: Wiley-Blackwell, 213–25.

Pasinetti, L. (1966) Changes in the rate of profit and switches of techniques. *Quarterly Journal of Economics* 80.

Pasinetti, L. (1977) *Lectures on the Theory of Production*, London: Macmillan.

Pasinetti, L. (1981) *Structural Change and Economic Growth*, Cambridge: Cambridge University Press.

Pavlik, C. (1990) Technical reswitching: A spatial case. *Environment and Planning A* 22: 1025–34.

Peck, J. (1996) *Work-Place: The social regulation of labor markets*, New York: Guilford.

Peck, J. (2002) Political economies of scale: Fast policy, interscalar relations, and neo-liberal workfare. *Economic Geography* 78: 331–60.

Peck, J. (2005) Struggling with the creative class. *International Journal of Urban and Regional Research* 29: 740–70.

Peck, J. (2009) Conceptualizing fast-policy space, embedding policy mobilities. Manuscript, available from the author.

Peck, J. (2010a) *Constructions of Neoliberal Reason*, Oxford: Oxford University Press.

Peck, J. (2010b) Zombie neoliberalism and the ambidextrous state. *Theoretical Criminology* 14: 104–10.

Peck, J. (2012a) Austerity urbanism. *City* 16: 626–55.

Peck, J. (2012b) Economic geography: Island life. *Dialogues in Human Geography* 2: 113–33.

Peck, J. (forthcoming) Pluralizing labor geography. In: Clark, G.L., Feldman, M., Gertler, M., et al. (eds) *The New Oxford Handbook of Economic Geography*. Oxford: Oxford University Press.

Peck, J. and Theodore, N. (2010) Mobilizing policy: Models, methods, and mutations. *Geoforum* 41: 169–74.

Peck, J. and Tickell, A. (2002) Neoliberalizing space. In: Brenner, N. and Theodore, N. (eds) *Spaces of Neoliberalism: Urban restructuring in North America and Western Europe*. Oxford: Blackwell, 34–57.

Peck, J., Theodore, N., and Brenner, N. (2012) Neoliberalism resurgent? Market rule after the Great Recession. *South Atlantic Quarterly* 111: 265–88.

Peet, R. (1985) The social origins of environmental determinism. *Annals of the Association of American Geographers* 75: 309–33.

Peet, R. (1987) *International Capitalism and Industrial Restructuring*, London: Allen & Unwin.

Peet, R. (2006) Book review: The end of poverty. *Annals of the Association of American Geographers* 96: 450–3.

Peet, R. (2009) Ten pages that changed the world: Deconstructing Ricardo. *Human Geography* 2: 81–95.

Peet, R. and Watts, M. (eds) (1996) *Liberation Ecologies: Environment, development, social movements*. London: Routledge.

Pesaran, M. (1987) *The Limits to Rational Expectations*, Oxford: Basil Blackwell.

Peters, K. and Oldfield, S. (2005) The paradox of 'Free Basic Water' and cost recovery in Grabouw: Increasing household debt and municipal financial loss. *Urban Forum* 16: 313–35.

Phelps, N. (2007) Gaining from globalization? State extraterritoriality and domestic economic impacts—The case of Singapore. *Economic Geography* 83: 371–93.

Pickering, A. (1995) *The Mangle of Practice*, Chicago: Chicago University Press.

Pike, A. (ed.) (2011) *Brands and Branding Geographies*, London: Edward Elgar.

Piketty, T. (2014 [2013]) *Capital in the twenty-first Century*, Cambridge, MA: Belknap Books.

Piore, M. and Sabel, C. (1986) *The Second Industrial Divide: Possibilities for prosperity*, New York: Basic Books.

Plummer, P. (1996) Competitive dynamics in hierarchically organized markets: Spatial duopoly and demand asymmetries. *Environment and Planning A* 28: 2021–40.

Plummer, P. and Sheppard, E. (2001) Must emancipatory economic geography be qualitative? A response to Amin and Thrift. *Antipode* 30: 758–63.

Plummer, P. and Sheppard, E. (2006) Geography matters: Agency, structures and dynamics. *Journal of Economic Geography* 6: 619–37.

Plummer, P., Sheppard, E., and Haining, R.P. (2012) Rationality, stability and endogenous price formation in spatially interdependent markets. *Environment & Planning A* 44: 538–59.

Polanyi, K. (2001 [1944]) *The Great Transformation: The political and economic origins of our time*, Boston: Beacon Press.

Polanyi, M. (1966) *The Tacit Dimension*, Chicago IL: University of Chicago Press.

Pollard, J. (1996) Banking at the margins: A geography of financial exclusion. *Environment and Planning A* 28: 1209–32.

Pollard, J. and Samers, M. (2007) Islamic banking and finance: Postcolonial political economy and the decentering of economic geography. *Transactions of the Institute of British Geographers* 32: 313–30.

Pollard, J., McEwan, C., and Hughes, A. (eds) (2011) *Postcolonial Economies*, London: Zed Books.

Pomeranz, K. (2000) *The Great Divergence: China, Europe, and the making of the modern world economy*, Princeton, NJ: Princeton University Press.

Poon, J.P.H, Thompson, E.R., and Kelly, P.F. (2000) Myth of the triad? The geography of trade and investment 'blocs'. *Transactions of the Institute of British Geographers* 25: 427–44.

Porter M. (1995) The competitive advantage of the inner city. *Harvard Business Review* 74: 55–71.

Porter, P.W. and Sheppard, E. (1998) *A World of Difference*, New York: Guilford Press.

Portes, A., Castells, M., and Benton, L.A. (eds) (1989) *The Informal Economy: Studies in advanced and less developed countries*. Baltimore, MD: Johns Hopkins University Press.

Powell, W. (1990) Neither market nor hierarchy: Network forms of organization. *Research in Organizational Behavior* 12: 295–334.

Pratt, G. (2012) *Families Apart: Migrant mothers and the conflicts of labor and love*, Minneapolis, MN: University of Minnesota Press.

Prebisch, R. (1959) Commercial policy in the underdeveloped countries. *American Economic Review* 49: 251–73.

Presbitero, A.F. (2006) Institutions and geography as sources of economic development. *Journal of International Development* 18: 351–78.

Prigogine, I. (1996) *The End of Certainty: Time, chaos and the new laws of nature*, New York: The Free Press.

Przeworski, A. (2004a) Geography vs. institutions revisited: Were fortunes reversed? Working Paper. New York: New York University.

Przeworski, A. (2004b) The last instance: Are institutions the primary cause of economic development? *European Journal of Sociology* 45: 165–88.

Pulido, L. (1996) *Environmentalism and Economic Justice*, Tucson, AZ: The University of Arizona Press.

Quesnay, F. (1753–58) *Tableau économique*, Versailles: privately printed.

Rankin, K.N. (2002) Social capital, microfinance, and the politics of development. *Feminist Economics* 8: 1–24.

Rauch, J. (1999) The role of transportation costs for people. *International Regional Science Review* 22: 173–8.

Ray, I. (2011) *Bengal Industries and the British Industrial Revolution (1757–1857)*, London: Routledge.

Raynolds, L.T. and Long, M.A. (eds) (2007) *Fair trade: The challenges of reforming globalization*, London: Routledge.

Rees, J.A. (1990) *Natural Resources: Allocation, Economics and Policy*, London: Routledge.

Ricardo, D. (1817) *The Principles of Political Economy, and Taxation*, London: John Murray.

Rickles, D. (2007) Econophysics for philosophers. *Studies in History and Philosophy of Modern Physics* 38: 948–78.

Rigby, D. (1990) Technical change and the rate of profit: An obituary for Okishio's theorem. *Environment and Planning A* 22: 1039–50.

Rigby, D. and Essletzbichler, J. (2006) Technological variety, technological change and a geography of production techniques. *Journal of Economic Geography* 6: 45–70.

Robbins, P. (2004) *Political Ecology: A critical introduction*, Oxford: Blackwell.

Roberts, A. (2014) Peripheral accumulation in the world economy: A cross-national analysis of the informal economy. *International Journal of Comparative Sociology* 54: 420–44.

Robertson, M. (2004) The neoliberalization of ecosystem services: Wetland mitigation banking and problems in environmental governance. *Geoforum* 35: 361–73.

Robins, K. (1995) Cyberspace and the world we live in. In: Featherstone, M. and Burrows, R. (eds) *Cyberspace/cyberbodies/cyberpunk: Cultures of technological embodiment*. Thousand Oaks, CA: Sage Publishers, 135–56.

Robinson, J. (1953–54) The production function and the theory of capital. *Review of Economic Studies* 21: 81–106.

Robinson, J. (1962) *Essays in the Theory of Economic Growth*, London: Macmillan.

Rocheleau, D., Thomas-Slayter, B., and Wangari, E. (eds) (1996) *Feminist Political Ecology: Global issues and local experience*, London: Routledge.

Rodrik, D. (1997) *Has Globalization gone too Far?*, Washington, DC: Institute for International Economics.

Rodrik, D. (2007) *One Economics, many Recipes: Globalization, institutions and economic growth*, Princeton, NJ: Princeton University Press.

Rodrik, D., Subramanian, A., and Trebbi, F. (2004) Institutions rule: The primacy of institutions over geography in economic development. *Journal of Economic Growth* 9: 131–65.

Roemer, J. (1981) *Analytical Foundations of Marxian Economic Theory*, Cambridge: Cambridge University Press.

Roemer, J. (ed.) (1986) *Analytical Marxism*, Cambridge: Cambridge University Press.

Romer, P. (1990) Endogenous technological change. *Journal of Political Economy* 98: S71–S102.

Roncaglia, A. (2000) *Piero Sraffa: His life, thought and cultural heritage*, London: Routledge.

Rose, G. (1993) *Feminism & Geography: The limits of geographical knowledge*, Minneapolis: University of Minnesota Press.

Rose, M. (2002) The seductions of resistance: Power, politics, and a performative style of systems. *Environment and Planning D: Society and space* 20: 383–400.

Rose, N. (1996) Governing 'advanced' liberal democracies. In: Barry, A., Osborne, T., and Rose, N. (eds) *Foucault and Political Reason: Liberalism, neo-liberalism and rationalities of government.* London: UCL Press, 37–64.

Rose, N. (1999) *Powers of Freedom: Reframing political thought,* Cambridge: Cambridge University Press.

Rosser, Jr J.B. (2000) Aspects of dialectics and non-linear dynamics. *Cambridge Journal of Economics* 24: 311–24.

Rossi-Hansberg, E. (2005) A spatial theory of trade. *American Economic Review* 95: 1464–91.

Rostow, W.W. (1960) *The Stages of Economic Growth: A non-communist manifesto,* Cambridge: Cambridge University Press.

Routledge, P. and Cumbers, A. (2009) *Global Justice Networks: Geographies of transnational solidarity,* Manchester: Manchester University Press.

Roy, A. (2009) Why India cannot plan its cities: Informality, insurgence and the idiom of urbanization. *Planning Theory* 8: 76–87.

Roy, A. (2010) *Poverty Capital,* New York: Wiley Blackwell.

Ruigrok, W. and van Tulder, R. (1995) *The Logic of International Restructuring,* London: Routledge.

Sachs, J,, Bajpal, N., and Ramiah, A. (2002) Understanding regional economic growth in India. *Asian Economic Papers* 1: 32–62.

Sachs, J. and McCord, G.C. (2008) Geography of regional development. In: Durlauf, S. and Blume, L. (eds) *The New Palgrave Dictionary of Economics Online.* second ed. London: Palgrave Macmillan. Available at: https://gps.ucsd.edu/_files/faculty/mccord/mccord_publications_palgrave.pdf accessed March 11, 2016.

Sachs, J. (2000) The geography of economic development. *Naval War College Review* LIII: 93–105.

Sachs, J. (2005) *The End of Poverty: Economic possibilities for our time,* New York City: Penguin Press.

Sadler, D. (2000) Concepts of class in contemporary economic geography. In: Sheppard, E. and Barnes, T. (eds) *A Companion to Economic Geography.* Oxford: Blackwell, 325–40.

Said, E. (1978) *Orientalism,* New York: Vintage.

Said, E. (1994) *Culture and Imperialism,* New York City: Vintage Books.

Samers, M. (2005) The myopia of 'diverse economies', or a critique of the 'informal economy'. *Antipode* 37: 875–86.

Samuelson, P.A. (1948) International trade and the equalization of factor prices. *The Economic Journal* 58: 181–97.

Samuelson, P.A. (1954) The transfer problem and transport costs, II: Analysis of effects of trade impediments. *Economic Journal* LXIV: 264–89.

Samuelson, P.A. (1967) Marxian economics as economics. *American Economic Review* 57: 616–23.

Samuelson, P.A. (1969) The way of an economist. In: Samuelson, P.A. (ed.) *International Economic Relations: Proceedings of the Third Congress of the International Economic Association*. London: Macmillan, 1–11.

Sandikci, Ö. and Rice, G. (eds) (2011) *Handbook of Islamic Marketing*. London: Edward Elgar.

Santos, B.d.S. (2008) *Another Knowledge is Possible: Beyond northern epistemologies*, London: Verso.

Sanyal, K. (2014) *Rethinking Capitalist Development: Primitive accumulation, governmentality and post-colonial capitalism*, London: Routledge.

Sargent, T. and Wallace, N. (1975) 'Rational' expectations, the optimal monetary instrument, and the optimal money supply rule. *Journal of Political Economty* 83: 241–54.

Sarkar, P. (1986) The Singer-Prebisch hypothesis: A statistical evaluation. *Cambridge Journal of Economics* 10: 355–71.

Sarkar, P. and Singer, H.W. (1991) Manufactured exports of developing countries and their terms of trade since 1965. *World Development* 19: 333–40.

Saxenian, A. (1994) *Regional Advantage: Culture and competition in Silicon Valley and Route 128*, Cambridge, MA: Harvard University Press.

Sayer, A. (1995) *Radical Political Economy: A critique*, Oxford: Basil Blackwell.

Sayer, A. (2007) Moral economy as critique. *New Political Economy* 12: 261–70.

Schaeffer, F.K. (1953) Exceptionalism in geography: A methodological examination. *Annals of the Association of American Geographers* 43: 226–49.

Schoenberger, E. (1997) *The Cultural Crisis of the Firm*, Oxford: Blackwell.

Schoenberger, E. (2015) *Nature, Choice and Social Power*, London: Routledge.

Schumpeter, J. (1939) *Business Cycles: A theoretical, historical and statistical analysis of the capitalist process*, New York and London: McGraw-Hill.

Schumpeter, J. (1954) *History of Economic Analysis*, Oxford: Oxford University Press.

Scott, A.J. (1988) *New Industrial Spaces: Flexible production organization and regional development in North America and Western Europe*, London: Pion.

Scott, A.J. (1989) *Metropolis: From the division of labor to urban Form*, Berkeley, CA: University of California Press.

Scott, A.J. (1998) *Regions and the World Economy: Territorial development in a global economy*, Oxford: Oxford University Press.

Scott, A.J. (2000a) Economic geography: The great half-century. *Cambridge Journal of Economics* 24: 483–504.

Scott, A.J. (2000b) Global city-regions and the new world system. In: Yusuf, S., Wu, W., and Everett, S. (eds) *Local Dynamics in an Era of Globalization: 21st century catalysts for development*. New York: Oxford University Press, 84–91.

Scott, A.J. (2006a) *Geography and Economy*, Oxford: Oxford University Press.

Scott, A.J. (2006b) *Global City-Regions*, Oxford: Oxford University Press.

Scott, A.J. and Storper, M. (2003) Regions, globalization, development. *Regional Studies* 37: 579–93.

Seligmann, L. (2001) *Women Traders in Cross-Cultural Perspective: Mediating identities, marketing wares*, Stanford, CA: Stanford University Press.

Semmel, B. (1970) *The Rise of Free Trade Imperialism: Classical political economy and the empire of free trade and imperialism 1750–1850,* Cambridge: Cambridge University Press.

Semple, E.C. (1911) *Influences of Geographic Environment,* New York: Henry Holt.

Sen, P. and Kolli, R. (2009) Delhi Group on Informal Sector—Contribution and present status. *Measuring the Informal Economy in Developing Countries.* Kathmandu, Nepal: International Association for Research in Income and Wealth.

Senior, M.L. (1979) From gravity modelling to entropy maximizing a pedagogic guide. *Progress in Human Geography* 3: 175–210.

Sevilla-Buitrago, A. (2015) Capitalist formations of enclosure: Space and the extinction of the commons. *Antipode* 47: 999–1020.

Shaikh, A. (1978) Political economy and capitalism: Notes on Dobb's theory of crisis. *Cambridge Journal of Economics* 2: 233–51.

Shaikh, A. (1979) Foreign trade and the law of value: Part I. *Science and Society* 43: 281–302.

Shaikh, A. (1980) Foreign trade and the law of value: Part II. *Science and Society* 45: 27–57.

Shaikh, A. (2010) The first great depression of the 21st century. In: Panitch, L., Albo, G., and Chibber ,V. (eds) *Socialist Register 2011: The crisis this time.* Pontypool: Merlin Press, 44–63.

Shalizi, C.R. (2002) Review of Kirill Ilinski. Physics of finance: Gauge modelling in non-equilibrium pricing. *Quantitative Finance* 4: 391.

Sheppard, E. (1978) Theoretical underpinnings of the gravity hypothesis. *Geographical Analysis* 10: 386–402.

Sheppard, E. (1980) The ideology of spatial choice. *Papers of the Regional Science Association* 43: 197–213.

Sheppard, E. (1990) Transportation in a capitalist space economy: Transportation demand, circulation time and transportation innovations. *Environment and Planning A* 22: 1007–24.

Sheppard, E. (2000) Geography or economics? Contrasting theories of location, spatial pricing, trade and growth. In: Clark, G., Gertler, M., and Feldman, M. (eds) *Handbook of Economic Geography.* Oxford: Oxford University Press, 199–219.

Sheppard, E. (2001a) How economists think: About geography, for example. Reflections on The Spatial Economy. *Journal of Economic Geography* 1: 131–6.

Sheppard, E. (2001b) Quantitative geography: Representations, practices, and possibilities. *Environment and Planning D: Society and Space* 19: 535–54.

Sheppard, E. (2002) The spaces and times of globalization: Place, scale, networks, and positionality. *Economic Geography* 78: 307–30.

Sheppard, E. (2004) The spatiality of limits to capital. *Antipode* 36: 470–9.

Sheppard, E. (2005) Free trade: The very idea! From Manchester boosterism to global management. *Transactions of the Institute of British Geographers* 30: 151–72.

Sheppard, E. (2006a) The economic geography project. In: Bagchi-Sen, S. and Lawton Smith, H. (eds) *Economic Geography: Past, present and future.* New York City: Routledge, 11–23.

Sheppard, E. (2006b) Positionality and globalization in economic geography. In: Vertova, G. (ed.) *The Changing Economic Geography of Globalization.* London: Routledge, 45–72.

Sheppard, E. (2008) Geographic dialectics? *Environment & Planning A* 40: 2603–12.

Sheppard, E. (2011a) Geographical political economy. *Journal of Economic Geography* 11: 319–31.

Sheppard, E. (2011b) Geography, nature and the question of development. *Dialogues in Human Geography* 1: 3–22.

Sheppard, E. (2012) Trade, globalization and uneven development: Entanglements of geographical political economy. *Progress in Human Geography* 36: 44–71.

Sheppard, E. (2014a) Globalizing capitalism and southern urbanization. In: Parnell, S. and Oldfield, S. (eds) *The Routledge Handbook on Cities of the Global South*. London: Routledge, 143–54.

Sheppard, E. (2014b) We have never been positivist. *Urban Geography* 35: 636–44.

Sheppard, E. (2015) Thinking geographically: Globalizing capitalism, and beyond. *Annals of the Association of American Geographers* 105: 1113–34.

Sheppard, E. and Barnes, T.J. (1984) Technical choice and reswitching in space economies. *Regional Science and Urban Economics* 14: 345–62.

Sheppard, E. and Barnes, T.J. (1986) Instabilities in the geography of capitalist production: Collective vs. individual profit maximization. *Annals of the Association of American Geographers* 76: 493–507.

Sheppard, E. and Barnes, T.J. (2000) *A Companion to Economic Geography*, Oxford: Blackwell.

Sheppard, E. and Barnes, T.J. (2015 [1990]) *The Capitalist Space Economy: Geographical Analysis after Ricardo, Marx and Sraffa*, London: Taylor & Francis.

Sheppard, E. and Curry, L. (1982) Spatial Price Equilibria. *Geographical Analysis* 14: 279–304.

Sheppard, E. and Glassman, J. (2011) Social class. In: Agnew, J .and Livingstone, D. (eds) *The SAGE Handbook of Geographical Knowledge*. London: Sage, 401–16.

Sheppard, E. and Leitner, H. (2010) Quo vadis neoliberalism? The remaking of global capitalist governance after the Washington Consensus. *Geoforum* 41: 185–94.

Sheppard, E. and Nagar, R. (2004) From east–west to north–south. *Antipode* 36: 557–63.

Sheppard E, Haining RP and Plummer P. (1992) Spatial pricing in interdependent markets. *Journal of Regional Science* 32: 55–75.

Sheppard, E., Maringanti, A. and Zhang, J. (2009a) Where's the geography? World Bank's WDR 2009. *Economic & Political Weekly* 44: 45–51.

Sheppard, E., Porter, P.W., Faust, D., et al. (2009b) *A World of Difference: Encountering and contesting development*, New York: Guilford Press.

Sheppard, E., Barnes, T.J., and Peck, J. (2012) The long decade: Economic geography, unbound. In: Barnes, T.J., Peck, J., and Sheppard, E. (eds) *The Wiley-Blackwell Companion to Economic Geography*. Oxford: Wiley-Blackwell, 1–24.

Shiozawa, Y. (2007) A new construction of Ricardian trade theory—A many-country, many-commodity case with intermediate goods and choice of production techniques. *Evolutionary and Institutional Economics Review* 3: 141–87.

Shiva, V. (1991) *Ecology and the Politics of Survival,* New Delhi: Sage Publications and United Nations University Press.

Sideri, S. (1970) *Trade and Power: Informal colonialism in Anglo-Portuguese relations,* Rotterdam: Rotterdam University Press.

References

Siebert, H. (1969) *Regional Economic Growth: Theory and policy*, Scranton, PA: International Textbook Company.

Signorini, L. (1994) The price of Prato, or measuring the industrial district effect. *Papers in Regional Science* 73: 369–92.

Simmons, C. (1985) 'Deindustrialization,' industrialization, and the Indian economy, c. 1850–1947. *Modern Asian Studies* 19: 593–622.

Simon, H.A. (1956) Rational choice and the structure of the environment. *Psychological Review* 63: 129–38.

Simon, J.L. (1998) *The Ultimate Resource 2*, Princeton, NJ: Princeton University Press.

Simone, A. (2004) *For the City Yet to Come: Changing urban life in four African cities*, Durham, NC: Duke University Press.

Simone, A. (2014) *Jakarta: Drawing the city near*, Minneapolis, MN: University of Minnesota Press.

Sismondi, J.C.L. (1827) *Nouveaux principes d'économie politique, ou de la richesse dans ses rapports avec la population*, Paris: Delaunay.

Sjoberg, G. (1960) *The Pre-industrial City*, Glencoe, IL: Free Press.

Slater, T. (2015) Planetary rent gaps. *Antipode* early publication online: DOI: 10.1111/anti.12185

Smith, A. (1776) *An Inquiry into the Nature and Causes of the Wealth of Nations*, London: A. Strahan and T Cadell.

Smith, A. and Stenning, A. (2006) Beyond household economies: Articulations and spaces of economic practice in postsocialism. *Progress in Human Geography* 30: 190–213.

Smith, D.A. and White, D.J. (1992) Structure and dynamics of the global economy: Network analysis of international trade 1965–1980. *Social Forces* 70: 857–93.

Smith, D.M. (1998) How far should we care? On the spatial scope of beneficience. *Progress in Human Geography* 22: 15–38.

Smith, M.E.G. (2010) *Global Capitalism in Crisis: Karl Marx and the decay of the profit system*, Halifax: Fernwood Publishing.

Smith, N. (1981) Degeneracy in theory and practice: Spatial interactionism and radical eclecticism. *Progress in Human Geography* 5: 111–18.

Smith, N. (1984) *Uneven Development: Nature, capital and the production of space*, Oxford: Basil Blackwell.

Smith, N. (1987) Gentrification and the rent gap. *Annals of the Association of American Geographers* 77: 462–5.

Smith, N. (1992) Geography, difference and the politics of scale. In: Doherty, J., Graham, E., and Malek, M. (eds) *Postmodernism and the Social Sciences*. London: Macmillan, 57–79.

Smith, N. (2004) Scale bending and the fate of the national. In: Sheppard, E. and McMaster, R. (eds) *Scale & Geographic Inquiry: Nature, society and method*. Oxford: Blackwell, 192–212.

Smolin, L. (1997) *The Life of the Cosmos*, Oxford: Oxford University Press.

Sober, E. (2006) Models of cultural evolution. In: Sober, E. (ed.) *Conceptual Issues in Evolutionary Biology*. Cambridge, MA: MIT Press, 535–54.

Soja, E. (1980) The socio-spatial dialectic. *Annals of the Association of American Geographers* 70: 207–25.

Solow, R.M. (1956) A contribution to the theory of economic growth. *Quarterly Journal of Economics* 70: 65–94.

Soper, K. and Trentmann, F. (eds) (2008) *Citizenship and Consumption*, Basingstoke: Palgrave Macmillan.

Sparke, M. (2013) From global dispossession to local repossession: Towards a worldly cultural geography of Occupy activism. In: Johnson, N.C., Schein, R., and Winders, J. (eds) *The Wiley-Blackwell Companion to Cultural Geography*. Oxford: Wiley-Blackwell, 385–408.

Spraos, J. (1983) *Inequalising Trade?* Oxford: Clarendon Press.

Sraffa, P. (1960) *The Production of Commodities by Means of Commodities*, Cambridge: Cambridge University Press.

Standing, G. (2011) *The Precariat: The new dangerous class*, New York: Bloomsbury Academic.

Steedman, I. (1979) *Trade amongst Growing Economies*, Cambridge: Cambridge University Press.

Steedman, I. and Metcalfe, J.S. (1979) Reswitching, primary inputs and the Hecksher–Ohlin–Samuelson theory of trade. In: Steedman, I. (ed.) *Fundamental Issues in Trade Theory*. New York: St. Martin's Press, 38–46.

Stengers, I. (1997) *Power and Invention: Situating science*, Minneapolis, MN: University of Minnesota Press.

Stiglitz, J.E. (2006) *Making Globalization Work*, New York: W.W. Norton.

Stiglitz, J.E. and Charlton, A. (2005) *Fair Trade for All: How trade can promote development*, New York City: Oxford University Press.

Stiglitz, J.E. and Walsh, C.E. (2006) *Principles of Macroeconomics*, New York: W.W. Norton.

Stiglitz, J.E., Sen, A., and Fitoussi, J.-P. (2010) Report by the Commission on the Measurement of Economic Performance and Social Progress. Paris: Commission of the Government of France. http://www.insee.fr/fr/publications-et-services/default.asp?page=dossiers_web/stiglitz/documents-commission.htm accessed March 11, 2016.

Stoker, G. (1998) Governance as theory: Five propositions. *International Social Science Journal* 50: 17–28.

Stolper, W.F. and Samuelson, P.A. (1941) Protection and real wages. *Review of Economic Studies* 9: 58–73.

Storper, M. (1997) *The Regional World: Territorial development in a global economy*, New York: Guilford.

Storper, M. (2013) *Keys to the City: How economics, institutions, social interaction, and politics shape development*, Princeton, NJ: Princeton University Press.

Storper, M. and Venables, A.J. (2003) Buzz: face-to-face contact and the urban economy. *Journal of Economic Geography* 4: 351–70.

Storper, M. and Walker, R. (1989) *The Capitalist Imperative: Territory, technology and industrial growth*, Oxford: Basil Blackwell.

Subasat, T. (2003) What does the Heckscher–Ohlin model contribute to international trade theory? A critical assessment. *Review of Radical Political Economics* 35: 148–65.

References

Sweezy, P. (1942) *The Theory of Capitalist Development*, London: Dobson.

Swyngedouw, E. (1997a) Excluding the other: The production of scale and scaled politics. In: Lee, R. and Wills, J. (eds) *Geographies of Economies*. London: Arnold, 167–76.

Swyngedouw, E. (1997b) Neither global nor local: 'Glocalization' and the politics of scale. In: Cox, K. (ed.) *Spaces of Globalization: Reasserting the power of the local*. New York: Guilford, 137–66.

Swyngedouw, E. (2004) *Social Power and the Urbanization of Water: Flows of power*, Oxford: Oxford University Press.

Taylor, P.J. (1996) Embedded statism and the social sciences: Opening up to new spaces. *Environment and Planning A* 28: 1917–28.

Teece, D.J. (1986) Profiting from technological innovation. *Research Policy* 15: 285–305.

ter Wal, A.L.J. and Boschma, R.A. (2011) Co-evolution of firms, industries and networks in space. *Regional Studies* 45: 919–33.

Thaler, R.H. and Sunstein, C.R. (2003) Libertarian paternalism. *American Economic Review* 93: 175–9.

Tharakan, J. and Thisse, J.F. (2002) The importance of being small. Or when countries are areas and not points. *Regional Science and Urban Economics* 32: 381–408.

Thomas, B. (1972) *Migration and urban development: A reappraisal of British and American long cycles*, London: Methuen.

Thrift, N. (1994) Inhuman geographies: Landscapes of light, speed and power. In: Cloke, P.J., Doel, M., Matless, D., et al. (eds) *Writing the Rural: Five cultural geographies*. London: Paul Chapman, 191–248.

Tickell, A. and Peck, J. (1992) Accumulation, regulation and the geographies of post-Fordism: missing links in regulationist research. *Progress in Human Geography* 16: 190–218.

Tobler, W. (1970) A computer movie simulating urban growth in the Detroit region. *Economic Geography* 46: 234–40.

Trentmann, F. (2008) *Free Trade Nation: Commerce, consumption, and civil society in modern Britain*, Oxford: Oxford University Press.

Tsing, A.L. (2005) *Friction: An ethnography of global connection*, Princeton, NJ: Princeton University Press.

Tugan-Baranowsky, M. (1901 [1894]) *Studien zur Theorie und Geschichte der Handelskrisen in England*, Jena: G. Fischer.

Turner, B.L., Kasperson, R.E., Matson, P.A., et al. (2003) A framework for vulnerability analysis in sustainability science. *Proceedings of the National Academy of Sciences* 100: 8074–9.

Tversky, A. and Kahneman, D. (1986) Rational choice and the framing of decisions. *Journal of Business* 59: 8251–78.

Unger, R. (2007) *Free Trade Reimagined: The world division of labor and the method of economics*, Princeton, NJ: Princeton University Press.

Van Staveren, I., Elson, D., Grown, K., et al. (eds) (2007) *The Feminist Economics of Trade*. London: Routledge.

van Zijp, R. (1993) *Austrian and New Classical Business Cycle Theories*, London: Edward Elgar.

Venables, A.J. (2006) Shifts in economic geography and their causes. *Federal Reserve Bank of Kansas City*, fourth quarter: 61–83.

Venables, A.J. and Limão, N. (2002) Geographical disadvantage: A Hecksher–Ohlin von Thünen model of international specialization. *Journal of International Economics* 58: 239–63.

Villar, O. (1999) Spatial distribution of production and international trade: A note. *Regional Science and Urban Economics* 29: 371–80.

Vinod, H.D. (ed.) (2012) *The Oxford Handbook of Hindu Economics and Business*. New Delhi: Oxford University Press.

Virilio, P. (1995) *The Art of the Motor*, Minneapolis: University of Minnesota Press.

Von Thünen, J.H. (1966 [1910]) *The Isolated State*, New York City: Pergamon.

Wackernagel, M. and Rees, W. (1998) *Our Ecological Footprint: Reducing human impact on the earth*, Gabriola Island, BC: New Society Publishers.

Wade, R. (1990) *Governing the Market*, Princeton, NJ: Princeton University Press.

Wallerstein, I. (1979) *The Capitalist World Economy*, Cambridge: Cambridge University Press.

Wallerstein, I. (2004) *World-Systems Analysis: An introduction*, Durham, NC: Duke University Press.

Walras, L. (1874) *Élements d'économie politique pure*, Lausanne: Corbaz.

Ward, K.G. (1997) Coalitions in urban regeneration: A regime approach. *Environment and Planning A* 29: 1493–506.

Waring, M. (1988) *If Women Counted: A new feminist economics*, London: Harper & Row.

Warren, B. (1980) *Imperialism: Pioneer of Capitalism*, London: New Left Books.

Watts, M. (1983) *Silent Violence: Food, famine and peasantry in northern Nigeria*, Berkeley: University of California Press.

Webber, M. and Rigby, D. (1996) *The Golden Age Illusion: Rethinking postwar capitalism*, New York: Guilford.

Webber, M. and Rigby, D. (1999) Accumulation and the rate of profit: Regulating the macroeconomy. *Environment and Planning A* 31: 141–64.

Webber, M., Sheppard, E., and Rigby, D. (1992) Forms of technical change. *Environment and Planning A* 24: 1679–709.

Weber, M. (2003 [1902]) *The Protestant Ethic and the Spirit of Capitalism*, New York City: Dover Publications.

Weeks, J. (2012) *The Irreconcilable Inconsistencies of Neoclassical Macroeconomics: A false paradigm*, London: Routledge.

Weeks, J. (2013) The fallacy of competition: Markets and the movement of capital. In: Moudud, J.K., Bina, C., and Mason, P.L. (eds) *Alternative Theories of Competition*. London: Routledge, 13–26.

Weintraub, E.R. (1979) *Microfoundations: The compatibility of microeconomics and macroeconomics*, Cambridge: Cambridge University Press.

Werner, M. (2012a) Beyond Upgrading: Gendered Labor and the Restructuring of Firms in the Dominican Republic. *Economic Geography* 88: 403–22.

Werner, M. (2012b) Contesting power/knowledge in economic geography: Learning from Latin America and the Caribbean. In: Barnes, T., Peck, J., and Sheppard, E. (eds) *Wiley-Blackwell Companion to Economic Geography*. London: Wiley-Blackwell, 132–46.

References

Werner, M. (2016) *Global Displacements: The making of uneven development in the Dominican Republic and Haiti*, New York: Wiley Blackwell.

Whatmore, S. (2001) *Hybrid Geographies: Natures, cultures, spaces*, Thousand Oaks, CA: Sage.

Whatmore, S. and Thorne, L. (1997) Nourishing networks: Alternative geographies of food. In: Goodman, D. and Watts, M. (eds) *Globalizing Food: Agrarian questions and global restructuring*. London: Routledge, 287–304.

While, A., Jonas, A., and Gibbs, D. (2010) From sustainable development to carbon control: Eco-state restructuring and the politics of urban and regional development. *Transactions of the Institute of British Geographers* 35: 76–93.

White, H. (1988) Varieties of markets. In: Wellman, B. and Berkowitz, S.D. (eds) *Social Structures: A network approach*. Cambridge: Cambridge University Press, 226–60.

Williams, C.C. (2005) *A Commodified World? Mapping the limits of capitalism*, London: Zed Press.

Williams, C.C. (2013) Out of the shadows: A classification of economies by the size and character of their informal sector. *Work, Employment & Society* 28: 735–53.

Williamson, J. (2003) From reform agenda to damaged brand name: A short history of the Washington Consensus and suggestions for what to do next. *Finance & Development*. September: 10–13.

Williamson, J.G. (1965) Regional inequality and the process of national development: A description of the patterns. *Economic Growth and Cultural Change* 13: 1–84.

Williamson, J.G. (2005) *Globalization and the Poor Periphery before 1950*, Cambridge, MA: MIT Press.

Williamson, J.G. (2011) *Trade and Poverty: When the third world fell behind*, Cambridge, MA: MIT Press.

Williamson, O.E. (1985) *The Economic Institutions of Capitalism: Firms, markets, relational contracting*, New York: The Free Press.

Wills, J. (1996) Geographies of trade unionism: Translating traditions across space and time. *Antipode* 28: 352–78.

Winch, D. (1996) *Riches and Poverty: An intellectual history of political economy in Britain, 1750–1834*, Cambridge: Cambridge University Press.

Wolfe, R. (2015) First diagnose, then treat: What ails the Doha Round? *World Trade Review* 14: 7–28.

Wong, K.-Y. (1995) *International Trade in Goods and Factor Mobility*, Cambridge, MA: MIT Press.

Wood, S. (ed.) (1992) *The Transformation of Work? Skill, flexibility and the labour process*, London: Taylor & Francis.

World Bank. (2009) *World Development Report 2009: Reshaping economic geography* Washington DC: The World Bank.

Wright, M. (2001) Asian spies, American motors and speculations on the space-time of value. *Environment & Planning A* 33: 2175–88.

Wright, M. (2004) From protests to politics: Sex work, women's worth and Ciudad Juarez modernity. *Annals of the Association of American Geographers* 94: 369–86.

Wright, M. (2006) *Disposable Women and Other Myths of Global Capitalism*, London: Routledge.

Wu, F. (2007) The poverty of transition: From industrial district to poor neighbourhood in the city of Nanjing, China. *Urban Studies* 44: 2673–94.

Wu, J. (1999) Hierarchy and scaling: Extrapolating information along a scaling ladder. *Canadian Journal of Remote Sensing* 25: 367–80.

Yaffe, D. (1973) The Marxian theory of crisis, capital and the state. *Economy and Society* 2: 186–232.

Yamamoto, D. (2008) Scales of regional income disparities in the United States, 1955–2003. *Journal of Economic Geography* 8: 79–103.

Yeung, H.W.-c. (2005) Rethinking relational economic geography. *Transactions of the Insititute of British Geographers* NS 30: 37–51.

Yeung, H.W.-c. (2012) East Asian capitalisms and economic geographies. In: Barnes, T., Peck, J., and Sheppard, E. (eds) *The Wiley-Blackwell Companion to Economic Geography*. Oxford: Wiley-Blackwell, 118–31.

Yeung, H.W.-c. (2014) Governing the market in a globalizing era: Developmental states, global production networks and inter-firm dynamics in East Asia. *Review of International Political Economy* 21: 70–101.

Yiftachel, O. (2003) Relocating 'the critical'? Reflections from Isreal/Palestine. *Environment & Planning D: Society & Space* 21: 137–42.

Young, A.A. (1928) Increasing returns and economic progress. *The Economic Journal* 38: 527–42.

Yuval-Davis, N. (1999) What is transversal politics? *Soundings: Journal of Politics and Culture* 12: 88–93.

Zein-Elabdin, E.O. and Charusheela, S. (2004) *Postcolonialism meets Economics*, London: Routledge.

Zook, M. (2005) *The Geography of the Internet Industry: Venture capital, dot-coms and local knowledge*, Oxford: Blackwell.

Zook, M. (2012) The virtual economy. In: Barnes, T., Peck, J., and Sheppard, E. (eds) *The Wiley-Blackwell Companion to Economic Geography*. Oxford: Wiley-Blackwell, 298–312.

Zook, M. and Grote, M.H. (2014) The microgeographies of global finance: High frequency trading and the construction of information inequality. Manuscript, available at SSRN 2401030.

Zoomers, A. (2010) Globalisation and the foreignisation of space: Seven processes driving the current global land grab. *Journal of Peasant Studies* 37: 429–47.

Index

Index

Sachs, J. 4–5, 6–7, 9–10, 21, 23, 25, 129
Samuelson, P.A. 97, 101–2
Sanyal, K. 94–5
savings and investment 69
Say's Law 74
scale 12–14, 15, 57, 58
  and bodies 8, 36, 139
  and firms/enterprises 85, 91
  global 6, 137, 152
  and globalization 12–13, 64
  household 136
  intra-urban 136–7
  jumping 14, 27, 60, 109
  local 48, 60, 61
  national 21, 27, 61, 62, 112
  politics of 14
  subnational/regional 26, 27, 49
  supranational 63, 65
Schumpeter cycles 72
Schumpeterian competition 83
Schumpeterian creative destruction 91
science and technology 128–9
Scott, A. 11, 18, 51
second industrial divide 51
self-interest 41, 45
Semple, E. 9
sexuality 128, 139
Shaikh, A. 75, 118–19, 121
Shenton, R.W. 24
Shiozawa, Y. 122
shock therapy 21
'smart' money 153
Smith, A. 33, 43, 44, 46, 54, 83n, 101, 108
Smith, N. 2–3, 79–80
social classes 38
social inequalities 28, 56–7
social network analysis (SNA) 14–16, 56
social ontology 35
social reproduction 133
societal norms 56
socio-cultural context 50–1
socio-ecological impacts 147
socio-ecological sustainability 63
socio-spatial dialectic 3, 9, 29, 36, 55, 81, 96, 157–8
socio-spatial equity/inequality xv, 20, 25, 26, 47, 98, 134
socio-spatial imaginaries xv
socio-spatial ontology 15, 29, 31–6, 44, 46, 98, 115, 118
  economic geography 29, 36
  evolutionary economic geography (EEG) 85–6
  mainstream (geographical) economics 32–6, 123
  mainstream trade theory 98, 105–7, 115

socio-spatial positionality 18–20, 25, 26, 27, 28, 37, 90, 125, 134, 135, 149
  capitalism 148, 149, 155–6
  commodity production 37–8, 45–6
  finance 152–3, 154
  free trade 111, 114, 116
  more-than-capitalist, entanglements with 135, 141
  more-than-economic, entanglements with 127
  space, entanglements of 125–6
socio-spatial structure 53
socio-spatial temporality 116, 132
socio-spatial theory 10, 21, 52, 101n
Soja, E. 3, 9
Solow, R. 69
South Africa 5, 112
  see also BRICS (Brazil, Russia, India, South Africa)
South America (southern cone) 5
South Asia 115
Southeast Asia 153
South Korea 125
sovereignty 63–4
space 57
  annihilation of by time 79, 87
  entanglements of 124–6
  -neutral policies 86
  producing: accessibility as commodity 39–43
  -time 86–7, 126
  see also spatio-temporality
spatial agglomerations 50–1, 60
spatial costs 11
spatial equilibrium *see* dynamic (spatial) equilibrium
spatial fetishism 2–3
spatial fix 79–80
Spatial History 1 27, 93–6, 97, 159
Spatial History 2 27, 93–6
spatial impossibility theorem 35, 54
spatialities 10–20, 36, 77–80
  entanglements 99–100, 129
  networks and connectivity 14–18
  place 10–12
  scale 12–14
  socio-spatial positionality 18–20
  see also spatialities of commodity production; spatio-temporality
spatialities of commodity production 29–46
  producing commodities: time, space (spatio-temporality) and relational economy 38–9
  producing space: accessibility as commodity 39–43
  socio-spatial ontology 31–6